THE ENGLISH BOOK TRADE

THE KING'S JOURNALIST

THE

KING'S JOURNALIST

1659 - 1689

STUDIES IN THE REIGN OF CHARLES II

BY

J. G. MUDDIMAN

[1923]

AUGUSTUS M. KELLEY · PUBLISHERS

NEW YORK 1971

First Edition 1923

(London: John Lane The Bodley Head, 1923)

REPRINTED 1971 BY
AUGUSTUS M. KELLEY · PUBLISHERS
REPRINTS OF ECONOMIC CLASSICS
New York New York 10001

. . . .

ISBN 0-678-00729-2
LCN 74-125774

. . . .

PRINTED IN THE UNITED STATES OF AMERICA
by SENTRY PRESS, NEW YORK, N. Y. 10019

GEORGE MONCK, K.G., DUKE OF ALBEMARLE, CAPTAIN GENERAL ON
LAND AND SEA OF ENGLAND, SCOTLAND AND IRELAND

From the portrait by Sir Peter Lely in the Guildhall, Exeter

THE KING'S JOURNALIST

1659–1689

STUDIES IN THE REIGN OF CHARLES II

By J. G. MUDDIMAN

(M.A., EXETER COLLEGE, OXFORD)

WITH FOURTEEN ILLUSTRATIONS

LONDON
JOHN LANE THE BODLEY HEAD LIMITED

PREFACE

WHEN the present writer took in hand the task of writing the life of Henry Muddiman, the first editor of the *London Gazette*, he had little more in view than a study of the origin of the oldest surviving European newspaper and an appreciation of the part played in English life by the written news-letters that eventually beat it out of the field. News-letters and their origin have not been understood in modern times, and the names of their writers, at all events up to the end of the reigns of the last two Stuart kings, had not survived. It was, however, obvious that " news-letters " could not exist before the Post Office was set on foot, and a lengthy search for the date of commencement of the " Letter Office of England " (which, alone, was the equivalent of our modern Post Office) elicited the fact that it did not exist before the month of April, 1637. The documents printed in the Appendix will afford ample evidence of this, as well as a great deal of curious information about the " Letter Office " and the various " post roads."

When this important sidelight on the times had been fully followed up, it was found that not only the history of the Press would have to be brought into relief, but also the extraordinary tale of the campaign of wilful and deliberate lying which culminated in Titus Oates's " Popish Plot." And in order to understand all this as well as to bring into relief the fact that Henry Muddiman's

news-letters stood by themselves, in a class apart, owing
to the fact that he was the King's journalist, and wrote
" with privilege," some account of the political history
of the times had to be written, commencing with the
restoration of the Rump, in May 1659. The result is
not a complete history of the reign of Charles II—that
has yet to be written—but a history of the careers of a
number of writers whose very names have been forgotten,
but who, nevertheless, very often played a prominent
part in the history of their own times. The somewhat
amazing story of Benjamin Harris, the first American
journalist, is one that deserved writing in full.

No attempt has been made to deal with the reign of
James II, for the simple reason that the official news-
letters are practically the only complete and consecutive
record in existence of that reign. To all intents and
purposes, there are no State Papers for the reign of
James II. The news-letters for that reign, therefore,
ought to be printed almost in their entirety.

For the years 1659 and 1660, the present writer has
quoted lavishly from the collection of tracts made by the
contemporary bookseller, George Thomason. As a rule,
the dates placed on his tracts by Thomason have been
found to be accurate, and, therefore, it has generally
been unnecessary to cite their press marks. The reader
will find them all (under the dates given) in the " Catalogue
of the Thomason Tracts."

A word should be said about the Calendar of Domestic
State Papers for 1665–1666. This is so inaccurate and,
at times, so untruthful even, that it has been discarded,
save only for the purposes of an index, and the original
documents have been cited in each case.

Lastly, the writer has had the benefit of access to the
hitherto unknown manuscripts of the whole of Henry
Muddiman's news-letters, from 1667 to 1689 inclusive,
generously placed at his service by the Marquess of Bath,

in whose library they have reposed since the year 1704. For obtaining permission for him to transcribe these MSS., he is indebted to the kind offices of Lady Cromer and of the late Sir George W. Prothero, by whose advice the present book was written.

CONTENTS

CHAP.   PAGE

I. INTRODUCTION—ENGLAND AND LONDON AT THE RESTORA-
TION—THE RUMP—THE ARMY AND THE SECTS . . I

II. THE "REPRESENTATIVE" 37

III. GENERAL MONCK—SIR RICHARD WILLYS, TRAITOR . . 50

IV. THE RUMP AGAIN EJECTED BY THE ARMY—MONCK TAKES
ACTION—HEWSON SENT AGAINST THE CITY . . . 66

V. HENRY MUDDIMAN AND GENERAL MONCK—CLUBS, SONGS,
AND BALLADS OF THE TIMES 82

VI. MONCK RESTORES THE LONG PARLIAMENT—MUDDIMAN AND
DURY OFFICIAL JOURNALISTS—MEETING OF THE CON-
VENTION PARLIAMENT AND RECALL OF THE KING . 99

VII. THE ANABAPTISTS AND THE KING'S JOURNALIST—VENNER'S
REBELLION 123

VIII. THE BOOKS OF THE PRODIGIES AND FRANCIS SMITH—THE
LONG PARLIAMENT OF 1661—ROGER L'ESTRANGE'S SER-
VICES TO THE GOVERNMENT—MUDDIMAN SUPERSEDED
BY L'ESTRANGE IN 1663—HIS COUNTRY HOUSE . . 144

IX. THE FARNLEY WOOD CONSPIRACY — TWYN AND THE
PRINTERS OF THE "SPEECHES AND PRAYERS" CON-
VICTED—WILLIAMSON'S DESIGN AGAINST L'ESTRANGE
AND MUDDIMAN — MUDDIMAN FOUNDS THE *LONDON
GAZETTE*—L'ESTRANGE APPEALS TO THE KING AND IS
PENSIONED—DEFEAT OF THE PLOT OF WILLIAMSON
AND JAMES HICKES—SIR WILLIAM MORICE PROTECTS
MUDDIMAN 168

CHAP.   PAGE

  X. NEMESIS AND JAMES HICKES—MUDDIMAN'S GREAT REPUTA-
        TION—THE KING AND MUDDIMAN   194

 XI. OATES'S AND SHAFTESBURY'S PLOTS — BENJAMIN HARRIS,
        FRANCIS SMITH AND OTHERS—NEWS-LETTER WRITERS
        AND THE PENNY POST   208

XII. THE OXFORD PARLIAMENT—THE KING'S VENGEANCE BEGINS
        —FATE OF THE PUBLISHERS OF NEWSPAPERS—DEATH
        OF CHARLES II — DEATH OF MUDDIMAN — BENJAMIN
        HARRIS, THE FIRST AMERICAN JOURNALIST—END OF
        HIS CAREER IN THE FOLLOWING CENTURY .   .   . 233

        APPENDICES   256

ILLUSTRATIONS

GEORGE MONCK, K.G., DUKE OF ALBEMARLE   .   .   . *Frontispiece*
                                                        Facing page
"ROME RUINED BY WHITEHALL"   24

PRAISE-GOD BAREBONE   102

SIR WILLIAM MORICE 122

THOMAS VENNER   136

SIR JOSEPH WILLIAMSON   144

FRONTISPIECE OF "MIRABILIS ANNUS"   .   . *between* 152 & 153

HENRY BENNET, K.G., EARL OF ARLINGTON   .   .   . 174

ROGER L'ESTRANGE, ESQ., AGED 68 234

ILLUSTRATIONS TO "PROTESTANT TUTOR" 246

FRONTISPIECE OF THE FIRST EDITION OF THE "PROTESTANT
        TUTOR"   246

ENLARGED TITLE-PAGE OF THE FIRST EDITION OF THE "PRO-
        TESTANT TUTOR"   248

ILLUSTRATIONS TO THE "PROTESTANT TUTOR" .   .   . 250

JOHN PARTRIDGE   252

THE KING'S JOURNALIST
1659–1689

CHAPTER I

INTRODUCTION—ENGLAND AND LONDON AT THE RESTORA-
TION—THE RUMP—THE ARMY AND THE SECTS

ONE of the most brilliant, but by no means the
most trustworthy, of English historians, Lord
Macaulay, has, with matchless literary skill,
depicted the condition of England at the close of the reign
of Charles II, by way of a background to the story of the
Revolution told by him.[1] Probably no part of Macaulay's
history of England has received more attention than the
introductory chapters dealing with England at and after
the Restoration.   But history nowadays has become an
exact science.   Each worker in his own chosen field
contributes his part to the picture of times gone by, and
the accredited tale of one generation becomes the exploded
fable of the next.   Macaulay was a Whig partisan, but a
Whig whose transparent honesty was one of his most
amiable traits, and if, in tracing the beginnings of certain
institutions and in telling a fuller story of certain indivi-
duals severely criticized by him, I reverse his facts and
dispute his conclusions, it is not because he misinformed
his readers, but because, as time goes on, new sources are
brought to light and fresh sidelights thrown upon England's past.   There is no finality in history, and over and
above this the history of the reign of Charles II has
never yet been written on a scale satisfactory to modern

---

[1] Macaulay's statistics, comparing England at the date when he
wrote, with the England of the Restoration, are, of course, thoroughly
out of date nowadays and have been revised by Mr. A. L. Bowley, in
his annotations upon the *Third Chapter of Macaulay's History of
England*, published in 1909.

requirements. I have but a miniature to paint in lieu of the wide canvas covered by the larger brush of Macaulay, but I am able to use materials unknown to him, and in doing this I must perforce alter the lights and shades of his detail.

The England and the Englishman of the Restoration by no means correspond to the England and the Englishman of to-day. Laws, government, social life and customs all differed widely from those of our own time, and in no respect was the contrast greater than in questions of religious and political toleration. Intolerance, political and religious, was the hall-mark of the times. No institution was quite the same as it is nowadays, and no sect, whatever its name or status, corresponded exactly to its present-day successor. When the King returned there were no " prime ministers " of the Crown; parliamentary government, as we understand it, did not exist, and religious hatred, mainly a hatred of what was comprehensively termed " Popery," was the dominant issue of the day. It is not possible, therefore, to write of the times of Charles II in terms of modern value; the language of the past must be used and, as we go along, we must, as far as is possible, differentiate its meaning from that of our own times.

In nothing is the contrast between the England of Charles II and the England of to-day more marked than in that of population. Owing to superstitious dislike to any " numbering of the people," the population of England during the seventeenth century can only be approximately stated. But, from rough calculations made from time to time, it appears that England at the time of the Restoration of 1660 contained no more than from five to five and a half millions of people, and that London accounted for nearly 390,000 souls in this total.[1]

[1] Edward Chamberlayne, F.R.S., in *Angliæ Notitia* (third ed., 1669, p. 79), basing his calculations upon the number of houses in each parish, estimated the population of England at 5,446,000.
John Graunt, in his *Natural and Political Observations . . . on the*

The population of Ireland, in 1659, had sunk to 500,091, thanks to Cromwell's ruthless measures against the Irish.[1] Of Scotland there is no record, but it is considered to have contained between 800,000 and 950,000 souls.[2]

The City of London, at the time of the Restoration, was largely a town of wooden houses crowded together in narrow courts and lanes. In Westminster, the houses clustering round the King's Palace of Whitehall and the Houses of Parliament were no better. Roger North tells us that in the year 1641 his father's house, " though but a sorry one," was remarkable for being the first and only brick-built house in King Street, Westminster, for many years.[3] King Street was at that time the main avenue from Whitehall to the Houses of Parliament, and was a narrow street flanked by courts and alleys on either side. Here, in King Street, at the sign of the Fountain, Oliver Cromwell lodged from 1648 up to the time when he set out for Ireland in the following year.

The City had extended itself outside its walls, along the river to Westminster and not towards the east. Drury Lane and the Strand were fashionable suburbs. North of Holborn and Clerkenwell there were open fields, and the modern West End was unbuilt. Piccadilly and " the Pell Mell " were really country roads. Kensington was a village with one hamlet between it and Chelsea—that of Earl's Court—which, including its Manor House, con-

---

Bills of Mortality (1662), put the population of London, including Westminster and other portions of the city outside the walls, at 383,998. Norwich, stated later on by Muddiman, in one of his news-letters, to be the second city in the kingdom, was known to have contained 30,000 inhabitants thirty years later on. Bristol came third with about 5000 less. The great manufacturing and shipping towns of the north were the creation of the eighteenth century.

[1] A census of Ireland was taken in 1659, and has been printed in the Transactions of the Royal Irish Academy, Vol. XXIV. Part III. 319.

[2] This is the opinion of Dr. Neilson, Stipendiary of Glasgow, kindly communicated to the present writer by the Rev. Dr. John Willcock.

[3] *Life of Sir Dudley North,* paragraph 2.

tained only nine houses.[1] Knightsbridge and Brompton were villages infested by footpads at night. Hyde Park was a country recreation ground, and the nearest resort for Londoners was the Spring Garden at Charing Cross, where Pepys and his wife went to gather pinks, and where the nightingales could still be heard in the " solemn grove."

In spite of all the praise by contemporary writers of London's opulence and of its splendid buildings, it must be confessed that the City, apart from the great stone houses of the aristocracy and a few public edifices, would present but a picturesquely sordid appearance to modern eyes. The great churches and religious houses of the Middle Ages had been miserably mangled and were falling into decay. Over all towered the gaunt skeleton of a religion the nation had been taught to hate, the great Cathedral of St. Paul; longer and loftier than the present church, but in a ruinous condition, defaced by Inigo Jones's Ionic portico and shorn of a lofty steeple, said to have been the highest in Christendom. St. Paul's was then used partly for warehouses and partly as a cavalry barracks and had horses stabled in it. Only the East End was reserved for religious worship.[2]

The streets of the City were horribly dirty, with central gutters filled with unsavoury garbage and holes full of water in bad weather. Wealthy people, journeying from Westminster to the City, or vice versâ, if they did not go

[1] See note to p. 167, *infra*.

[2] *University Queries, in a gentle touch by the by*, Cambridge, published on June 6, 1659, inquired :
"Whether the soldiers are garrisoned in St. Paul's that the sanctity of the place might protect them from the Devil, or that their lewd actions might affright him from entering there, for fear of contracting from their bad society a greater measure of iniquity, it being impossible that the Devil should go beyond them in that point ? "
Martin Parker, the ballad-writer, wrote a striking lament over St. Paul's in *Mercurius Melancholicus* for Dec. 25 to Jan. 1, 1649; but it must be remembered that the Nave had been a public walk for gossips and newsmongers for many years previous to the Rebellion.

in their own coaches or hire a hackney-coach [1] or sedan-chair, journeyed to and fro by boat; for there was no other means of crossing the river between London and Kingston bridges, and the Thames was then a popular highway. Thus between London and Staines many thousands of watermen plied their craft.

The sanitary condition of the City was terrible. The Fleet river was then open to the sky, half sewer and half ditch. Each house had its cesspool, the graveyards round the churches and even the churches themselves were overcrowded with the bodies of the dead, and the water supply too often consisted of a well in dreadful proximity to the churchyard. The very reek of the City made strangers ill, so that a contemporary writer actually compared London to villages on the West Coast of Africa, which could be smelt for miles out at sea. [2]

Ever since the great visitations of 1603, when 30,000 persons died, and of 1624, when 35,417 died in London alone, the plague had lurked in the insanitary courts and alleys of London. Year by year deaths from plague were recorded in the " Bills of Mortality "; thirty-six dying from it in 1659; and the greatest visitation of all was to come in 1665, [3] and to be followed by the great fire of the following year.

[1] There were about 400 hackney-coaches in London. Their owners were entitled to charge 10s. a day for hire, or 1s. 6d. for the first hour and 1s. for the second (Thos. Delaune's *Present State of London*, 1681). There was keen competition between the hackney-coachmen and the watermen on the Thames.

[2] In *The Golden Coast ; or, A Description of Guinney* (1665), p. 12 : " It's true indeed that upon some showers of rain there is such a stinck sometimes, as forceth strangers to go some leagues off into the sea, but it is as true that there is such a stinck in London that there was a man I knew upon the Exchange, who never could stay in town above an hour, insomuch that he rid twelve miles every day he came to the Exchange and tied his horse to a pillar there, took a turn or two, grew sick, and immediately took his horse and rid Post out, and this at least three times a week."

[3] Annual statistics of the plague were given in the 1669 edition of Henry Peacham's *Worth of a Penny*, from 1642 to the date of the book. From 1661 to the date of 1696, by which time the plague had

The social customs of the times were abominable, and in 1659, owing to the absence of the Court, politeness was at its lowest ebb. Evelyn, the diarist, published his translation of a *Character of England* by a French Protestant visitor in 1659, describing the people in the most unfavourable terms. Drunkenness, said by Camden to have been unknown in England before the days of Elizabeth and to have then been imported from Holland, was rife amongst all classes, and in 1668 another diarist tells us that Sir William Stanley of Hooton, Lancashire, having invited " Lord M, the three T's and I think some few more " to stay with him three or four nights, the party drank sixteen dozen bottles of wine, two hogsheads of beer and two barrels of ale.[1]

Religious services before the Restoration, when not conducted by anabaptists or the minor sects—in which case they frequently degenerated into Saturnalia—were dull and dreary in the extreme. Men sat through them with their hats on and slept through dull and stupid sermons, or listened to prayers termed " canting, a term by which they do casually express the gibberish of beggars and vagabonds." The organs had all been taken away and were set up in taverns for the benefit of boon companions. The Sacraments, particularly baptism, had fallen into disuse. Foreigners were saluted with stones and dirt by the uncivil people.[2]

---

vanished, the statistics are to be found in a *Catalogues of books . . . since the fire of* 1666. In 1660, 14 persons died; in 1661, 20; in 1662, 12; in 1663, 9; in 1664, 6, and in 1665 the appalling total of 68,596 in London was reached. The " Bills of Mortality," week by week, for 1665 are reprinted in Vol. II. of the *Antiquarian Repertory.*

[1] *Crosby Records : a Cavalier's Note-book.* By William Blundell, p. 94 (ed. T. E. Gibson).

[2] *A Character of England*, by Gallus Castratus. Evelyn published his translation of this in May 1659, prefixing an apologetic preface to it. Of the prayers of the clergy, John Fry, a member of the Rump, wrote in 1650, in his *Clergy in their Colours*, " What wry-mouths, squint eyes and scru'd faces do they make, that in that garb they are not like the men God and Nature hath made them."

On the other hand, institutions without which our modern life could not be carried on were slowly developing. Two of these will bulk largely in the story I have to tell, so that it is necessary to devote some space to their history. The first is the modern Post Office.

The Post Office as we know and term it was utterly unknown in England before the year 1637, when Thomas Witherings, having " found out the true and exact way of correspondency, not formerly understood," received a grant for life of the inland Post Office. Then only, and for the first time, in April, was the public " Letter Office," which we now term " Post Office," set up and called " The Letter Office of England." [1]

At first, there was but one post a week for the public. Every Tuesday night, postmen rode forth from London on their various roads and returned answers by the Monday following. In 1649 the posts were increased to two a week, another one being added on Saturdays. [2] And a few years later on (probably in 1655) a third post was added, on Thursdays. So that during the reigns of Charles II and Jas. II there were in existence three general posts a week for inland letters.

To send a letter was not the simple matter it is nowadays. There were no envelopes, so that when the letter

[1] There is a brief history of the subject in a tract published in the reign of Charles II and entitled " *A View of the Fallacies contained in a late printed paper, entitled the Lord Stanhope's case and title to the office of Postmaster of the Posts and Messengers.*" This is reprinted in Vol. VII. of the Somers Tracts. A great deal of erroneous history on the subject has been written, and has been due to writers confusing the duties of the " Postmaster of the Posts and Messengers " and the " posts " set up in Elizabeth's days or earlier, with the receipt and transmission of letters by the general public through a " Letter Office " —carried out under the same official at a later date. Hickes's statements in his petition to the Secretaries (Appendix C) also prove that there was no public conveyance of letters before 1637.

[2] " The nation is desired to take notice that whereas the weekly post went out every Tuesday night from London and returned answers by Monday following, that the same post sets out likewise every Saturday night and returns answers every Friday following. So that the conveniencie is now of sending twice a week, whereas it was once before."—*The Moderate* for March 27—April 3, 1649.

was written on three sides of a folded sheet of paper, the fourth was left blank as a cover. The ink was dried with fine sand (in lieu of blotting-paper), still to be seen sparkling in old documents, and then the writer folded over his missive at each end, placed one end within the other, sealed the resulting packet with sealing-wax on one side and addressed the other. As there were no adhesive stamps (and no postmarks until 1681), the next step was to take the letter into the City to the solitary " Letter Office " and hand it through the window to James Hickes, who usually received the letters. This last step was so inconvenient to people outside the City that, in 1661, when it was found that persons were representing themselves as having been authorized to receive letters, with the accompanying postage, and were charging an additional penny for delivery at the " Letter Office," five sub-offices were, for the first time, set up.[1] If the letter was not prepaid the recipient paid for it at the other end, but the usual course was to prepay, and then Hickes initialled it.

The minimum charge (for the shortest distance) was twopence for each sheet sent. Only writs, deeds, etc., were charged for by weight, and then the rate was eightpence an ounce. It is generally considered that the penny or shilling of those days should be multiplied by four to four and a half, in order to compare prices with modern values, so that these rates for postage were very high.[2]

[1] Notice in the *Kingdomes Weekly Intelligencer*, for Aug. 12–19, 1661. The sub-offices were " Westminster, Mr. Parker, at Mr. Grincil's shop, a grocer next door to the Sanctuary gate. Strand, Mr. Roberts, a grocer at the Bay Tree, over against York House, Covent Garden. Mr. Magnet, stationer in Russel St., Holborn. Mr. Place, stationer at Gray's Inn Gate. Fleet St., Mr. Eales and Mr. Marriot, at Mr. Marriot's shop in St. Dunstan's churchyard."

[2] The charges are set out in the Post Office Act of 1660 (12 Car. II, c. 35). Richard Blome's *Britannia*, of 1673, gives a full description of the Post Office at that date, from which it appears that there were then 172 deputy postmasters in England. It is difficult to be quite certain about the value of money, owing to the high prices realized

From its first commencement, in 1637, the public carriage of letters had proved immensely remunerative, so that in 1653 the Post Office (which, of course, comprised also the means of transport) was farmed out, the revenue from it being stated at that time to have been £10,000 a year. This policy was continued after the Restoration, in 1660, and many improvements then took place. In October 1660 three vessels were appointed to take letters to and from Ireland twice a week, the post for this purpose leaving London every Tuesday and Saturday, and Dublin every Wednesday and Saturday.[1] And, in the same year, one Van der Heyden, with the King's consent, and notwithstanding the opposition of the Postmasters at the Hague and at Antwerp, set up a new post between Amsterdam and England, commencing on the 22nd of June. The time of transit by this post was three or four days. Letters from Italy came by this post in eleven days, and from Hamburg, whence Van der Heyden established a separate service, the time of transit was six days. Van der Heyden's packet set out from Dover to Sluys every Saturday at three in the afternoon, and carried passengers.[2]

Another growing institution was the newspaper, then represented by weekly pamphlets of " two sheets " (*i. e.* sixteen pages quarto) termed " diurnalls," " news-books," or sometimes " books," simply. One of my objects is to show the origin of the first newspaper, name and thing,

---

by some common articles and to the cheapness of others; but, taking food as a standard, we are frequently told that the cost of an " ordinary," or dinner at a tavern, was fourpence, so that from four to four and a half seems to be a fair multiple by which to ascertain the modern equivalent. The salaries of the letter carriers (6s. to 8s. per week) and other salaries mentioned in Hickes's letter of July 2, 1667 (set out in the Appendix) will also afford a useful basis of comparison. See also Appendix B for a list of postage charges to various places, in and outside the kingdom.

[1] *Parliamentary Intelligencer*, Oct. 15–22, 1660.
[2] *Ibid.*, Aug. 20–27, 1660.

so attention should be given to this terminology,[1] as well as to the fact that before the Restoration the word " advertisement " usually meant news or notice, and did not begin to receive its modern limitations until after the Restoration. In the month of November, 1641, the " diurnalls " of domestic news first began and, naturally, their circulation was much helped by the weekly post. In the seventeenth century there were no printers outside London, save at Oxford and Cambridge and (after the Restoration) at York, so that with occasional exceptions, printed at Oxford, no sort or kind of a newspaper was printed outside London until the year 1701, when the first country newspaper, the *Norwich Post*, of Francis Burges, began. Previous to 1641, therefore, " intelligencers " had supplied domestic news in letters to their patrons, and after the institution of a public post in 1637, " intelligencers " who multiplied their " news-letters " for public sale (and thus evaded the censorship incurred by printed matter) first began to exercise their calling. The two pioneers in this species of journalism were Samuel Pecke, a scrivener with a little stall in Westminster Hall, who traded in Parliamentary speeches and proceedings, and ultimately wrote the printed *Perfect Diurnall* of 1642–1659, and Captain Edmund Rossingham, who lived at the sign of the Lamb at the Temple Gate.[2]

---

[1] There is a discussion of this subject (by the present writer) in *The Times Tercentenary* " Handlist of English and Welsh Newspapers " (1920).
[2] There is a discussion of the subject of Parliamentary reporters in connexion with Samuel Pecke in the introduction to *The Commons Debates for* 1629, edited by Wallace Notestein and Frances H. Relf (University of Minneapolis, 1921). Pecke's " authorship " of the *Perfect Diurnall* is shown in the Stationers' Registers, under July 1, 1643.
A number of Captain Rossingham's news-letters are summarized in the Calendars of State Papers for 1637, 1639 and 1640, and are for the most part addressed to Lord Conway. He is mentioned as a public news-letter writer (under the name of Rashingham) in Wither's *Great Assizes of Apollo, holden on Parnassus*.

The calling of an " intelligencer," therefore, developed *pari passu* with that of a writer of the printed news, and both were often united in one and the same person. The only difference between a " news-letter " and a " news-book," or pamphlet of news, was that the " news-letter " contained little or no comment on its news and was necessarily free from the interference of a licenser. Of the two, therefore, the news-letters are the most valuable to historians.[1]

Of the most famous of all the " news-letter " writers, Henry Muddiman, the one "intelligencer" almost the whole of whose work has survived and has until the present day been hidden in a private library, almost nothing has been known until recently, but the first outline of the history of English newspapers, written by a journalist in 1712, mentioned him in terms which prove that his memory was still green in those days.

Writing in 1712, the author of the *British Mercury* [2] gave a history of English newspapers, in which he says :

" It does not appear that this method of spreading news in print was much in use before the reign of King Charles I, and even then it had its beginning with those calamities which involv'd the whole nation; and, no doubt, contributed much toward them. The Rebellion then set all the presses at liberty, and the two contending parties attacked one another as fiercely in paper as they did in the Field. *Mercurius Politicus, Mercurius Aulicus, Intelligencer,* and many more, under several denominations, flew about in the cities and towns, as the bullets did in the open country. The Restoration, bringing back

---

[1] A satirical account of an " intelligencer's " news-letters is contained in Samuel Butler's *Characters*, etc. (ed. A. R. Waller), pp. 86–7.

[2] *The British Mercury.* " Publish'd by the Company of the Sun Fire Office," etc., No. 369. From Wed., July 30 to Sat., Aug. 2, 1712." For a continuous series of references to " Muddiman's Letters " see Anthony à Wood's *Life and Times* (ed. A. Clark), *passim*.

the blessing of Peace, for a time put a period to that dis-
temper, suppressing that furious run of news and slander.
The famous Muddiman was then the only news-monger,
supplying the nation with some intelligence as to publick
affairs, by written letters. This furnish'd him with a
plentiful maintenance and satisfied the then less curious
people, nothing of that nature being yet in print, except,
I think, for some time a single paper, by the name of an
intelligence."

The odd thing about this otherwise fairly accurate
piece of history is that, even then, Henry Muddiman's
career as journalist to General Monck, and afterwards as
the first editor of our oldest newspaper, the *London
Gazette*, had been forgotten, together with all the conflicts
and struggles with which he had met in both capacities.
It is not necessary to say more of him at this juncture
than that he did not put pen to paper before December
1659, and that it is necessary to describe most of the
preceding events of that year in order that his life's work
may be properly understood.

There had been an immense output of duly licensed
news-books from 1641 to 1655, when Cromwell suppressed
them all in favour of his own bi-weekly, licensed by his
Secretary of State, John Thurloe, and written by Marchamont Nedham. This periodical was entitled *Mercurius
Politicus* on Thursdays and the *Publick Intelligencer* on
Mondays. The two overlapped, each giving the news for
the whole of the week preceding its publication, so that
a reader was as well served by purchasing the one as he
was by the other, though, of course, by subscribing to
both he would receive his news earlier than if he only
purchased one of the two. And, as each pamphlet consisted of two sheets in quarto (*i. e.* sixteen small pages),
" advices," as advertisements were then termed, were
few in number and confined to books, runaway appren-

tices and servants, and lost or stolen horses. Trade advertisements only began to creep in about the year 1655. But, in 1657, Marchamont Nedham commenced a separate pamphlet, wholly confined to " advices," and termed the *Publick Adviser*.[1] This brought him into conflict with an anabaptist gunsmith called Oliver Williams. On Dec. 13, 1637, Charles I had granted Captain Robert Innes and his assigns a patent for an " Office of Intelligence " to bring buyers and sellers together. Those who had goods to sell or houses to let, etc., were to register their names and the particulars of the things they offered in a register book, and, in similar fashion, those who wished to buy or to rent houses could also enter their names for inspection. The patent was for the term of forty-one years, but was hampered by the singular restriction that Innes was not to charge any fees. He was to be remunerated as his clients thought fit.[2] When Innes died in battle Oliver Williams purchased his patent from his widow. The important point to note in this patent, a point to which I shall have to draw attention later on, is that it conferred no right to publish anything whatever in print. When, therefore, Marchamont Nedham issued his *Publick Adviser* in 1657, Oliver Williams, as assignee of Innes's patent, contested his right to do this; for registry offices all over London had been set up by Nedham in connexion with this pamphlet of advertisements. As a result of the legal proceedings which took place, it was decided that Oliver Williams had no right to publish anything in print, so that a pamphlet of advertisements issued by him and entitled *The Weekly Information from the Office of Intelligence* was suppressed. On the

[1] This is sometimes misdescribed as the *Publick Advertiser*—the term of course was not in use.

[2] The patent is summarized in the Calendar of State Papers for 1637–8, p. 19. On pp. 20 and 21 there is a long letter from Innes. There are many notices of Oliver Williams in the State Papers of Cromwell's time, for he and others had purchased other patents, and he was, besides, employed by Cromwell as a gunsmith.

other hand, it was held that Nedham had no right to set
up " Offices of Intelligence." Thus, both schemes col-
lapsed. The *Weekly Information* was confined to one
number, and the *Publick Adviser* lasted only for four
months.[1] Oliver Williams's " Office of Intelligence " was
revived in 1659, under the circumstances to be narrated
later on, and with extraordinary results.

The career of the journalistic " Vicar of Bray," called
Marchamont Nedham, has been fairly well known, owing
to his connexion with Cromwell. Nedham attracted an
amount of angry denunciation, never meted out to any
journalist since his time. Never has such a turncoat
been seen. He had written against Charles I in *Mercurius
Britanicus* [*sic*] from 1644 to 1646; for the King in
Mercurius Pragmaticus from 1648 to 1649; for the Rump
Parliament in *Mercurius Politicus* from 1650 onwards,
and for Cromwell and his son in the same periodical and
its supplement, the *Publick Intelligencer* (1655) to 1659.
In turn he had been imprisoned for nearly every periodical
he had written. In turn he had attacked and angered
every party in the kingdom. He was the " Goliath of
the Philistines," wrote Roger l'Estrange, " whose pen
in comparison of others was like a weaver's beam." John
Cleiveland, the Royalist poet, compared him to an Italian
bravo, ready to be hired for any crime, and suggested
that he should be thrown into the sea, like the Roman
parricides, tied up in a sack with a cock, an ape and a
serpent. But it was reserved for John Goodwin, the
independent preacher, to sum Nedham up in a master-
piece of vituperation. He was, said Goodwin, " *Fax
hominum, atque fax causarum*, one that blesseth what
God curseth and curseth whatever God blesseth, an
infamous and unclean person, next the hangman."

[1] The latter, nevertheless, is a most interesting publication, and
affords valuable sidelights on the life of the times. The first advertisements of coffee and chocolate are to be found in its pages.

From all that has been said, it will be realized that the times I am describing differed very much from our own, both in institutions now a necessity for the well-being of the community, and also in the terms used to describe them. In nothing is this more evident than in the so-called " Parliament " of the times, and in the Army— the Monster which the Presbyterians, like Frankenstein, had built up during the Great Rebellion. Charles II's old " bear " Hobbes, the philosopher, has left us a very convenient summary of the changes of government during the Great Rebellion and Interregnum.[1] When discussing the question of in whom the actual sovereignty reposed during that troubled period, Hobbes traced it as follows :

" First," said he, " from 1640 to 1649, when the King was murdered, the sovereignty was disputed between King Charles I and the Presbyterian Parliament. Secondly, from 1648 to 1653, the power was in that part of the Parliament which voted the trial of the King, and declared themselves, without King or House of Lords, to have the first and supreme authority of England and Ireland. For there were in the Long Parliament two factions, Presbyterian and Independent; the former whereof sought only the subjection of the King, not his destruction directly; the latter sought directly his destruction; and this part it is which is called the ' Rump.' Thirdly, from April the 20th to July the 4th, the sovereign power was in the hands of a Council of State constituted by Cromwell. Fourthly, from July the 4th to December the 12th of the same year [1653] it was in the hands of men called unto it by Cromwell, whom he termed men of integrity and fidelity, and made them a Parliament; which was called, in contempt of one of the members, ' Barebone's Parliament.' Fifthly, from December the 12th, 1653, to September the 3rd, 1658, it was in the

---

[1] *Behemoth ; or, The Long Parliament* (ed. Tönnies), p. 195.

hands of Oliver Cromwell with the title of ' Protector.'
Sixthly, from September the 3rd, 1658, to April the 25th,
1659, Richard Cromwell had it as successor to his father.
Seventhly, from April the 25th, 1659, to May the 7th of
the same year it was nowhere. Eighthly, from May the
7th, 1659, the Rump, which was turned out of doors in
1653, recovered it again, and shall lose it again to a
Committee of Safety and again recover it, and again lose
it to the right owner."

The history of the year 1659 from 7th May, therefore—
at which time my story opens—is largely the history of
the " fag end " of a House of Commons in coarse contempt
termed " the Rump." [1]

Again, answering the question of what this Assembly,
pretending to be a Parliament, really was, Hobbes says :

" It is doubtless an oligarchy. For the supreme
authority must be in one man or more. If in one it is
monarchy; the Rump therefore was no monarch. If the
authority were in more than one, it was in all, or in fewer
than all. When in all, it is democracy; for every man
may enter into the assembly which makes the sovereign
Court; which they could not do here. It is therefore
manifest, that the authority was in a few, and consequently
the State was an oligarchy."

This oligarchy, as is well known, at one time termed
itself the " Commonwealth of England." But the

---

[1] This term did not come into general use until 1659, though it was
asserted by Heath to have been conferred by Clement Walker, the
author of the *History of Independency*, in 1649. It, however, was
derived from the coarse jests told about Alderman Atkins, M.P. for
Norwich City from Nov. 10, 1645, one of the most unpopular members
of the Rump. These stories probably had no better foundation in
fact than the anagram of his surname. It would be a mistake to
suppress the explanation of this given in a pamphlet, published on
April 11, 1660, and entitled *Free Parliament Queries* (Thomason
tract E, 1019 (24)). " 30. Whether Atkins be the anagram of a stink,
or a stink of Atkins, etc., etc." Compare with this the anecdote of
Atkins in *Nicholas Papers*, iv. 197. A pamphlet devoted solely to
ridicule of Atkins appeared on June 14, 1648, as " Reverend Alderman
Atkins " (the full title is unquotable) " his speech."

majority of the members of the Parliament of England
were of the opinion that it was nothing of the kind. For,
said they, in their temperately worded " Apology," published in 1660, " the Commonwealth of England hath
been long interrupted," so that " the shadow and name
of a Commonwealth, all the essential parts of it being
condemned and vanished, hath been set up instead
thereof." [1]

An analysis of the membership of the House of Commons in 1659 amply justified the contention. The House
of Commons of the Long Parliament contained 508
members in all. Of these the Rump, in 1659, consisted
of 89 members and no more (for some who at one time or
another had sat with them now refused to do so any
longer). Out of this maximum of 89 " seldom 50 appeared
at once together."

Again, we find that 16 only of the members of the
Rump were " knights of shires," out of a total of 78 for
England and 12 for Wales. Twenty-six English and
eleven Welsh counties were totally unrepresented in the
Rump Parliament. Among these unrepresented counties
were such important shires as Essex, Bedford, Devon,
Cornwall, Middlesex and Oxford.[2] Others had but one
representative. Coming to the cities of the kingdom,
York, Westminster, Bristol, Canterbury, Chester, Exeter,
Oxford, Lincoln, Worcester, Chichester, Carlisle, Rochester,
Wells and Coventry had no members. And of its four
members, London was represented by but one; Norwich,

[1] *An Apologie and Vindication of the major part of the Members of Parliament, excluded from sitting and speaking for themselves and the Commonwealth.* Published Jan. 27, 1659/60 (Thomason tract E., 1013 (18)).
[2] I have taken my statistics from the very complete account given
in the book published on Jan. 30, 1660 (Thomason tract E, 1013 (22)),
and entitled *A Full Declaration of the True State of the Secluded Members*,
etc. Lists of names, etc., are given from p. 55 to the end of this tract.
Ludlow, in his Memoirs, untruthfully puts the total number of the
Rump at 150. None of the many printed lists ever put the total higher
than 129 *entitled to sit*, and of course these include people not entitled
to sit in the House of Commons at all.

the second city in the kingdom, also having but one member. A still closer analysis proves that the bulk of the members of the oligarchy had been elected between the years 1645 and 1648, most of them through intimidation of the electors by the Army.[1]

Ever since Pride's Purge in 1648 the key to power had reposed in the Army of 10,000 horse and 20,000 foot, by which the nation was ruled by main force. Nominally the servant of the Rump, it was really its master, and in the end in 1653 its general, Cromwell, had treated the Rump with contempt. Now it was without a General, and had reinstalled the Rump. We must search a little deeper, therefore, for an explanation of the root cause of the renewed quarrels between the Rump and its Army in 1659, and for the reason why the Army steadfastly refused to be disbanded.

This can be briefly stated in one word—money !

The rates of pay received by the Army, quite apart from its " free quarter " and other exactions from time to time, were simply outrageous. A Colonel of a foot regiment received, in all, 45s. a day—somewhere about £3500 a year in our money. A Lieutenant-Colonel received 30s. a day, and a Major 24s. If these officers were " lobsters " or " ironsides," as the regiments of horse were nicknamed, they each received an additional allowance of 21s. a day for six horses each. Even a Captain received 24s. a day, with the additional 21s. if his regiment was one of horse.[2] No wonder so many Parliament men obtained commands in the Army.

[1] In Dec. 1648 Pride's Purge at first left 46 members in the Commons, of whom not more than 26 (according to Sir Orlando Bridgeman, who presided at the trial of the regicides in 1660) or 27 (according to Philip Henry, the nonconformist, and father of Matthew Henry, the biblical commentator) could be found to vote an " Act " for trial of the King. " The King can be tried by no Court," said the republican Algernon Sidney, to Cromwell, " and this Court " [that is, the pretended " high court of justice "] " can try no man." ·

[2] The rates of pay are stated in Sir Thomas May's *Arbitrary Government displayed to the life, in the tyrannic usurpation of a Juncto of Men*

THE ARMY

No wonder, also, that, as a result of the confusion the recent political changes had brought about, the Army's pay was in arrear. A career in the Army offered to penniless adventurers, as well as to the fanatics by whom it was officered, the easiest possible means of accumulating a fortune rapidly. Skippon, one of Cromwell's " Major-Generals," of whom the satirists said that " Godliness was great gain," for he had obtained the Manor of Acton, Middlesex, and incidentally " acquired " most of the Guildhall plate, was originally a waggoner in Vere's Army in the Low Countries. Thomas Pride, notorious for " Pride's Purge," was a Sedgemoor swineherd, who had found fortune in London as drayman to Robert Triplet, a brewer of Islington (still living in 1649) and could neither read nor write. Another Colonel, Hewson, infamous for the butcheries at Drogheda, was commonly described as a " translator of old boots," or cobbler. Colonel Okey was a brewer's stoker.[1]

---

called the Rump Parliament (first edition 1682), p. 96. May was Recorder of Chichester and member for that city in James II's Parliament. In the last edition of his book, printed in 1690, he drew a parallel between James II's standing Army and that of Cromwel and the Rump.

Under Cromwell, the rates of pay, though excessive, were lower. According to a tract published in February 1658, and entitled "*A Narrative of the late Parliament (so-called). . . . With an account of the places of profit, salaries, etc.*" (E 935 (5)), a Colonel of horse received £474 10s. and a Colonel of foot £365 per annum. Nothing was said about the allowance for horses.

The "Articles" signed by Cromwell on Jan. 2, 1654, contained a proviso for a "standing army" of 30,000. A pamphlet entitled *The Unhappy Marksman ; or, 23 Queries*, published on June 13, 1659, inquired : "Whether any accomptant be able to compute which of the two, viz. the maintenance of the kingly office, or 30 thousand soldiers, be most chargeable to a nation." There seem to have been thirty regiments in all.

[1] " Of a famous brewer my purpose is to tell,
        Now mighty roaring Oliver and Pride are gone to Hell,
        The Noble stoker Okey, that doth the rest excel,
        And give him more ale and grains."

("Colonel John Okie's lamentation. To the tune of ' A begging we will go.' " Published March 26, 1660.)

This list might be multiplied to infinity, if it were possible to ascertain the antecedents of the minor officers, but it is quite evident that men of these classes, pleased with their fine clothes and the (to them) unlimited supplies of cash and opportunities for plunder their new occupations afforded, were plastic material in the hands of a really gifted and cunning leader like Cromwell.

The actual heads of the Army, in 1659, were second-rate men compared with Cromwell, " Major-General " Fleetwood, the " Weeping Anabaptist," was a poor creature—a fanatic whose rise to power is in great part explained by his marriage to Cromwell's daughter. He was not a regicide and fell into oblivion after the King's return. Desborough, a Cambridgeshire farmer and Fifth Monarchy man, owed his position as " Major-General " to his marriage with Cromwell's sister. The only Army leader who was not likely to play the rôle of the Ass in the Lion's skin was Major-General Lambert, a gentleman by birth, endowed with a keen intellect, one who was not a regicide and who was never identified with any of the sects of the times. Indeed, he (untruthfully it

---

As regards Thomas Pride, his " signature " to the death warrant of Charles I should be noticed, only the two letters " th " being formed. At the end of 1649, three men in his regiment were sentenced to " run the gauntlet " for " forging his mark." He obtained the monopoly of the supply of beer to Cromwell's Army, and (as appears from his will, proved in 1658, and still preserved at Somerset House), had obtained the King's park of "Nonsuch," Surrey. His brewhouse was at Brentford. His chaplain was Samuel Oates, the infamous father of a still more infamous son, Titus Oates.

Cromwell's father purchased a brewery, and his mother brewed and sold beer at Huntingdon. So also did most of his ancestors on his father's side. See, in this connexion, Miss Louise Imogen Guiney's article on " Cromwell's nickname, the Brewer," in the *Dublin Review* for April 1914. A licensed news-book—the *Moderate Intelligencer* for March 22–29, 1654, remarked, " His highness the lord protector being not very well takes the morning ayr often; he lies again at the Cockpit, but intends ere long for his new palace (Whitehall) as soon as all things can be made ready for him. The old trade still goes on, and *a brew house is erecting*." The writer appears to have been punished for this. (Cal. S. P. Dom., 1654.)

would seem) was said to have ended as a " Papist."[1] Lambert was a brilliant soldier who had won the respect and affection of his men. He had been living in retirement at Wimbledon for some time past, but was now recalled to the Army, and thus free to give full play to his ambition to follow in Cromwell's footsteps.

The Army now had no " General," with power to appoint or cashier officers at his own will, and the Rump was determined it never should have one again. This was the first bone of contention between the Rump and the Army. The second and by far the most important issue was the question of the militia. The Army sat upon the back of the nation, like the old man of the sea, strangling the life out of it. The Rump was determined to get rid of the Army by gradually substituting a militia in its stead. On the other hand, the Army did not intend to be disbanded and was determined not to be deprived of its easily earned pay.

The whole quarrel between the Army and the Rump, therefore, soon resolved itself into the questions of " A general or no general," and of the control of the militia. And in the background was a strongly Presbyterian city which loathed both the Army and the Rump, and yet would have to find the cash for both.

It is not possible to understand either the history of the Rump Parliament or, indeed, of the plots during the whole of the reign of Charles II without some knowledge of the political history of the congeries of sects known loosely, and perhaps inaccurately, as the anabaptists. The question of baptism played no part in the political history of these sects, and to term them Baptists is to obscure the history of the time and to bring a modern

[1] Lambert died a prisoner on St. Nicholas Island, Plymouth, in March, 1684, and was buried on the 28th (*News-letter of 1st April*, 1684). Oates involved him in his Popish Plot.

denomination into disrepute.[1] The terminology of the times must be adopted, with the whole of its connotation and denotation.

No statistics about them are available, but the facts prove that the anabaptists largely officered Cromwell's Army, and there can be no doubt whatever that in the year 1659 they formed the dominant sect in the Army. Most (though not all) of the anabaptists and many of the other sects were " Fifth Monarchy Men." [2] Here again no statistics are available, and in but few cases can it be proved how far individual believers in this latter religion put into practice the worst of its doctrines.

The Fifth Monarchists literally interpreted the prophecies in the Book of Daniel to mean that the four great monarchies of Antichrist were those of Assyria, Persia, Greece and Rome, and that they were to be succeeded by a fifth monarchy: the reign of Christ on earth for a thousand years. As a speculation, or heresy, this opinion is nowadays of little interest to the general reader, who will be inclined to conclude with Butler, that " Nothing comes so near the Kingdom of Darkness as the Fifth Monarchy, that is nowhere to be found but in dark prophecies, obscure mythologies and mystical riddles, like the visions Æneas saw in Hell of the Roman Empire."[3]

It is in the fact that the anabaptists were the propagators of this opinion, and in the unexpectedly horrible use they were prepared to make of it, that the whole interest of their story lies. For they concluded that

[1] This is the mistake made by Miss Louise F. Brown in her *The Political Activities of the Baptists* [sic] *and Fifth Monarchy Men in England during the Interregnum*, published in 1912. This writer's knowledge of the tracts of the times was necessarily limited, and her work is very misdescriptive.

[2] Thus, even Thomas Goodwin, a blameless divine who has been claimed as a Congregationalist, published a sermon on the Fifth Monarchy, in 1654, in which he asserted that it must come in " by the sword."

[3] Samuel Butler's " *Characters and Passages from his Note-books* (ed. A. R. Waller) : Character of a Fifth Monarchy Man."

this fifth monarchy was to come into being at once, after the destruction by themselves of all that they held to be typified by the Church of Rome, that is to say, not merely the Papacy but also the " Prelatists " and even the " Presbyterians " and regular clergy of all sects. All magistrates and ministers who would not comply with them were to be put to the sword all over the world. Then their own rule, the rule of the self-styled " Saints," would begin and there would be no need for laws or ordinances of any kind for a thousand years; for the " Saints " could not sin, all that they did being under the direction of the " light within."

The world had already seen what the anabaptist millennium meant in actual practice. As the result of the introduction of Protestantism into his city of Münster, in Westphalia, in 1533, by Franz von Waldeck, bishop and temporal lord of the city, the anabaptists from Holland obtained control of the town through Bernard Rothmann, a chaplain, and Knipperdolinck, a cloth merchant of the city. After a few months these were joined by two Dutchmen, Jan Matthiessen, a baker, and Jan Bockold, a tailor, of Leyden, commonly called John of Leyden. Knipperdolinck was elected burgomaster in February 1534, and the quartette of miscreants then initiated their millennium. Münster was renamed the " New Jerusalem " or " New Sion," John of Leyden was proclaimed king, and communism, polygamy and community of women were enforced. John of Leyden took to himself sixteen wives (one of whom he beheaded in the market-place) and Rothmann four. A reign of terror then began. All the literary and art treasures of the city were destroyed and indescribable orgies took place. The bishop had been compelled to call other temporal princes to his aid and to besiege his own city in 1534, and when John of Leyden found that his tenure of it was becoming desperate, he decided to set fire to it and destroy the town. Fortunately, Münster was delivered from this fate by its unexpected capture, after a bloody assault, on June 24, 1535. John of Leyden, Knipperdolinck and their Chancellor Krechting were seized, and after being imprisoned and tortured for six months, they were put to death and their bodies hung in iron cages on the steeple of the Lamberti-kirche. The steeple has since been rebuilt, but the cages were replaced and can still be seen upon it.[1]

Many of the Dutch anabaptists, including some refugees from Münster, fled into England. Henry VIII burnt some of them and Elizabeth executed others, but their subsequent history is obscure.[2] In the Civil Wars the anabaptists came out into the light again. The murder of Charles I, and Cromwell's massacres of Irish Papists at Drogheda and Wexford, proclaimed the Fifth Monarchy Men, were evidence that their millennium was at hand and that the Rump was to initiate it. At the end of 1649, therefore, John Spittlehouse dedicated his work on this subject to the Rump's then " Council of State." This was entitled *Rome ruined by Whitehall ; or, The Papall Crown demolished ; containing a confutation of*

---

[1] Full accounts of the Münster anabaptists have been printed in German. C. A. Cornelius published his *Geschichte des Münsterschen Aufruhrs* at Leipzig in 1855 (Vol. I.) and 1860 (Vol. II.). Dr. Ludwig Keller's *Geschichte der Wiedertäufer und ihres Reichs zu Munster* was published at Münster in 1880, and Bahlmann's *Widertäufer zu Münster* at Munster in 1894. The Presbyterians published a number of pamphlets about Münster, by way of warning against the English anabaptists. A little book published on March 28, 1661, after Venner's rising (Thomason tract E, 1086 (1)), and entitled *Semper Iidem ; or, A Parallel betwixt the Ancient and Modern Phanaticks*, contains a large number of quotations from ancient chronicles, and these (in refreshing contrast to most of the writers of the times) the author has duly referenced. See also Janssens' *History of the German People at the close of the Middle Ages* (ed. Christie, Vol. V.).

[2] The chief authorities are Richard Blome's *The Fanatick History ; or, An exact relation and accompt of the old Anabaptists and New Quakers* (1660), and Ephraim Pagitt's *Heresiography* (sixth edition, 1662). In his *Beam of Light*, published on May 2, 1659, Christopher Feake sketched the past history of his sect from 1640 onwards. Edwards's *Gangraena* is largely devoted to the anabaptists.

FRONTISPIECE TO ROME RUINED BY WHITEHALL.

(From a copy at the British Museum)

Papacy, Prelacy, and Presbitery. The engraved frontispiece to this book is worth noticing, and the whole proves plainly the measure of toleration the anabaptists wished to be meted out to these three forms of religion. They soon found that the oligarchy had every intention of perpetuating itself after its conquest of Ireland and Scotland and, therefore, hailed Cromwell as the inaugurator of their millennium, when he and the notorious anabaptist, Thomas Harrison, turned out the Rump in 1653 and set up Barebone's Parliament in their stead.[1]

But, on February 28, 1650, a number of ministers of the anabaptist congregations who, very properly, objected to the immoral teaching and practices of some of the Fifth Monarchy Men, thought it their duty to publish a manifesto against them in the shape of a " General Epistle," signed, amongst others, by William Kiffen and Thomas Patient. Kiffen is remembered because he was a wealthy City merchant who afterwards was on friendly terms with Charles II; so much so that the King endeavoured to obtain a loan of £40,000 from him. Kiffen made the King a present of £10,000 and afterwards boasted that he had saved £30,000. Patient—or Patience—was co-pastor with Kiffen, after the Restoration, of the Devonshire Square " conventicle." These two, with fourteen other but not so well known preachers,[2] signed

---

[1] Thomas Harrison, a " Major-General," was the son of a butcher at Newcastle-under-Lyme. Coming to London he became clerk to one Hulker, an attorney of Clifford's Inn (brother-in-law of Richard Smythe of the " Obituary "). He married the daughter of a " Colonel Harrison " of the City of London, by whom he had had an illegitimate child (*A Paire of Spectacles for the City,* Dec. 4, 1647; *Mercurius Elencticus* for Dec. 25–Jan. 4, 1648-9). Hence, in all the satires of the times he is termed " Noverint Universi," because he had " taken bond " for the woman's marriage to himself. At the capture of Basing in 1645, finding that three prisoners who had surrendered to him were players, Harrison murdered all three in cold blood, remarking, " Cursed be he that doeth the work of the Lord negligently."

[2] This " General Epistle," was headed *Heart-bleedings for Professors' Abominations* (Thomason tract E, 594 (13)), and the signatories were " John Spilsbury, William Consett, Tho. Waters, Thomas Patience,

the "General Epistle" of 1650. No specific mention of
the Fifth Monarchy Men was made in this epistle, probably because the signatories themselves were not prepared
to say that the millennium was not about to take place.
But they definitely disowned the practices of their own
followers. The epistle accused the millenarians of
teaching that they were "perfect and as in as happy an
estate as could be," and said that they alleged that man's
light was his only law; "that is to say, whatever that
Spirit which dwells therein (which they call God within)
dictates to them, that ought to be done by them." As
a result "they follow the law of their own mind," and
"whatever their evil hearts were naturally inclined to"
they put into practice, even murder, adultery, and similar
crimes. They added, "It is a great mistake to judge
that these persons were all of our societies, for this we can
clearly evince, that many if not most of them were not
members with us." [1] Thus the anabaptist doctrine of

William Kiffen, Edw. Drapes, Hen. Forry, John Pearson, Solomon
Saffery, John Vernon, Tho. Young, Ralph Francis, Hugh Gosnell,
Theo. Vane, John Watson and Joseph Sanson."

[1] I believe that this is the first occasion in which attention has been
drawn to this tract. It clearly separates the modern "baptists"
from the anabaptists. For the actual trial of a "perfect" Saint by
Fairfax, for adultery, acknowledged by him to have been dictated by
the "light within," see the trial of Lieut. William Jackson, set out by
Mr. C. H. Firth in the Appendix to his *Cromwell's Army*. In 1651,
Christoph Arnold, a German, wrote a letter from London to a friend
at Nuremberg in which he says : "The enthusiasts and fanatics hold
their exercises of private piety on the Lord's Day in the evening when
sermon is over. This week I have heard four workmen of this order of
preachers in an obscure street called S. Laurence Lane near the Thames,
vulgarly nicknamed the street of the heretics, who call themselves
eminent (κατ' ἐξοχην) Christians. At a place called Clerkenwell Green,
near the City, the Ranters, whom I consider to be real schismatics or
breakers of religion, have been imprisoned. These people call their
fellows not a man but a 'fellow-creature.' There also is that blas-
phemer whose wife is about to bring forth the Messiah; another has
joined to himself a certain maid who is to be the mother of the Author
of our salvation, and commends her in a wonderful manner to all who
come to see her." Arnold then goes on to describe other Chiliasts at
some length (Georg Richter's *Epistolæ Selectiores* (Nuremberg, 1662,
p. 488). Compare with this *A List of some of the Grand Blasphemers
and Blasphemies, which was given in to the Committee for Religion,*

the " light within " had very different results from that of the Quakers, and it is not surprising to find that the two sects were continually in conflict.[1]

Some mad blasphemers announced that this or that woman was about to give birth to the King of the Millennium. One of these sects, termed the " Ranters," had its headquarters in Clerkenwell, and there John Robins, in 1651, proclaimed himself the Ranters' " God," and asserted that his wife Joan was about to bring forth the New Messiah.[2]

Barebone's Parliament, many, if not most, of whose members were fanatics of this type, was hailed with delight by the anabaptists, and the chief step taken by it to further the millennium was the institution of civil marriage. For the solemn vows taken before a minister of religion a bare " promise " before a Justice of the Peace was substituted, it being declared that no other marriage should be valid. The " promise " in the case of the man was to be " loving and faithful," and for a woman to be " loving, faithful and obedient." Thus, in the eyes of the common people, Christian marriage had been abolished—with the inevitable results. Numbers of bastard children were murdered by their mothers, and so great did the evil become that in 1655 the Lord Mayor ordered a precept on the subject to be read in all the

---

published as a broadside on March 23, 1654 (Thomason tract 669, f. 17 (80)). This tract contains the names of a number of women preachers who were about to give birth to the New Messiah. It has never been quoted.

[1] A good example of these controversies is Edward Burrough, the Quaker's, " Something in answer to a book called ' Choice Experiences.' Given forth by J. Turner." See also the tracts exchanged between Martin Mason and Jonathan Johnson.

[2] The tracts published about this sect abound in offensive details and are sometimes illustrated with objectionable illustrations. See *The Routing of the Ranters* (Nov. 19, 1650); *The Ranters Ranting*, with examinations of some of them (Dec. 2, 1650); and John Holland's *Smoke of the Bottomless Pit*. Many tracts about them were printed at this time.

churches of London, on Sunday, February 11, together
with the Statute against child murder of 21 James I.[1]

By 1658 the crime had increased to such an extent that
a writer seriously proposed to Cromwell that he should
introduce polygamy as a remedy.[2] Every assize, said he,
with perfect truth, recorded the murders of children by
their own unnatural mothers, and then suggested that
the fathers should be allowed to legitimatize them, by
the introduction of polygamy, pointing out as an inducement how the Turks had extended their empire by this
means. " You shall want no other Ram to batter the
walls of Rome," added he, foreshadowing a final victory
over the Papists if polygamy was introduced. On
June 22, 1658, Cromwell ordered a committee to " consider of the book concerning polygamy," and to report.[3]
No disapproval was expressed and the report did not
afterwards transpire.

When, therefore, Barebone's Parliament came to an

---

[1] This precept is set out in full in " Severall Proceedings " for
February 8–15, 1654/5, and the Statute is annexed to it. When the
news-books of the times detailed proceedings at Assizes, as they
invariably did when news was scanty, cases of murder of bastard
children continually appeared in them.

[2] *A Remedy for Uncleanness ; or, Certain Queries propounded to his
Highness the Lord Protector*, etc. " By a Person of Quality." Published on June 14, 1658.

[3] Cal. S. P. Dom., 1658–1659, p. 71. I need hardly draw attention
to the hypocritical " Adultery Act " of the Rump, carried through,
as the Commons Journals prove, by the aid of Marten and other
members of like character, for this was exposed by the late Mr. Inderwick, Q.C., in his *Studies in the Interregnum*. The solitary conviction
Mr. Inderwick could find, and for which he inspected the Somerset
records, was that of a woman convicted of adultery with a " priest,"
and Mr. Inderwick made the mistake of thinking that this meant
" seminary priest." But this case was reported in one of the news-
books, as the date proves, and the " priest " was probably a Presbyterian, to which class of ministers the term " priest " was more usually
applied than to a Prelatist. The *Weekly Intelligencer of the Commonwealth*, No. 1, for July 16–23, 1650, p. 7, reports it as follows :

" July 20. By letters from Somersetshire it was this day advertised
that a woman was there indicted (according to the late Act) for incon-
tinence with a priest, who had heretofore been displaced from his
Rectorship for his scandalous life. The Jury found her guilty, and
she stands convicted according to the Act." This news-book was
Presbyterian in tone.

end and it was realized that Cromwell had taken all power into his own hands, and that he intended that no further " reformation " should take place, the anabaptists considered him as an enemy, and openly advocated his destruction. Cromwell's supervision of the Press was as effective as it was severe, and it is probable, therefore, that the first Fifth Monarchy manifesto at this time was issued in manuscript. This professed to be the explanation of an allegorical engraving (which has not been traced) entitled the " Panther Prophecy," and was first circulated at the end of 1653 or beginning of 1654. The objects of this document were to advocate the extermination of the magistrates and of the clergy of the times and the destruction by fire of the City of London.[1] The tract was printed or reprinted in 1662, and again, in Holland, in 1688. Personal " revelations," therefore, became the order of the day, and at this time one of the most dangerous fanatics of this type was Anna Trapnell, the " prophetess." Fired by the example of Christopher Feake, one of their leading preachers, who had composed a " hymn," in 1653, forecasting the triumph of the " Saints "—to the glory of Barebone's Assembly [2]—this

[1] The British Museum contains a copy of both the editions of 1662 and of 1688 (" Het gezight van den Panther "). From these it appears that the author was Owen Lloyd, who communicated his " vision " to John Rogers in 1653 (or 1654). The later version of the tract, therefore, is catalogued under " Owen Lloyd."

[2] "With cheerful spirits raised to Heaven
We sing our song of praise.
For generations past the Saints
Saw no such blessed days.
How pleasant are the days of joy
To Sion's children all;
With trembling we rejoice to see
Proud Babylon downfall.

" A new sharp threshing instrument
With teeth make Mount Sion,
And let the meek worm Jacob now
Be as a strong Lion,

madwoman now specialized in " extempore " hymns.
When Cromwell assumed the style of " Protector " she
came to the house of one Roberts, who kept an " ordinary "
(or restaurant) at the entrance to Whitehall, and remained
there for a whole fortnight, existing on toast and small
beer and indulging in extempore hymns, sung, no doubt,
to extempore tunes.   Her doggerel rimes were taken
down by her followers and printed.   No doubt Cromwell,
as he went in and out of Whitehall, must have heard
this weird performance going on.[1]   Her discourses are
" desperate " against you and your government, wrote
Marchamont Nedham to Cromwell on Feb. 7, 1654.
When, however, she travelled as far afield as Cornwall,
endeavouring to stir up the people, Cromwell had her
arrested and sent her to Bridewell to be flogged.   This
seems to have ended her career.   Nevertheless, she found
successors in her art of extempore hymn singing, for
Mr. Broderick, writing to Clarendon on June 24, 1659,
told him that Lord Pembroke, the Chief Justice St. John's
wife and others were accustomed to meet three times a
week in order to sing extempore in rime, and that,
basing themselves upon a passage in the Book of Revelation, they blasphemed and cursed for a time, then preserved silence for half an hour, before the person who,

---

The tyrants of the earth to tear,
Their power to take away,
The Dragon, Beast, the False Prophet
In the Lord's strength to slay."

(George Thomason's MS. in E. 710 (13). This is headed " Mr. Feakes
hymne.   August ye 4th, 1653.   Christ Church."   Several verses in
denunciation of the Dutch follow.)

[1] Trapnell's tracts, containing autobiographical matter as well as
her rimes (which I forbear from inflicting upon my readers) were
as follows : *The Cry of a Stone* (Jan. 7, 1654), *Strange and Wonderful
Newes from Whitehall* (March 11, 1654), and *A Legacy for Saints* (July
24, 1654).   All these were published by Thomas Brewster.   See more
of her in *Severall Proceedings* for Jan. 12–19, 1654, and the Calendars
of Domestic State Papers under the dates of July 25, 1653; Feb. 7,
1654; April 7, 1654; June 2, 1654; and July 26, 1654.

they supposed, was inspired commenced extempore hymn singing.[1]

To such a pass was the Christian religion brought by the Rump's " Reformation."

Not without reason did the old English rime run :

> " Tack tent to my saw, my sonnes three,
> Rob, Will and Tavy.
> Keepe well your ' Pater ' and your ' Ave,'
> And if your mind your fathers reed
> Stand close to your old creed.
> But for my daughter Gyllion,
> I wad shee were well bolted with a bridle,
> That leaves her warke to play the Clarke
> And lets her wheele stand idle.
> For it sawes not for shee Ministers,
> Farriers, nor Furriers,
> Cobblers nor Button-makers
> To descant on the Bible." [2]

In 1657 the Fifth Monarchy Men decided once more that the time predicted for their millennium had arrived (after some slight disagreement about the exact month), and made their chief meeting-place in Swan Alley, Coleman Street, where Thomas Venner, a wine cooper, was the chief preacher. Eventually, April 9 was fixed as the day, a standard was prepared with a red lion "couchant" on it, and the text "Who shall rouse him up?" and a manifesto signed by the Secretary of their Army, or "Scribe," as they termed him, William Medley, Venner's son-in-law. This was printed and published as "A Standard set up, whereunto the true seed and Saints of the Most High may be gathered together." [3] It is

[1] Clarendon's State Papers, III. pp. 505–6. St. John is said to have built his new house out of the stones of Peterborough Minster, which he commenced to pull down (*Arsy Versy ; or, The Second Martyrdom of the Rump*, published on March 23, 1659/60).

[2] Quoted by Richard Brathwaite, in his *Mercurius Britannicus ; or, The English Intelligencer. A tragi-comedy*, printed in 1641, as " that old and wittie rhime commonly chanted in the Isle of Britaine."

[3] Thomason tract, E. 910 (10). Thomason's date to this is May 17, which does not seem to be correct. Perhaps he could not obtain it before this date. A full account of this rising appears in Mr. C. H. Firth's *Last Years of the Protectorate*, Vol. I. pp. 208–17. Many details and lists of prisoners can be gathered from *Mercurius Politicus*, for April 16–23, 1657. See also the Commons Journals and Thurloe State Papers.

unnecessary to describe the document further than to
note that it termed Cromwell " an apostate and a mur-
derer " and ordered his destruction. Cromwell's spy
system was the most perfect ever seen, and he had been
aware from the first of all that was going on. All the
leaders, including Harrison, Lawson (an admiral), Rich
and Danvers, with many minor " Saints," were imprisoned and the affair was nipped in the bud. Thus
the " Saints " had perforce to postpone their millennium.
They had made a mistake in the date for its inception.

Two anabaptist ministers, both of them Fifth Monarchy
Men, do not seem to have been imprisoned by Cromwell
but became very prominent by their printed publications in 1659 and 1660. The first was John Canne, the
biblical commentator, who became a journalist in 1659,
and the second Henry Jessey, who issued lying and
seditious tracts in 1660.

" Old Father Canne,
    That Reverend Man,"

as the " Psalm of Mercy," in a lampoon of 1661,[1] terms him,
was an educated man, but, unfortunately, no trustworthy
account of his birthplace and antecedents has come to
light, with the exception of some information about his
ministrations to an English congregation at Amsterdam
previous to the Great Rebellion.

On June 13, 1653, in anticipation of Barebone's Parliament, John Canne had written *A Voice from the Temple
to the Higher Powers*, dedicating it to Cromwell and to
Colonel Overton—then a Fifth Monarchy man—in which
he " explained " the prophecies of the Book of Daniel,

---

[1] The " Psalm of Mercy—Sing it in the Nose " was printed at the
end of a tract entitled *The Holy Sisters' Conspiracy against their husbands
and the City of London, designed at their last farewell of their meeting in
Coleman Street* (Thomason tract E, 1055 (20)), published on Jan. 26,
1661, after Venner's rising. This scurrilous tract is some indication
that Canne may have been the writer of Venner's manifesto entitled
" The Door of Hope."

to mean that the fifth monarchy was about to begin, and asserted on unconvincing grounds that there was no parallel between his sect and the anabaptists of Münster. He added that the " Ancient of Days " had " set up his throne in England by the dissolution of the late Parliament."

His views upon " tolleration " were that everyone was to be " tollerated " who was not a Papist, Prelatist, Royalist, or Presbyterian.   So he was in favour of " tolleration " for all sects, however much they differed. As the vast majority of the educated people of England belonged more or less to the parties excluded from toleration, it is quite evident that " tolleration " was something utterly opposed to religious toleration as we know it.

And on August 15 in the same year John Canne published his *Second Voice from the Temple*, dedicated to Barebone's Parliament. This practically ordered them to take away all decrees of Popes and Popish institutions. Amongst the latter he reckoned (1) the National Ministry of the Church of England, even as it was then, and (2) Tithes, by which it was maintained.   Finally, he contended that in lieu of regular ministers everybody should be allowed to preach, even though he or she possessed no qualifications at all.   Thus the " tolleration " of which we hear so much in 1659 meant toleration for all sects, however squalid or immoral, and the destruction of all forms of the Christian Church, Catholic or Protestant, as the nation had up to that time known them.

The career of Henry Jessey or " Jacie " (as he sometimes spelt his name), on the other hand, is well known but has not been accurately described.   Jessey graduated from St. John's College, Cambridge, in 1623, was ordained and obtained preferment, but was deprived of his living in 1634 for nonconformity.   It has been suggested that Jessey was not a Fifth Monarchy Man, but of this there can be no doubt whatever, for he was one of the preachers at the Coleman Street meeting-house in Swan Alley,[1] reserved entirely for the Fifth Monarchy sect. A true appreciation of Jessey's character can only be obtained by perusing the tracts written by him in 1660.

After the defeat by Cromwell of their projected rising of 1657, a fresh date had to be fixed for the millennium. The first word of warning to his sect to be ready was given by Christopher Feake in his *Beam of Light*, published on May 2, 1659. He told them to " wait the word of Command " from their Leader " to execute the vengeance written against Babylon," and concluded his tract with " You are invited to be in a readiness and at an hour's warning," for, so he said, the Fifth Monarchy was about to begin.

Great alarm was caused by this incitement to indiscriminate slaughter. "An Alarum to the City and Soldiery " was issued on June 6, printed as a broadside and placarded about the City :

" The Fifth Monarchy Men are armed, officered and every man in a readiness to surprise and suppress the Army, to fire the City and to massacre all considerable people of all sorts, whom they suspect averse to what they impiously designed," ran this poster. " Feake hath lately given them the alarum in print; Sir Henry Vane

[1] Marchamont Nedham (in the original of his letter to Cromwell, dated Feb. 7, 1654, summarized on p. 393 of the Calendar of Domestic State Papers) says that after the arrest of the two leading Fifth Monarchy preachers, Feake and Simpson, of All Hallows, he attended the meeting there on the sixth, and that the three preachers who took their places were " Highland, John Spencer and Mr. Jessey, these (your highness knows) are no Boanerges men (and men) that carry no thunderbolts." He added that though " the bellows seem (comparatively) to blow but very gently, yet I perceive it keeps the coales alive, and the humours boiling which were first heated by others." After a description of the sermons of Highland and Spencer, who prayed for the two fellow-sufferers and talked of " serving up the flesh of Captains at the great feast of the Lord," he concluded, " Mr. Jessey being a soft low man, I could not hear him in the crowd and departed."

is chief in the design. . . . Beware Tuesday next, we say, Beware ! "

On the third of June the Royalist Major Wood had written as follows :

" Three days since, about 5000 of the Fifth Monarchy men met at Horsham in Sussex, and dispersed after eight hours' consultation. There are two or three thousand of them well armed, and officers appointed to every thousand and every hundred; Harrison is their General and Vane their Chancellor : they say they must begin at the altar and with fire and sword prepare the coming of Christ. We daily expect a massacre; it was deferred this week and is to be performed again Tuesday night next. Sometimes the redcoats and they are agreed, and the next hour at difference. It's like they may go on in this massacre, and Lambert may advance it, since it is but a few days ago he said that there would be no settlement till all the Cavaliers' throats were cut." [1]

Add to this the warnings given that a rising of the " Papists " was to be expected, with the same results, namely, the firing of the City and the cutting of the throats of the Protestants.

Jeffery Corbet had already announced this in his *England's Warning Piece*, published in 1654, and on Nov. 8, 1656, had issued another caution, printed as a broadside and entitled *The Protestants' Warning Piece*. Both these tracts were based on Prynne's " Romes Masterpeece," and both served to keep before the affrighted minds of the people of London, the fact that the firing of the City and the destruction of orthodox religion (as it was then understood) was contemplated by one sect or the other. There is no better reason to be offered why such a plot in the days of Titus Oates must have seemed probable in the eyes of the average Englishman.

[1] Clarendon's State Papers, III. 479.

The design of the Fifth Monarchy men to fire the City and set on foot a general massacre was, of course, denied in the news-books, *Mercurius Politicus* and the *Publick Intelligencer*. But (as I shall prove later on) the news-books were, at the time of these denials, written by John Canne, and therefore their denials may be dismissed as worthless.

Had the Presbyterian and Royalist rising planned for August 1659 really taken place, there can be no doubt that the Fifth Monarchy men, probably with the complicity of the Rump, would have set on foot a general massacre, as the means for the introduction of their millennium. It is to the credit of General Monck, who must have been perfectly well aware of all this, that he sternly discountenanced all attempts for a rising, and thus frustrated all opportunities of putting counter-measures into effect. When these facts are all borne in mind the history of the events of the year 1659 will be better understood.

CHAPTER II

THE " REPRESENTATIVE "

O N Saturday, May 7, 1659, the oligarchy, expelled
by Cromwell in 1653, returned to power once
more at the invitation of the Army whose General
had turned it out. At the summons of Speaker Lenthall,
such members of the so-called " Commonwealth " as
could be got together assembled, in the first instance, in
the Painted Chamber of the Houses of Parliament. Of
all that followed on that day we have three accounts,
two in printed pamphlets published within a week or
two, and written respectively by Arthur Annesley, afterwards Earl of Anglesey, and by Prynne; and another
in a letter written by Mr. Miles, Sir Edward Nicholas's
" intelligencer." [1]

Prynne tells us that there were then " about eighty
secluded members " of the Long Parliament in London
and Westminster; " being near double the number of
those sitting that day, and above three hundred members
of all sorts still living, chosen, or sitting in the House of
Commons, before December 1648, over and above those
that now sate."

A slight initial difficulty proved the wisdom of the
preliminary meeting in the Painted Chamber. Forty
members were essential in order to form a " quorum "

---

[1] *England's Confusion*, a pamphlet published anonymously on May 30,
1659, but written by Annesley (Halkett and Laing's *Dictionary of
Anonymous and Pseudonymous Literature of Great Britain*), and *Loyalty
Banished*, published on June 16, 1659, by Prynne.   Miles's letter is
in the recently published fourth volume of the *Nicholas Papers*, p. 134.

of the House of Commons, and apart from the Speaker, forty members were not present. So the assembled members sent an order to the gaols for the liberation of two of their leaders who happened to be in prison under execution for debt. These were Harry Marten [1] and William, Viscount Monson, of Castlemaine in Ireland.

When Marten and Monson arrived, the total number of members present, including the Speaker, was forty-two, so failing to find any other mace, that from the Court of Chancery was borrowed, and with this at their head and with Lenthall and Monson leading them, the little band proceeded by two and two from the Painted Chamber into the House of Commons. Just like the animals into the Ark, wrote Miles to Nicholas, adding, " All of them say they return to the House by the Hand of God; but Marten was brought hither (in his blasphemous phrase) by *both* Hands."

During these proceedings Prynne, Annesley and others of the members of the House of Commons excluded in 1648 had been forcibly prevented from entering the House.

Probably no more scathing description of those who sat was ever penned than that which has been left us by one of their own paid writers—the poet, John Milton. The aberrations of genius are many, and Milton's conception of an ideal republic, ultimately to be evolved from the mock " Commonwealth," had led him to publish books in their favour which will always brand his name with infamy. He had scolded like a Billingsgate fishwife in

---

[1] On January 15, 1652, Thomas Gower wrote to John Langley as follows : " Heert, the Spanish Ambassador, is discontented at the carriage of most of the English ladies who were at his entertainment, and they as much at him, for giving the chief place and respect to Col. H. Martin's mistress . . . they are also much displeased at her for being finer and more bejewelled than any. . . . 'Tis no small argument of the greatness of the ' Hogen Mogen Heeren Staten ' of England that the Ambassador of the great Monarch of Spain should make such an entertainment for such a property belonging to one of the Parliament of England."—(*Hist. MSS. Comms. Fifth Report, App.*, p. 192.) Monson was a little man, and it was frequently said that his wife used to beat him for his infidelities to her.

their service, he had lied even on their behalf, and last of all, he, the advocate of the freedom of the Press from licensing, had actually licensed *Mercurius Politicus*.[1] The author of *Areopagitica* became a licenser of the Press for a year for the Rump.   Ten years after the Restoration, when he had had time to reflect and to consider how it came about that no republic had ever been set up, Milton pointed to the men he had supported as the cause of this.

" Liberty hath a sharp and double edge," wrote Milton in 1670, " fit only to be handled by just and virtuous men; to bad and dissolute it becomes a mischief unwieldy in their own hands; neither is it completely given but by them who have the happy skill to know what is grievance and unjust to a people and how to remove it wisely; what good laws are wanting and how to frame them substantially, that good men may enjoy the freedom which they merit and the bad the curb which they need. But to do this and to know these exquisite proportions, the heroic wisdom which is required, surmounted far the principles of these narrow politicians. . . . Hence did their victories prove as fruitless as their losses dangerous, and left them, still conquering, under the same grievances that men suffer, conquered; which was indeed unlikely to go otherwise, unless men more than vulgar bred up, as few of them were, in the knowledge of ancient and illustrious deeds, invincible against many and vain titles, impartial to friendships and relations, had conducted their affairs; but then, from the chapman to the retailer, many, whose ignorance was more audacious than the rest, were admitted with all their sordid rudiments to bear no mean sway among them, both in Church and State.

" From the confluence of all their errors, mischiefs and misdemeanours, what in the eyes of man could be

---

[1] During 1651. This is proved by the recently printed *Transcript of the Stationers' Registers*. John Hall (the minor poet), however, and not Nedham, was writing it at the time.

expected, but what befell those antient inhabitants [of Britain before the Conquest] whom they so much resembled? Confusion in the end." [1]

Of the men " bad," and " dissolute " or " sordid," present on that day, Marten, Monson, Thomas Scot, Nevill, Heveningham, Sir Peter Wentworth and Chaloner were representatives. They form a formidable minority (out of the forty-two) who were unfitted to lead in any religious reformation. And of mere " chapmen and retailers," disguised for the most part by military titles, who could not have possessed any idea of the " rudiments " of government, Salwey, the smart City apprentice recently set up in business as a grocer, Walton, the draper, who supplied the " blacks " for Cromwell's mock funeral, Dennis Bond, the City woollen-draper, Alderman Pennington, the fishmonger, Cornelius Holland, originally Sir Henry Vane's serving-man, John Jones, originally servant to Sir Thomas Middleton, but who married Cromwell's sister, were types of men hardly qualified to shape a new constitution for the Commonwealth of England. For there was not one man among them all who ever gave evidence of any real ability, even in his own calling.

[1] This passage of Milton's prose has a remarkable history. Originally written in 1671 as part of a character of the Long Parliament and the Assembly of Divines, and inserted by way of parallel in Book III. of his *History of Britain to the Conquest*, the licenser of the Press, Sir Roger l'Estrange, struck the whole parallel out, as he states, " out of tenderness to a Party " (the Presbyterians) " for some harshness " therein. (The Declaration of Indulgence was in contemplation at the time, and one of the Secretaries of State, to whom l'Estrange would naturally refer, was Sir John Trevor, who had Nonconformist leanings.) Philips, Milton's nephew, states that his uncle gave the passage struck out to Arthur Annesley, Earl of Anglesey. And it must have been by arrangement with l'Estrange, who, quite obviously wrote the preface, that the passage in question was issued by l'Estrange's publisher, Henry Brome, immediately after Charles II had crushed his last Parliament at Oxford in 1681. The title of the resulting tract is " Mr. John Milton's Character of the Long Parliament and Assembly of Divines in 1641. Omitted in his other works and never before printed and very seasonable for these times " (1681). There is a reprint of the whole tract in the Harleian Miscellany, Vol. V. pp. 576-9.

And the strong men, the real leaders of this motley band, were Sir Henry Vane, junior, the crack-brained advocate of a qualified " fifth monarchy " religion, Scot, and Sir Arthur Hesilrige, the " Church thief," a North-country territorial magnate who had possessed himself of most of the lands of the Bishopric of Durham, including the bishop's house and Manor of Bishop Auckland, and who had done his best to deface the Cathedrals of Wells and Bristol.[1] Hesilrige had most to lose if the oligarchy was to be ousted from power and compelled to refund the property it had stolen.

On the same day a " Committee of Safety " was appointed, part of which was selected from the Army leaders, but on May 14 this was replaced by a " Council of State." This Council consisted of twenty-one members, chosen from those sitting in the House of Commons, and of ten persons who were not members. Some of the latter refused to act.[2] Thus there was a legislative body sitting in the House of Commons and an administrative body sitting in Whitehall, termed the " Council of State."

In the meantime, the members sitting in the House of Commons, following the precedents set by themselves in the year 1649, flooded England with a " Declaration," printed as a broadside, to be attached to all the church doors throughout the kingdom.[3]

[1] Clarendon credits Vane with the ambition to be the King of the proposed millennium. Hesilrige's religious views were never prominent, but *University Queries*, published on June 6, 1659, asks, " Whether Sir Arthur Hesilrige ought not to invert the sentence, The zeal of Thy House hath eaten me up,' into, ' My zeal hath eaten up Thy House.' " Scot, like Marten, had no religion at all.

[2] The ten outsiders were John Bradshaw, Lambert, Desborough, Lord Fairfax, Berry (" the worst of Cromwell's Major-Generals, with the exception of Butler "), Anthony Ashley Cooper (" a gentleman too wise and honest to sit in such company "), Sir H. Townshend (" of too good an estate to be hazarded with such a crew "), Sir Robert Honeyhood (Vane's brother-in-law), Sir Archibald Johnston (" never advanced before Argyle till he came to England "), and Josiah Barners (Josias Berners) (" the fool of the play "). The comments are by Annesley.

[3] It is also set out in the Commons Journals.

They described themselves in this as having been
" blessed by the eminent favour and mercy of God,"
termed themselves the " Representative of the People,"
and complained that they had been " forced out of doors "
from 1653 up to that time.   But, they added, the officers
of the Army, calling to mind that the members thus
forced out " were assertors of the Good Old Cause, and
had a special presence of God with them," had, through
their leaders, the " Lord " Lambert, and the " Lord "
Fleetwood, invited them to return to their trust.   And
therefore they were resolved to " endeavour the settlement of this Commonwealth " without " a single person
[i. e. protector], Kingship, or House of Peers," and would
" carry on the Reformation " so much desired, to the
end that there might be " a godly and faithful magistracy
and ministry, to the glory and praise of our Lord " and
" to the reviving and making glad the hearts of the upright
in the Land."

A pamphleteer sarcastically asked, " Whether perfectly
to effect this long-expected work of Reformation it be
not very expedient to have all laws, ordinances, declarations, etc. tending thereto penned in a more intelligible
speech than English ? " [1]—and assuredly all the catch-
words of the times need a great deal of translation and
explanation.   One fact, however, can be recorded to
the credit of the " Representative."   It never pretended
to be a Republic.   It was going to be a Republic—indeed
had stated as much in its first manifesto in 1649, but the
people did not see eye to eye with its " Representative "
in that matter; so that until the political problem of
how to build up a Republic in which the members of the
Representative should still wield complete power, but
in which the people should have no predominant part,
could be solved, the people would have to be content

[1] *The Unhappy Marksman ; or, Twenty-Three Queries*, published on
June 13, 1659.

with a "Representative." So that the people at once
began to clamour for a "Free Parliament"; that is to
say, a Parliament which they themselves should be free
to elect, and whose members, when elected, should be
free to sit without molestation from either a "single
person," the Army or any other outside power whatsoever. That such a Parliament would restore the King
everyone knew, though whether on terms or not was a
question.

The "Representative" was fully aware of the place
it held in the affections of the "People," and from the
first day of its sitting had been protected by a guard
of soldiers, to whom, on May 31, it voted an additional
penny a day in the case of foot-soldiers and threepence
in the case of troopers.[1] These soldiers, of course, were
supplied by the Army, and though they might protect
the members from the vengeance of the people they would
not protect them from the Army. So, on June 16, a
separate "life-guard" of 120 horse was set up, in emula-
tion of Cromwell's "life-guard," and with an equally
extravagant rate of pay. Each man received 3s. a day,
each captain 20s., a lieutenant 14s., a cornet 12s., and the
quartermaster 9s.[2] Presumably, all this was in addition
to lodging and food. The "life-guard's" duties were
to attend and protect the "Representative," and also
the "Council of State" when the former body was not
sitting. Both could hardly sit at the same time, for in
that case there would have been no quorum of the
"Representative."

Before it commenced its labours the "Council of State"
proceeded to wreak its vengeance upon Cromwell's
memory. A huge monument to Cromwell had been
erected at the east end of Henry VII's Chapel in West-

[1] Commons Journals, under date cited.
[2] Cal. S. P. Dom., 1658, p. 376. Rugge, in his diary, draws great
attention to this life-guard.

minster Abbey, and (apparently) had barely been completed, for no illustration or description of it has survived. During the week ending June 7, 1659, the Council of State destroyed this monument and ordered Cromwell's crown and sceptre to be broken and sold.[1] These were not unpopular steps, though, no doubt, they irritated the Army, but at the same time the " Representative " and its Council perpetrated a series of grave mistakes in policy.

Nearly everyone who had served Cromwell was dismissed from his post. Thurloe, the very able Secretary of State, was dismissed, and fell into such contempt that he was even arrested by a bailiff; and on June 9, John Barkstead, the Fleet Street thimble-maker who had been Cromwell's Lieutenant of the Tower, was supplanted by one Fitch, a tailor, and, of course, a Colonel of the Rump's promotion. Two days previously, Barkstead had been arrested on the Exchange by Overton, the Fifth Monarchy man (imprisoned in the Tower by Cromwell), in an action for trespass and, followed by a jeering crowd of street boys, had been taken prisoner to the Counter.[2]

Cromwell had chosen men for places, the Rump chose places for men. Instead of Thurloe, the Council of State selected as its Secretary, Thomas Scot, the regicide, elected M.P. for Aylesbury in place of Sir Ralph Verney in 1645. Scot, therefore, was the penman of the Rump's manifestoes in 1659, as he had been in 1649, and no doubt the Declaration I have just cited must have been his handiwork.

[1] *The Weekly Post*, No. 5, for May 31 to June 7, 1659, announced that, " The stately and magnificent monument of the late Lord Protector, set up at the upper end of the chancel in the Abbey at Westminster, is taken down by order of the Council of State, and publick sale made of the Crown, Sceptre and other Royal ornaments, after they were broken. The inscription set upon the wall is said to be, ' Great in policy, but matchless in tyranny.' It was put up by one of the Royal party, but pulled down by one of the soldiery."
[2] Commons Journals, June 9, 1659; *Mercurius Politicus*, June 2–9, 1659; and *Nicholas Papers*, iv. p. 155.

It is essential to point out that the private character of this man will not bear investigation. He was not merely vicious like Marten and others, but he was criminally vicious, a man whose constant claims in his manifestoes to the " visible protection " of the Almighty for himself and his colleagues in their worst actions thus became nauseating in the highest degree.[1]

Even before this the " Representative " itself had turned its attention to the official bi-weekly *Mercurius Politicus* and the *Publick Intelligencer*. It was felt that any writer who had identified himself so thoroughly with Cromwell's policy as Marchamont Nedham could no longer be suffered to write these journals. So they decided to employ John Canne, who published a *Seasonable Word to the Parliament Men* on May 10, in which he warned them against the danger of " Single persons," and not obscurely set forth the claims of his own sect for consideration. He seems to have been destitute of humour; for, on page three of his tract, he assured the " Representative " that " My prayer to God is that this Parliament may do worthily in Ephrata and be famous in Bethlehem "—an aspiration which the wits of the times did not fail to construe as meaning that the Rump ought to seek for the approbation of the inmates of the Bethlehem Hospital for Lunatics, vulgarly called " Bedlam." And he actually wound up his booklet with the admonition to " go and sin no more, lest a worse thing " should befall them. The necessity for conciliating Canne's sect, therefore, must have been very great, for, on May 13,

---

[1] To cite all the stories told of Scot would be to quote all the Royalist and Presbyterian pamphlets from 1649 onwards. Details too offensive to describe are given in the Royalist Mercuries in 1649, and the satires by Sir John Berkenhead and Samuel Butler, the author of *Hudibras*, thenceforward constantly refer to Scot's private life. Throughout the year 1659 the enemies of the Rump never fail to refer to Scot's character. When Scot was executed in 1660, Muddiman remarked that he " dy'd as he lived, there's few in England but know how that was."—(*Parliamentary Intelligencer*, Oct. 15–22, 1660.)

the " Representative " itself authorised John Canne to write the weekly intelligence and " prohibited " Nedham.[1]

Canne celebrated his appointment by a manifesto of his own, printed in the *Publick Intelligencer* on May 16. This was signed by himself, Henry Jessey and H. Harrison. Of Harrison, who was probably a relation of Thomas Harrison, the regicide, nothing is known. The heading of their manifesto deserves citation :

" An Invitation to the Lord's People throughout the three Nations, to provoke them to a holy rejoicing in the Lord and exalting His Name for the late Salvation begun, and the good hopes of reviving the work again in the midst of us."

The authors of the " late Salvation " then commenced to scramble for the deer Cromwell had preserved in the Royal parks. Venison pasties, a great delicacy of the times, must have been quite common in London in 1659. As a " bonne bouchée " for the " Lord " Lambert, the " Council of State " presented him with " two brace of bucks " on June 13, and, in order to prevent unfairness in sharing the spoils, made an order on June 15 that " no member was to have more than two bucks before each member had one." Warrant after warrant followed in favour of members of the " Parliament " and Council.[2] Some members were enabled to stock their own grounds, particularly the bankrupt Wentworth.

[1] Commons Journals, May 13, and *Publick Intelligencer*, May 9–16. An anti-Cromwell but non-Royalist Tract, published on May 26, and entitled *Eighteen New Court Queries*, suggested that Nedham should be punished, and asked, " Whether Mr. Nedham the curranto-maker, the Court pamphleteer, being an impudent fellow, a lyer and a forger of foreign letters, a mercenary informer [see his letter to Cromwell about Anna Trapnell in the Calendar of State Papers, Domestic Series, for 1653–4, p. 393], an abuser and base vilifier of worthy and eminent persons, an insulter over gallant men's afflictions and miseries, a murtherer of men's fame, credit and reputation, does not very well deserve to forfeit his ears in the pillory ? "

[2] Cal. S. P. Dom., 1658–1659, p. 374. The lists of warrants for the delivery of deer will be found on page 583 of this Calendar, and on pages 561 to 571 of the Calendar for 1659–1660.

When all this was over, the "Representative" set seriously to work upon the preliminaries for ridding itself altogether of the Army, which at any time might strangle the life out of it once more. First of all, it cashiered a number of officers, replacing them by anabaptists. As each new commission was issued the recipient was forced to attend and receive it from the hands of the Speaker, for there were to be no more generals with unlimited powers. Fleetwood himself was compelled to attend the House of Commons, and received a new commission as Major-General and Chief Commander.

Next they turned their attention to the General of the Army in Scotland, George Monck, who, in a letter to Fleetwood dated from Dalkeith on May 8, had signified his acquiescence in the restoration of Parliamentary control typified by the Restoration of the Rump.[1]

They, therefore, sent him their commission, and also commissions for new officers, ordering him to cashier a number in whom he trusted and to replace them by their own nominees. In return they received an unpleasant surprise in the shape of a "peremptory letter" refusing to do anything of the kind. Monck "knew no reason why he should disband old officers, just and faithful, to admit others whose fidelity and principles he knew not." So, some in the House, indignant at his tone, said his letter "ought to be burnt by the common hangman for his incivility to the commission sent him." [2] The "Representative" pocketed this affront, but ever afterwards watched Monck with suspicion. He was potentially as dangerous as Lambert.

In the meantime, the Army in England was becoming mutinous. As far back as April 29 it was noted that the inferior officers thought themselves the equals of

[1] This letter was printed in *Mercurius Politicus* for May 19–26.
[2] *Nicholas Papers*, iv. p. 162. Cal. S. P. Dom., 1659–1660, p. 19, and Commons Journals, June 9, when Hesilrige was ordered to prepare a reply.

Desborough and Fleetwood, and were quite as willing to turn them out as they had been to turn out Richard Cromwell.[1]

Mr. Miles, Sir Edward Nicholas's " intelligencer," then wrote a series of letters to him, depicting the growing strife between the English Army and the " Representative."

On June 3 Miles wrote that the Rump " would fain raise the militia in City and country," and " thus new model the Army, and had dismounted some scores of officers." [2]

On July 1, he said that the new militia was to be distinct from the Army, and to have vast powers conferred on them to judge of men's estates of all kinds and their affection, and to force them by oaths, distresses and imprisonment to arbitrary contributions; " a practice of dangerous consequence, as to the creation of jealousies both in the people and Army. Greater oppression this nation hath scarce known, vast sums of money must by the like violent means be levied." [3]

When the common soldiers heard of this they feared the loss of their arrears, threatened to turn out the Rump again, and were with difficulty appeased by their officers. The " Representative " discontinued its debates for the moment, but finding that all was quiet after all, set to work again, sitting " even in the afternoons," endeavouring to settle the militia " post haste." On July 22 Miles wrote, " the City is sick of its new militia," but by the

[1] A Cambridge wit asked, " Whether the promotion of gentlemen cobblers, etc., to places of the highest dignity and greatest trust, and the dethronizing of Kings, ignobleizing Peers, cashiering Lords and all well-deserving loyal heroes be not therefore done that the Scripture might be fulfilled, ' The first shall be last, and the last first ' ? "—(*University Queries, in a gentle touch by the by*, published on June 6.)

[2] *Nicholas Papers*, iv. p. 158. The Commons Journals at this time are full of displacements of officers and orders about the militia, but the fullest record is to be found in *Mercurius Politicus* and the *Publick Intelligencer*.

[3] *Nicholas Papers*, iv. p. 164.

27th, thirty-nine officers and six regiments for the City
of London had been nominated by the " Representative."
As far as can be ascertained, all the officers were anabaptists or fanatics.[1]

On the King's side, Sir Edward Nicholas wrote to
Major-General Massey in August that the new militia
would be the absolute ruin of the Army, but would reduce
the nation to the condition of slaves. Other Royalists
were of a different opinion and thought that the Army
and the " Representative " would come to blows as a
result. " If we keep our swords in their sheaths, they will
soon cut their own throats," Colonel Gervase Holles had
written in May.

This was a wise opinion, but the Royalists were not
acting upon it. While the Rump and the Army were
preparing for an inevitable struggle, the Royalists and
their quondam enemies, the Presbyterians, were doing
their best to unite the two by themselves uniting and
preparing for a gigantic rising in favour of the " known
laws " of England. In this rising it was hoped that
General Monck would take part.

[1] *Nicholas Papers*, IV. *passim*. The lists are printed in *Mercurius
Politicus* for July 21–28. William Kiffen was Lieutenant-Colonel of
the " Red " regiment. The officers for the Tower Hamlets and the
Borough of Southwark, forty-one in all, were agreed upon on the same
day. A fuller and slightly altered list was made out on August 5,
and printed in *Mercurius Politicus* for August 4–11. Over all Skippon
was made " Major-General." He was hated by the City Presbyterians.

CHAPTER III

GENERAL MONCK—SIR RICHARD WILLYS, TRAITOR

EVER since the days of Henry III the Moncks of Potheridge had ranked among the great families of Devon, and though their estates were encumbered by the time when George Monck was born in 1608, and the boy himself was brought up by his maternal grandfather, Sir Thomas Smith, of Maydford, Heavitree, yet George Monck could boast of Royal descent. For his father's grandmother, Frances Plantagenet, was a daughter of Arthur Plantagenet, Viscount Lisle, and the genealogists tell us that still further back his kinship with King John can be traced through Richard, King of the Romans, and his son the Earl of Cornwall.

The bearer of such a name could not, therefore, have been other than loyal at heart, and Monck's loyalty must have been kept alive in his breast throughout all the dismal years of the Interregnum by his relations in Devonshire and Cornwall. The cross-relationships of the great county families of the seventeenth century were numerous and reveal clanships and family ties unknown nowadays. And if this was the case in all the counties of England, it was peculiarly so in Devon and Cornwall, isolated as they are by the sea from all the other counties of England, save on one side. There is no nobler name in all the annals of England than that of Grenvile or Granville,[1] the direct

---

[1] " Grenvile " was the spelling adopted by Sir Bevill. The variations, however, have been confusing. Archbishop William Grenvile of York (1304 to 1315), who was also Chancellor of England from 1302 to 1305, and was consecrated by the Pope himself, appears to have spelt his

line of which family was seated at Stowe, in the parish of Kilkhampton, Cornwall, between Bude and the borders of Devon.   In a county where, to this day, copies of the letter of thanks from Charles the First to his faithful Cornishmen can still be seen in parish churches, the name of Grenvile has always been held in great honour.

Though the direct line of the great Cornish and Devon house of Grenvile died out in the eighteenth century, still on winter evenings tales are told in remote " sanctuary " (parsonage) or lonely farmhouse of the great sailor Sir Richard, who, in Queen Elizabeth's days, fought the whole Spanish Fleet in his little ship, the *Revenge*.   But the memory of Sir Bevill, the Bayard of the West, and George Monck's uncle, is greener still.   This noblest of all the combatants in the Civil Wars " could not contain himself within doors when the King of England's standard waved to the field in so just an occasion."   Sir Bevill rallied to himself and to Sir Ralph Hopton, the King's General in the West, an army of Cornish pikemen who scattered the Roundheads before them like chaff.   At Stratton Hill, on May 16, 1643, in Sir Bevill's own parish and upon his own land, where the great Earl of Stamford had entrenched himself with vastly superior forces, Sir Bevill and Hopton, with their pikemen, ignominiously routed the Parliamentary rebels, captured all their cannon and stores, and drove them out of Cornwall.   For this victory Sir Bevill received a warrant for an Earldom and Hopton was created Baron Hopton of Stratton.[1]   Victory after victory

---

name " Greenfield."   No doubt the right spelling was " Granville," from which place in Normandy the family (descended from Rollo, the first Duke) took its name.   The spelling " Granville " was resumed by Dennis Granville, Dean of Durham, Sir Bevill's youngest son.   There is an excellent history of the Granville family by the Rev. Prebendary Roger Granville, formerly Rector of Bideford.

[1] S. R. Gardiner asserts that Hopton's barony was conferred on him for yielding the governorship of Bristol (captured by the King's forces on July 26) to Prince Rupert, and this has been corroborated by the fact that the actual grant of Hopton's barony was dated Sept. 4, 1643.   As a warrant invariably preceded a grant, often by many months, this

followed. The Cornish pikes drove on through Devon
into Somerset until at last, on July 5, 1643, the end came,
in the crowning triumph over Sir William Waller at Lansdown Hill, near Bath. Sir Bevill, mortally wounded by
a blow from a pole-axe, when he had captured the hill, was
carried to Cold Ashton Parsonage, where he died. So the
Cornish foot " drooped for the loss of their lord, whom they
loved," and the fortunes of the " White King " fell with
the blue-eyed and auburn-haired champion of his cause.
Stories of Sir Bevill's victories at Stratton and at Lansdown still abound in Cornwall, and the name of Sir Bevill's
giant henchman, Anthony Payne, has become a legend.
Payne, mounted on his horse " Samson," hewed down the
rebels with his mighty broadsword and protected his
master's son, " Jacke," then a boy of fifteen, who also
fought at Lansdown. When King Charles heard the tale
a month later on, at Bristol, he knighted John Grenvile.[1]

Sir Bevill had been educated at Exeter College, Oxford,
and members of the University combined to publish a
book of elegies after his death. One of the Oxford poets,
Martin Lluellin, asked a question :

> " Where shall the next famous Grenville stand ?
> Thy grandsire fills the seas, and thou the land."

Sir John Grenvile was to supply an answer to this question.

Boy as he was, Sir John Grenvile became a redoubtable
soldier, and was Governor of the Scilly Islands from 1649
to 1651, when he was compelled to surrender to Blake, on

corroboration is worthless, and, as a matter of fact, Hopton's barony
was announced in the Parliamentary news-books before Bristol was
captured.   Sir Bevill did not live to take up his grant, but his daughters
were granted the rank and precedence of an Earl's daughters.   See
more of this in the autobiography of Mrs. Mary Delany.

[1] The legends of Anthony Payne, who was eight feet high and broad
and strong in proportion, are numerous.   One Christmas at Stowe he
picked up the donkey bringing in the Yule Log, and throwing it over his
shoulders marched into the great hall with the cry of " Ass and fardel ! "
" Ass and fardel, for my Lady's Yule ! "   There is a portrait of Payne
at Truro, in the museum of the Royal Cornwall Institution.

terms so favourable that the so-called Parliament refused to ratify them until Blake threatened to throw up his commission. The " fag end " of a House of Commons had three months previously sent orders to the brutal boor Desborough to imprison Sir John's brothers and sisters until he surrendered.

When George Monck was starving as a King's officer, imprisoned by the Long Parliament from 1644 to 1646, and even later, when he fought in Ireland against the Scots for the " Parliament," he could not have thought of his uncle Sir Bevill and his cousin " Jacke " without being moved. And that he was continually reminded of his loyal cousin we have ample proof. Sir Bevill's executor and trustee was William Morice of Churston Ferrers, Devon, who was kinsman to the Grenviles and to the Moncks through his mother, who was a Prideaux. Like Sir Bevill, Morice had been educated at Exeter College. The sole heir of his father, and thus well endowed with this world's goods, William Morice was an excluded member of Parliament, who devoted his time to his books and to his estates. He bought Werrington from Sir Francis Drake in 1651, and though elected for all the various pseudo-parliaments of Oliver and Richard Cromwell, was still excluded from his seat. Thus he had led the life of a wealthy Devonshire gentleman of scholarly tastes, and had managed his kinsman George Monck's property as well as that of Sir John Grenvile. On William Morice's advice Sir John Grenvile presented his cousin Nicholas Monck, the brother of George and future Bishop of Hereford, with the valuable family living of Kilkhampton, on the death of Parson Rouse in 1653. Thus, George Monck, directly or indirectly, was in continual communication with his cousin, Sir John Grenvile, through their joint trustee, William Morice. Nor did these family ties alone indicate Monck's political sympathies.

Sir John Hinton, the King's physician, in his little

known *Memoirs*, addressed to Charles II after Monck's death, told the King the following story.

" The day before he went into Scotland," wrote Hinton of Monck, " he dined with me, for I had contracted a great friendship with him when he was of our party. And after dinner he called me into the next room, and after general discourse, taking a lusty glass of wine, he drank an health to his ' black boy ' (as he called your Majesty), and freely declared to me, that if ever he had power he would serve your Majesty to the utmost of his life. At which I was astonished, he being in so great a station."

General George Monck, despite his popularity with all classes—a popularity evinced by his nicknames of " Old George " or " Honest George "—was the " wariest man in England," [1] in days when it was dangerous to trust to friends. He is said to have held in high honour a maxim of Duke George of Saxony, to the effect that "if he thought his shirt knew his thoughts and intentions, he would take it off and burn it."[2] That so many conflicting accounts of Monck's restoring the King to the throne should have been published by contemporaries was inevitable with anyone of Monck's disposition and training, for he had had no " education but Dutch and Devonshire," and was first and last a professional soldier who remembered above all things that he came of a great English house, and had nothing in common with the men who composed the " Representative " and officered the Army. Restoration of Parliamentary Government was Monck's goal, and this he ever kept steadily in view, for, in order to restore the King, the people, in the person of their Parliament, must first be restored. No other explanation of a policy which was straightforward throughout is needed.

The King's affairs in England during the Interregnum

[1] Lady Mordaunt to her husband, on March 30, 1660. Clarendon State Papers, iii. 711.
[2] *Fragmenta Aulica*, by T. S. (1662), p. 45.

had been managed by a committee of seven gentlemen known as the " Sealed Knot," or " Secret Cabinet," [1] but in 1659, just before Richard Cromwell was turned out by the Army, the King and his advisers considered the moment opportune for a great national rising, in which the Presbyterians were to join. The " Sealed Knot," therefore, was dissolved and a Royal Commission granted, on March 11, 1659, to Arthur Annesley, a Presbyterian (whose tract has already been quoted), Sir Thomas Peyton (a Roman Catholic), Colonel William Legg, whose son was created Earl of Dartmouth, and to John Mordaunt (afterward Lord Mordaunt of Avalon) and Sir John Grenvile (afterwards Earl of Bath), both of whom had been members of the " Sealed Knot."

These five were given plenipotentiary powers and could treat with all but the regicides.

In the projected rising the Presbyterians were given the initiative. The Earl of Stamford, who had fought against Sir Bevill in Cornwall, now undertook to raise Leicestershire for Charles II, and Sir William Waller, who had been routed by Sir Bevill at Lansdown, actually kissed the paper appointing him and said, " Let him be damned that serves not this Prince with integrity and diligence." [2] Waller was appointed Lieutenant-General by the King, and the Marquess of Hertford General. Even Fairfax, the old Parliamentary Commander-in-chief, accepted a commission from the King.

All this could not be done without the knowledge of what was taking place leaking out, and, on June 2, one pamphleteer, writing under the very noses of the Rump, publicly advised the Royal party to desist and, as he put it, to " make all they can for an oligarchy, however a

[1] Aubrey de Vere, Earl of Oxford; John, Lord Belasyse; Sir William Compton, son of the Earl of Northampton; Colonel John Russel; Sir Richard Willys; John Mordaunt, and Sir John Grenvile.
[2] Clarendon State Papers, iii. 446.

democracy will do it, and let the soldiers alone and be quiet. For let them have a common enemy, or any power to oppose, they'll join and be unanimous in such a business. But let them rest and have nothing to do and they'll make something to do. Let them be idle and they'll be busy, and if they can find no business, they'll make some. Give them no occasion of fighting with others and, my life for it, they'll fight with themselves. And when thieves fall out, honest men will come by their own." [1] The army was reduced to a fine pass when prints like these could openly flout it in the streets of London.

The very next day after this tract was published, a startling warning was given to the Royalists.

On the third of June, a notice was found to have been posted on the Royal Exchange and in several other places in London. It ran as follows :

" These are to advertise all loyal hearts whom these may concern that Sir Rich. Willys, knight, is a traitor· and false to the trust his King and Master putteth in him, having of late been several times followed to divers places, to a tavern in Shoemaker's Row, the Indian tavern and sundry other holes where he hath met with Mr. Secretary Thurloe and his creatures to discover the secrets (which) were committed to him, and, when time would not permit a rendezvous, he hath sent letters to the above named, as hath been confessed by one Davy, a porter, his own confession.

" By Order." [2]

The effect of this warning was twofold. By the Royalists it was generally believed to be impossible that Sir

---

[1] Concluding words of a pamphlet, published on June 2, 1659, and entitled *A Word to Purpose; or, A Parthian Dart shot back to 1642 and from thence shot back again to 1659*, etc.

[2] See Sir Richard Willys's Defence, printed in *Notes and Queries*, Series 12, x. p. 123 (transcribed by the present writer). The actual notice itself is printed in the fourth volume of the *Nicholas Papers*, edited by Sir G. F. Warner for the Historical Society.

Richard Willys, of the " Sealed Knot," had been a traitor. His poverty, his friends, and his frequent imprisonments by Cromwell all militated against such a sweeping reversal of all that was known of him. By the Presbyterians, however, who knew no more of him than that he was a former enemy, the warning seems to have been taken seriously and in most instances they seem to have relaxed their efforts and to have adopted a waiting attitude.

But right down to the end of the year, long after all question of a rising had been put aside, Lord Clarendon's correspondence proves that the Royalists still refused to believe Willys a traitor, in spite of the King's own assurances of the fact. An inquiry into the matter even had to be held after the Restoration, with the result that Willys was condemned and banished from the precincts of the Court for ever.

Willys had been a traitor ever since the commencement of the year 1655.[1] In connexion with the Royalist rising of 1655, Willys had been imprisoned from Jan. 14 to Oct. 12 and " detained " to the following February—this period of imprisonment and detention having been arranged to keep his friends from asking inconvenient questions. Again, in 1658, in connexion with a rising only projected, but which never took place, he was arrested on Good Friday (April 9). This imprisonment also was a subterfuge. Willys was not the only traitor at this time, and the blood with which Cromwell then terrorised London was due as much to others as to Willys.

In sharp contrast with his behaviour to the Fifth

---

[1] This date has been a matter of some dispute. In 1903, the late Sir Reginald F. D. Palgrave published his *Oliver Cromwell, H. H. Lord Protector, and the Royalist Insurrection against his Government of March* 1655. In Sir Reginald's opinion Lord Clarendon's statements (*Autobiography*, ii. 30, and *Great Rebellion*, xvi. 931 of the edition of 1839) point conclusively to the beginning of 1655. The present writer has brought to light corroboration of this view in the shape of a petition from Willys to Cromwell in 1654. This was transcribed and annotated in *Notes and Queries*, Series 12, x. p. 101.

Monarchy men, who directly aimed at his life, and yet received no punishment worse than imprisonment or a flogging, Cromwell took the lives of the Royalists universally asserted to have been deliberately " trepanned " by him.

Fully aware that no jury would convict anyone for attacking himself, confronted by the fact that all the judges, even of those days, refused to act as his executioners,[1] Cromwell found but one man sufficiently servile to condemn the flies in his net.   This was John Lisle, president of the bogus " high court of justice."   On Tuesday June 8, 1658, Sir Henry Slingsby and the Rev. Dr. Hewitt were beheaded on Tower Hill by Lisle's order, and on July 7, Colonel Ashton was drawn on a sled to the Mark Lane end of Tower Street and there hanged and quartered, with the same cruelty as if he had been guilty of high treason.   In Cheapside, John Bettley was butchered in like fashion on the same day.   A third man, Fryer, was drawn to Smithfield, but was reprieved when he was on the ladder.   The cat then began to play with his

[1] Petition to the House of Commons of Lady Mary Hewitt, widow of John Hewitt, D.D. :
" Humbly sheweth : That Oliver late pretended Protector, thirsting after innocent blood, did, in May 1658, by the advice of his Council contrary to the known fundamental laws of the land (whereto every freeborn Englishman hath an inherent birthright, and according to which laws the said bloody, tyrannical, pretended protector at his instalment swore to govern the three kingdoms), erected a high court of justice (or rather injustice) to try several persons for supposed crimes against the said pretended protector, whereof he appointed John Lisle, Esq., President."
The Petitioner adds that her husband was accused by Lisle of " treason," and " offered to plead to any such indictment as the judges of the land (who were also commissioners in the said commission, but refused to act) should declare to be legal, or according to any Act of Parliament, and therefore appealed to their judgment " . . . " that all the judges refusing to sit and join in any such proceeding, the said John Lisle did, notwithstanding, without jury or witness procured, sentence your petitioner's said husband to death," etc., etc.
Printed in full in *Perfect Occurrences of the most Remarkable Passages in Parliament*," etc. No. 4, for May 11–18, 1660 (Burney, 54, A.).   See Commons Journals for May 15.
This petition has hitherto been unknown.   There is no copy of it in the State Papers.

victims. On July 9 Sumner and Stacy were drawn to Cornhill, Sumner being carried to the " Black Boy " Inn while Stacy was hanged. After this Sumner went for a further journey on the sledge to a gallows in Bishopsgate Street. Here he was reprieved. Next, Oliver Allen was drawn to the " Four Spouts " at the upper end of Gracechurch Street; at the gallows he also was reprieved.[1] Yet no rising had taken place and no blood had been shed.

All this had taken place only a year before, and whatever excuse might be found for Cromwell in all these cruelties, the Royalists must have felt that none could be found for Willys, who, if he was guilty, was the worst of traitors. So they steadfastly refused to believe in his complicity, and preparations for the intended rising still continued.

In the meantime, directly he was " posted," Willys followed the previous precedents, procured his own arrest, and when he found it convenient to be released, on July 22, entered upon the darkest and most dangerous scheme he had yet attempted. He arranged for a squadron of horse to be posted before his own door " the whole summer long," and also for a summons for himself to attend the " Council of State " daily, in order to keep off his Royalist friends and to enable him to plot fresh villainy with Scot and Vane.[2]

[1] Details are given in *Mercurius Politicus* and the *Publick Intelligencer* under the dates cited.

[2] Thanks to the blunders of the eighteenth-century historian, Eachard, the inner history of the posting of Sir Richard Willys and of the plot that followed has been thoroughly obscured. I should point out, therefore, that I refer to the original documents and have disregarded Eachard.

These documents are as follows. The three narratives of Sir Samuel Morland, the earliest of which has recently been published in the fourth volume of the *Nicholas Papers;* the second (in the MSS. at Lambeth Palace) was printed by the Rev. Dr. John Willcock, in his *Life of Sir Henry Vane the Younger*, and transcribed by the present writer; and the third, written seventeen years after the event, printed in *Notes and Queries*, Series 12, x. p. 145; also by the present writer. The Lambeth MS. is the fullest of these. See also Historical Manuscripts Commission's Seventh Report, Appendix, Part I, p. 245 (*b*).

The biography of George Paule has been taken from the Historical

When the " Representative " discharged Thurloe earlier
in the year, Thurloe's clever under-secretary, Samuel
Morland, lost his employment. At that time Morland
was well-to-do. He had, as he says, an income of £1000
a year, a house and garden in " the Pell Mell," a coach
in his stables, a round sum in ready cash, and a " beautiful
young woman " for his wife. Mrs. Morland was Suzanne,
daughter of a French Protestant nobleman, Daniel de
Milleville, Baron de Boissay in Normandy. One of their
friends at this time was George Paule, who had made their
acquaintance as a redeemed captive from Algiers. Paule
was the son of the Registrar of the High Commission
Court, who died in 1635, and he had been a sailor.
Captured at sea by the Algerian pirates, Paule was a slave
for six years before he was redeemed.

At the time of Thurloe's downfall, Morland, whose
character seems to have been pusillanimous, had made up
his mind to quit England and settle in France, but his
ambitious French wife and the sailor, Paule, had other
plans in view for him. It was fairly evident that, sooner
or later, the King would return, and the two knew enough
of all that had taken place in Thurloe's offices to be aware
that it was in Morland's power to render the King services

Manuscripts Commission's Sixth Report, Appendix, pp. 79 (b) and 87 (b)
and from his petitions to the King in January 1666 (Calendar of 1665–6,
p. 299). Paule's narrative was printed by Mr. C. H. Firth in the Appendix to the last volume of the Clarke Papers, and seems to have been
attached to one of his petitions in 1666.

A hitherto unknown account by Dr. James Welwood (explaining the
passage in his memoirs about Cromwell and Morland) was transcribed
by the present writer in *Notes and Queries*, Series 12, x. p. 281.

The list of traitors sent by Morland to the King is as follows : " A
List of the names of those who received salaries for betraying the King
and his loyal subjects to Cromwell and the Rump." " Mannering, who
was shot to death. Sir Richard Willis. Sir John Marley. Col.
Barnfield. Col. Rogers. Col. Thomas Howard. Mr. Gardiner. Mr.
[Rev. Dr.] Corker. — Robotham. Mr. Vernatti. Mr. Risdon. L.-Col.
Malcom Smith. Dr. Janson, a civilian. Mr. Hanckitt. Mr. Charles
Wheeler. Mr. Rob. Rookwood. Isaack Allen. — Lollier " (S.P.,
Dom. Interregnum, vol. 220, No. 70 (I)). This list is noted, with others,
on p. 411 of the Calendar of State Papers, Domestic Series, for 1659–1660,
but the names are not set out).

which might end in great honour and rewards in return. Suzanne, therefore, helped Paule to ransack her husband's papers, and when Paule found out the treachery that had been going on in the Royal party for years past, he acted without Morland's knowledge and " posted " Sir Richard Willys in the manner described.   After this had been done there was a scene at the " neats house " in the garden in " Pell Mell."   Suzanne and Paule there told Morland of what they had done, and insisted upon his abandoning his plans to go abroad, and that instead he should offer his services to Bradshaw and the " Council of State," in order to keep the King informed of all their projects.   Eventually they succeeded in persuading the reluctant under-secretary.   Paule crossed to the Continent, saw the King and the rising was postponed.   The King required further proof, and at last Major Thomas Henshaw was sent across with original letters placing the treachery of Sir Richard Willys and other Royalists beyond question.   These only arrived a few days before the date of August 1, finally fixed for the general rising throughout England.   In the meantime, Sir Richard Willys, driven desperate by Paule's action in " posting " him, had, in conjunction with Vane and Scot, contrived a plan to rid the "Representative " of the Royal family for ever.

The King and his brothers were to come over to head the rising in person, and Hythe had been fixed upon as the spot where they would disembark.   Not far from Hythe there was at the time a famous old castle, that of Westenhanger.   It was a splendid pile, containing 126 apartments, and, by report, 365 windows, moated all round, its walls being very high and thick, and fortified with nine towers.   One tower was called after Fair Rosamund, mistress of Henry II, who was kept here for some time before she was removed to Woodstock.[1]   This

---

[1] There is a full description of Westenhanger in the third volume of Hasted's *Kent*.

castle belonged to the Poynings family and passed to the Champneys, who pulled it down in 1701. Nowadays all that remains of Westenhanger is a farmhouse in the village of Stanford.

Here the King and his brothers were to have been entrapped and murdered, for once inside the castle there would have been no escape for them. The news and the proofs of all this arrived at Brussels from Morland just as the King was " putting on his boots " to start for the coast. The rising, therefore, did not take place. Notices were sent out in all directions two or three days before August 1, and the preparations the Council of State had made were defeated. They had stationed troops of horse in every direction—at Tonbridge, Redhill, Salisbury, Lansdown(near Bath), Gloucester, Hereford and Chichester. Those of the Royalists and Presbyterians whom the notices did not reach and who arrived at their rendezvous were all arrested.[1] In London the Royal Commissioners, who, of course, were known, were watched and imprisoned at the latest possible date, in order that the main plot to capture the King might come to a head.[2] Only in Cheshire did the notice postponing the rising arrive too late, and then the Presbyterian, Sir George Booth, met, at first, with some success when he appeared in arms and was joined by Lord Derby and others at the appointed time, near Chester. They found that they had four thousand men in all and at once seized the city, where they were joined by a decided Royalist, Sir Thomas Middleton. Booth then printed a manifesto, in which he declared that his objects were a " free Parliament " and relief from " unsupportable taxes and payments unknown to our ancestors." No mention of the King was made in this

[1] Deane's letter to Lockhart, dated August 8/18 in Cal. S.P. Dom., 1659–1660, p. 87.
[2] Trusted leaders of the militia in every county were ordered to be ready on July 9. Forty-two letters of warning were sent out by the Council of State (Cal. S. P. Dom., 1659–1660, pp. 15–16).

proclamation, partly because it was unnecessary, for everyone knew that a " free Parliament " would at once restore the King, and partly, no doubt, because the Presbyterians would have brought him in on the terms of 1648.[1] Chester Castle, in spite of the capture of the city, still held out when the " Representative " took action, and despatched Lambert against the insurgents with a train of artillery and a vastly superior force of three regiments of horse, one of dragoons and three of foot. As Chester Castle had not surrendered the insurgents had no artillery, and when, on August 19, the two opposing forces drew up in battle array near Northwich, Booth found that by an absurd mistake all his powder had been left behind in Chester. " Sauve qui peut " was the order of the day. About thirty of Sir George's men were killed, while Lambert had only three men wounded and not one killed,[2] Booth made his escape southwards, disguised in woman's apparel, as " Mistress Dorothy," and on August 24 was detected by a sharp-eyed servant girl at the Red Lion Inn at Newport Pagnell, Bucks.

In the meantime, Monck had been approached by his cousin, Sir John Grenvile, who sent Nicholas Monck to Scotland, ostensibly to settle details about the marriage of the latter's daughter, who was then staying in Scotland with her uncle. Nicholas took with him a letter from the King, which Monck refused to receive, and altogether received an unsatisfactory reception. Monck had warned the Council of State in a somewhat perfunctory letter of July 5 that a rising was about to take place, but betrayed no one, and when Fairfax sent Colonel Atkins to him to ask him to join, had roundly declared that if a rising in the North took place he would send a force to suppress it.

[1] Booth's manifesto was reprinted in *A Happy Handfull; or, Green Hopes in the Blade*. The absence in it of any specific mention of the King gave umbrage to Middleton.
[2] Lambert's despatch in *Mercurius Politicus*, August 18–25. His letter winds up by pointing out that his soldiers needed boots and stockings and had only received sixpence each of their arrears.

A message from William Morice, however, delivered to his brother by Nicholas, induced the General to wait until he heard of the success or failure of Booth's rising " for a Free Parliament and the known laws of the land." [1]

Monck's chaplain, John Price, afterwards asserted that a letter to the " Representative " in London was drawn up and signed by Monck and some of his principal officers on Sunday, August 23, calling upon them to fill up their numbers and settle the " qualifications " for electors, but that at the last moment it was decided to wait for the Monday's post, in order to hear the news about Booth. When that arrived all was over. Nicholas Monck was entrusted with a sharp verbal reply to Grenvile, and George Monck, thinking that the King's cause was now definitely ended, wrote a letter of resignation to the Speaker and prepared to leave for his estates in Ireland. [2]

Fortunately, the letter was sent by Monck to his brother-in-law, Clarges, who was the agent in London of his Army, in order that Clarges might hand it to Lenthall, and Clarges knew that great changes were about to happen in London. So the two decided to detain the letter and not deliver it until it was seen what would take place. On August 5 a secret committee of the Army had commenced to sit. [3] The Army leaders did not intend to be superseded by a militia, and when Lambert returned to London matters would come to a head at once.

In the meantime Sir George Booth's fiasco elicited one vote from the " Representative " which ought not to pass without record.

[1] These episodes have been fully treated in Sir Julian S. Corbett's *Monk*, in the " English Men of Action " Series.

[2] Monck was even compelled to hold a " mirth and thanksgiving dinner," to celebrate Booth's defeat.   One of the officers present, a Captain Poole, expressed the opinion that nothing would go well in England " until all the steeplehouses were destroyed and the ' priests ' abolished." " Fair and softly, Captain Poole," cried Monck. " If you come to pluck there, I will pluck with you " !

[3] The record of this Committee's proceedings begins on August 5 in Cal. S. P. Dom., 1659–1660, p. 78.

On Friday, September 9, a " representation " and " petition " was presented in the House of Commons by thirty-eight ministers of the County of Leicester, congratulating the Rump on its great victory over Booth. This document was read, and the reply returned through Lenthall that the House " found in it a gospel spirit of Meekness, Sincerity and Holiness," and therefore thanked the ministers. Whether the " gospel spirit of meekness," etc., had been evinced by the fact that, as the minister presenting the petition assured the House, " some of us marched along with your forces to suppress the late rebellion," did not transpire,[1] but the House wound up the day's proceedings by sending one of its members, Peter Brook, to the Tower for joining in Booth's rising.

[1] Commons Journals. *Mercurius Politicus*, for Sept. 8–15, gives fuller particulars and a list of the names of the ministers.

CHAPTER IV

THE RUMP AGAIN EJECTED BY THE ARMY—MONCK TAKES
ACTION—HEWSON SENT AGAINST THE CITY

A NOTHER journalistic change now took place. John Canne had not given entire satisfaction as official journalist, as, indeed, it was hardly to be expected he would, and in the meantime Marchamont Nedham, with his customary agility, had " proved his good affection " by writing a book on behalf of the " Representative " against the King. This was entitled *Interest will not lie*.[1]

Such a timely piece of work could not pass unrewarded, and it was accordingly resolved, on Aug. 15, " That Marchamont Nedham, gentleman, be, and is hereby, restored to be writer of the public intelligence." [2] For the moment, therefore, John Canne's journalism ceased.

[1] The full title will give an excellent idea of its scope : " Interest will not lie. Or a view of England's true interest. In reference to the Papist, Royalist, Presbyterian, Baptized, Neuter, Army, Parliament, City of London. In refutation of a treasonable [*sic*] pamphlet entitled ' The Interest of England stated ' [By Dr. John Fell, afterwards Bishop of Oxford]. Wherein the author of it pretends a way how to satisfie all parties before mentioned and to provide for the public good by calling in the son of the late King. Against whom it is here proved that it is really the interest of every party (except only the Papist) to keep him out," etc.

[2] Commons Journals. The book had evidently been submitted to Scot for licence, and this prompt order was the result, two days before it was published.

William Kilburne's *New Year's Gift for " Mercurius Politicus,"* published Dec. 29, 1659, remarked :

> " . . . Mar. Nedham, Gent.
> Retracts his cursed perfidie
> And says that ' Interest will not lie.'
> And who but he ! (for old John Canne
> No more can do then can a man).

In the meantime, the City of London had not obscurely intimated its intention of refusing to pay taxes and of supplying no money for the Army until a " Free Parliament " was called.   As luck would have it, John Ireton, brother of Cromwell's son-in-law, Henry Ireton, was Lord Mayor during this year, and the Rump could count upon him to aid them in coercing the City.   So it was resolved on Sept. 2 that Ireton should continue to hold office during the ensuing year.   A few days later the Rump heard news about Lambert which caused them to postpone their plans for coercing the City.   Therefore, on Sept. 28, they revoked their order by allowing the City to proceed according to their Charter.   The City at once retorted by electing one of the Rump's most intrepid opponents as Mayor, Thomas Alleyn, who at once entered into communication with Monck.

Elated by his easy victory over Sir George Booth, Lambert returned to London on Tuesday, Sept. 20.   It was commonly said that Cromwell had promised him the succession to himself, and in any case he now " got up a petition " for a General to be appointed over the Army, " as being unfit that the Army should be judged by any power extrinsic to itself," an axiom, Hobbes adds, which was also that of Sir Henry Vane.   If the petition had been granted it would, of course, have at once solved the controversy between the Army and the Rump over the militia, and would have perpetuated the Army's ascendancy and left the way clear for Lambert.   This petition (by Lambert and his officers) was debated in the House on the 23rd

---

He writes against the Cavaliers
And pulls the Presbyterians' ears;
He cured the wounds which late he gave
To the Parliament's repute. . . ."

Another comment, not so unfriendly, was : " Whether Mr. Nedham's writing the Currant (Coranto) again be not a plain confutation of the book he lately published and entitled *Interest will not Lie*" (*One and Twenty Queries*, published Sept. 13, 1659).

September, and the " Representative " then voted that : " To have any more general officers in the Army than are already settled by the Parliament is useless, chargeable and dangerous to the Commonwealth." The day before this vote they had ordered another petition in preparation by Fleetwood and his officers to be brought to them, and, on Saturday the 24th, compelled them to " sign their intent to forbear any further proceedings in the said paper." [1] This did not suit Lambert at all, and he induced Fleetwood and the others to draw up a new petition; presented to the House by Desborough on the 5th October and printed and published the next day. The House decided to consider this petition on Saturday the 8th, and on that day, and the following Monday and Tuesday, debated the petition, clause by clause.

On Tuesday night Nicholas Monck arrived in London. He brought a verbal message from General Monck to his brother-in-law, Clarges, telling him " that he was resolved if the Parliament would be resolute in asserting their own authority against the Army, he would assist them in it, and if required thereunto march into England in their defence." Clarges was up with the dawn the next morning and went off to Walton, Hesilrige and Scot before the Rump met. Thus, when the House met, it " promptly resumed its spirits," revoked Fleetwood's commission, and cashiered Lambert, Desborough, and their supporters Colonels Kelsey, Barrow, Cobbet, Berry and Ashfield and Major Creed. Henceforward these persons became known and were celebrated in song as the " Nine Worthies." The House then placed the command of the Army in the hands of commissioners, viz. Fleetwood, Ludlow, Monck, Hesilrige, Walton, Morley and Overton (the Fifth Monarchy man). As three members of this Commission were to form a quorum, some at once set to work and sat

[1] *Mercurius Politicus*, Sept. 22–29.

up all night on the 12th October, in the Speaker's Chamber, in order to fill up the vacant places in the Army.

Then Lambert " got upon his horse," and drew down part of the Army to Westminster, where the soldiers " possessed themselves of the Hall, Palace Yards and Avenues leading to them."

But Hesilrige summoned his own regiment and the " Representative's " life-guard, and planted them in King Street and in and around the Abbey. There the two opposing forces faced each other, with loaded muskets and lighted matches, ready for a conflict which the merest accident might have precipitated. A piquant situation was created when Lenthall came down on the morning of the next day, the 13th, to open the House of Commons. As Speaker, Lenthall united in himself a variety of offices. He was " Lord Keeper of the Great Seal," " Lord Warden of the Cinque Ports," " Guardian (or gaoler) of the Liberties of England," " Lord Admiral of the Navy," and " Master of the Rolls "—this last office conferring upon him the right to reside at the Rolls House in Chancery Lane.[1] Finally, he, and he only, was the " Lord General of the Army," from whom Lambert and the rest had received their commissions. So that when he left Chancery Lane in his coach there must have been a curious crowd eager to see what would happen when he met his own men at the Houses of Parliament. The soldiers in King Street, of course, suffered him to pass, but when he reached the House of Commons, Colonel Duckenfield stopped him and refused to allow him to enter. " So the House sat not."

By nightfall the soldiers on both sides had fraternized, and drew off in one another's company. Hesilrige's own men had failed him. Next day Lambert set a guard upon the House of Commons.[2]

[1] *Seven Additional Queries on behalf of the Secluded Members*, published Jan. 4, 1660.
[2] Nedham's news-books contain very untruthful accounts of all this. Rugge's *Diurnall* (Add. MSS. 10,116,f. 31) should be substituted for them.

Thus, for the second time, the oligarchy that had terrorized three nations was turned out of doors by its own creator, the Army, and the delight of London was instantly expressed in songs and satires. Butler, the author of *Hudibras*, published his " *Acts and Monuments of our late Parliament*. By J. Canne, intelligencer generall," on the 19th of October, ridiculing it in unsparing terms and comparing it to Barebone's Parliament.[1]

A more ominous indication of public feeling was found in the songs, printed as broadsides, to be posted in taverns and sung to well-known tunes. One of the first of these was issued on November 11 and began :

" Good-morrow, my neighbours all. What news is this I heard tell?
    As I pas't through Westminster Hall, by the House that's near to
    Hell [a tavern in Palace Yard],
    They told me John Lambert was there, with his bears, and deeply
    did swear
    (As Cromwell had done before) those Vermin should sit there no
    more.
    Sing Hi, Ho, Will. Lenthall, who shall our General be ?
    For the House to the Divel is sent all, and follow, gid faith, mun ye." [2]

But the " Council of State " still continued to sit, and an amusing conflict of jurisdictions took place between it and the Army's " Committee."

On the 14th October the officers chose Fleetwood as Commander-in-Chief, and on the 18th appointed a " Committee of Ten " to manage the kingdom. This Committee included Lambert, second in command, Vane, who now deserted the Rump, and Desborough. Monck they attempted to supersede by appointing Lambert Major-General of England and Scotland and Desborough Commissary-General of the Horse in both countries. On the 26th the Committee was increased in number to twenty-

---

[1] Butler opened his satire by an imaginary debate in which the Rump, like Barebone's Parliament, was represented as discussing the question of what it was and what it should call itself.
[2] " *A Proper New Ballad on the Old Parliament*. To the tune of, ' Hi, Ho, my honey, my heart shall never rue.' " Published Nov. 11, 1659. Twenty-four verses follow, deriding different members in turn.

three, another member of the Rump, Ludlow, being added, with Colonel Hewson, amongst others, and was renamed a " Committee of Safety " once more. On October 29 the Army published a Declaration rendering null and void all the Acts and Declarations of the Rump on the 10th, 11th and 12th of October,[1] and afterwards issued a proclamation ordering the people to obey them. This was " sent into every county," to be proclaimed in every market town and city " throughout England." It failed, dismally.[2]

In the midst of all this confusion John Bradshaw died, of a " quartan ague." Though he was not really the cause of the death of Charles I, yet he was marked out by a wickedness and a cowardice peculiarly his own. When made serjeant-at-law on October 12, 1648, he had not scrupled to take the *ex animo* oath, that he did " abjure the damnable doctrine of deposing and murdering Kings by their own subjects "; and yet, within four months, he had allowed himself to be the instrument in doing this very thing. Wearing a hat lined with sheet-iron (still to be seen in the Ashmolean Collection of the Taylorian Museum at Oxford), he had " sentenced " the master he had sworn to protect to death, receiving for his reward a thousand pounds in cash and two thousand a year in land (out of Lord Cottington's estates).[3] The Chancellorship of the Duchy of Lancaster and the King's Manor and Park at Eltham were among his other perquisites given him by his accomplices. Ever since that time he had lived in a perpetual state of fear of poison or assassination, and had never ventured to go anywhere without protection. King Charles voiced the universal contempt felt for this man when, at the end of the attempts to " try " him, he

[1] *Mercurius Politicus* for Oct. 13–20, 20–27, and Oct. 27–Nov. 3, 1659.
[2] Rugge's *Diurnall*, Add. MSS. 10,116, f. 31.
[3] Commons Journals, June 19, 1649. See also Sir Thomas May's *Arbitrary Government*, etc.

terminated the proceedings with the remark to Bradshaw, " Pish !   I care not a straw for you." [1]

Nedham, who had once been imprisoned by Bradshaw for nearly two years, now printed a panegyric on his former enemy.   He ended this feat of journalistic agility with the words, " I cannot but sprinkle a few tears upon the corpse of my noblest friend, and leave the Commonwealth to put on mourning for so great a loss." [2]

The Commonwealth took the advice and began to mourn, but it mourned for the fact that Bradshaw had escaped the hangman.   Pieces of paper containing epitaphs for Bradshaw were scattered about the streets of London.[3] Several songs were also published, and one of these alluded to the real mourners :

> " Accusers there will be,
>   Bitter ones, bitter ones,
> Hangman and tree so tall,
> Bridge, Tower and City wall,
> Kite and Crow, which were all,
>   Robb'd of their right."[4]

Meanwhile, by the time when Monck's letter to Clarges ordering him to give the Rump verbal assurances that he would support them against the English Army had been

---

[1] On Tuesday, Jan. 23, 1649.   No historian has noticed this remark, recorded only in the *Moderate Intelligencer* (for Jan. 18–25) of John Dillingham (the sole licensed journalist with the courage to be loyal at that time), and in *The Moderate* of Mabbott, the licenser.

[2] *Mercurius Politicus* for Oct. 27–Nov. 3.

[3] Rugge quotes one of these :
> " If any near this grave dare appear,
> Ask but the Prince of Darkness who lies here.
> King-killing murderer he'll tell thee—that
> He hath made him his dear associate."

[4] " *The Arraignment of the Divel for stealing away President Bradshaw.* To the tune of ' Well-a-day, Well-a-day.' "   Published on Nov. 7. On Nov. 9 *A Guildhall Elegie*, etc., followed, in which the following verse occurs :
> " He was couragious even to impudence,
>   A virtue lately deemed cardinal.
> Needful as jacks [quills] are to a harpsicall [harpsichord],
> He and his Nedham, Peters and John Canne
>   Wholly engrossed it."

sent off, the " news-books " had arrived in Scotland, as well as private letters. Monck, therefore, decided that his hour had come, and that the destiny of England lay in his hands, and acted with startling rapidity. His Army was full of anabaptist officers. All the principal garrisons in Scotland were in the hands of Lambert's friends. His own regiment of foot was officered by anabaptists, and Talbot's " Black Colours " was a hotbed of this sect. Fortunately, Talbot was in London, and the second in command, Hubblethorne, was a man whom he could trust, as also was Ethelbert Morgan, at the head of his own regiment of foot. Both regiments were at Edinburgh. So an officer was despatched post haste to order Hubblethorne and Morgan to come at once to Monck at Dalkeith. Others were ordered thither in like fashion from Leith, arrived in a few hours and, with Monck, sat up all night perfecting his plans, after they had stopped all the posts. At dawn two captains were galloping to secure Perth and Ayr, Hubblethorne and Morgan were off with secret orders, the regiments of horse were being concentrated, and small parties of them stationed to arrest on their way to Dalkeith all the dangerous officers, who had in the meantime been summoned to meet their general at headquarters.

At midday Monck rode off for Edinburgh, escorted by a troop of horse. When he arrived, his own regiment of foot and Talbot's " Black Colours " were paraded to meet him, and he then rode to his quarters and proceeded to cashier nearly all the officers of both regiments. Morgan was appointed head of Monck's own regiment and Hubblethorne of Talbot's. Then Monck went back to the regiments, placed himself at their head, marched them down to Greyfriars, and before the astonished soldiers could dream of opposition, promptly had the whole of the cashiered officers arrested.

Then he addressed the men, asking them if they would

submit to the insolence of the English Army, and (in words which were the key to and justification for all his actions) said, " I think myself obliged by the duty of my place to keep the military power in obedience to the civil." Finally, he offered to allow those who dissented from his views to leave the service.

The effect of this speech was electric. Shouting that they would " live and die " with him, the men cheered " Old George " to the echo. Edinburgh was won, and no hitch followed in the gaining of the other garrisons or in the arrests of the anabaptist officers. Johnson was sent galloping away to secure Berwick, after the receipt of an appeal from Myers, the governor there, who was outnumbered by anabaptist officers, and the same night these anabaptist officers were arrested and Berwick secured. Thus General Monck had all Scotland in his hands. And that was a Presbyterian Scotland by no means displeased by the tramp of regiments, now cleared of anabaptists, rapidly concentrating into a formidable army at Edinburgh.

The most dramatic exploit of all, however, took place at Berwick. When the anabaptist Colonel Cobbet, one of the " nine worthies " cashiered by the Rump on Oct. 12, arrived there with the comparatively easy task of securing the garrison of Berwick, and instructions from the " Committee of Safety " to gain over the Scotch Army and arrest Monck, if necessary, he found that he had been anticipated by a few hours and was himself arrested.

Monck then wrote three letters, one to Speaker Lenthall, to let him know that the Army in Scotland was at the Rump's disposal in their quarrel with the Army, the second to Fleetwood, imploring him to restore the " Parliament," and a third to Lambert—short and sharp in tone— as to an " ambitious person " on whom he had his eyes. " The nature of England will not endure any arbitrary power," said he to Lambert, " neither will any true

Englishman in the Army." Therefore he begged him to
restore the Parliament to its freedom.

The consternation of the " Committee of Safety " at
the two last letters can well be imagined. That second-
rate men like Fleetwood and Desborough should have
miscalculated the calibre of their great adversary in
Scotland was natural, but for Lambert, who was not an
ordinary man, to have done so was a fatal error. Monck's
letters arrived in London by the post of Friday, the 28th
October, and the next day a council of the field officers
was called. Their decision was to send Lambert against
Monck, but with orders " to beget an understanding." [1]

Lambert rapidly got together an army of some 7000
men, and on Thursday, Nov. 3, began his march towards
Scotland.[2] Before he set out, the doomed " Committee
of Safety " had sent for Monck's brother-in-law Clarges,
the " Commissary " in London of his Army, and took
counsel with him what to do.

Of one thing Clarges was perfectly well aware, and this
was that there was no money for Lambert's Army, and
that the angry City of London would not provide a penny
for it. Monck's Army, on the other hand, was well paid,
and he knew full well that the Scots would smooth over
the financial side of his struggle with an Army of anabaptists, whom they hated. So, on Clarges's advice, the
Committee sent Colonels Talbot and Sewell to Scotland
to Monck with instructions to ask for an armistice, in
order that they might treat with him. This, they thought,
would divert any more of the lightning blows by which
Monck had upset all their calculations, and while the

---

[1] *Mercurius Politicus*, Oct. 27–Nov. 3.

[2] *Ibid.*, Nov. 3–10. A satire upon Harrington's Rota Club, printed
on Nov. 12, 1659, and entitled, *Decrees and Orders of the Committee of
Safety, by the Commonwealth of Oceana*, suggested :
    " That Politicus be appointed to make threnothriambeuticks (this
word will puzzle the lay elders) upon the Lord Lambert and the other
Maccabees that accompany him, in regard he was so happy in his
eulogium upon the pious and loyal Bradshaw."

negotiations were going on they hoped, by coercion if necessary, to squeeze pay for their own soldiers out of the City.

Nothing loth, and knowing full well that delay was in his favour, Monck consented to negotiate, and on Nov. 12 the three Commissioners appointed by him to treat arrived in London,[1] after an unsuccessful attempt by Lambert to detain them on the way, and thus to end the matter quickly.

In the meantime, there was a good deal of insubordination in Scotland. Captain Poole had headed a movement among the officers to correspond with those in England. Monck summarily terminated this by clapping up Poole in prison and sent most of the officers of Colonel Fairfax's regiment to join him.[2]

" Counsellor I have none to rely on," Monck said. " Many of my officers have been false, and that all the rest will prove true is too much gaiety to hope. But religion, law, liberty and my own fame are at stake. I will go on and leave the event to God." [3]

The " Committee of Safety " then began their own attack upon the City of London, on Nov. 11, by appointing a commission of seventy-five for the militia, with Skippon and the Lord Mayor at its head.[4] The militia officers received fresh commissions from Fleetwood, as General of the Army.

John Canne now recommenced his journalism. Oliver Williams, who, as was pointed out in the introduction, " revived " his " Office of Intelligence " this year, had taken advantage of Scot's permission to issue licensed news-books by publishing a bi-weekly, the first number of which had appeared on June 30, as *A Particular Advice*

---

[1] *Mercurius Politicus*, Nov. 10–17.
[2] *Ibid.*, Nov. 17–24.
[3] John Price : *Mystery and Method of His Majesty's Restoration.*
[4] *Mercurius Politicus*, Nov. 10–17.

from the Office of Intelligence, and had been supplemented
by *Occurrences from Foreign Parts* on July 26. These
two periodicals, concerned chiefly with advertisements
from Williams's " Office of Intelligence," were appearing
on Fridays and Tuesdays respectively. Canne now
undertook to edit them both. In a long notice published
on Nov. 15, Canne announced his assumption of the editorship by stating that " in the *Publick Intelligencer* and
Mercurius Politicus I have no hand," but that he had
" condescended to the desire of friends " and would
henceforth write Oliver Williams's two periodicals. Anyone who desired anything to be published in them was
directed to write to him at his own address, the " Three
Stills, without Bishopsgate." [1]

About the same time Monck's Commissioners in London
had been summoned back to Scotland, and had refused
to stay, says Rugge, despite the entreaties of the " Committee of Safety."

On Nov. 15 Monck addressed the Commission of the
Counties and Boroughs of Scotland, which he had previously assembled at Edinburgh, stating that he was
about to march into England to assert the freedom of
Parliaments and the " freedom and rights of these three
nations from arbitrary and tyrannical usurpations upon
their consciences, persons and estates," and requesting
them to preserve order during his absence [2] in England.
And on Nov. 23 Lord Mayor Alleyn and the Common

[1] *Occurrences from Foreign Parts*, No. 38, for Nov. 8–15, 1659.

[2] The only commonly truthful narrative of all that took place is
to be found in *The Faithful Intelligencer from the Parliament's Army
in Scotland*, No. 1, Nov. 29–Dec. 3, 1659. Printed by Christopher
Higgins at Edinburgh (Thomason tract E, 1010 (20). It contains a
detailed refutation of Nedham's falsehoods.

This is the only number extant at the British Museum. With No. 2,
for Dec. 8–15, this periodical was entitled *Mercurius Britannicus*, and
lasted up to and inclusive of No. 6 for Jan. 4–6. These last numbers
are to be seen at Worcester College, Oxford.

See more of this periodical in Mr. W. J. Couper's *The Edinburgh
Periodical Press* (1908).

Council of London had received and read a letter from him on the same subject, with which they had been very well satisfied. But Nedham described their reading of this letter as follows : " Which being read, it was so disliked by the Common Council that not one spake anything to second it." [1] This falsehood angered the City intensely and Monck himself still more, for he now saw plainly that unless he found a journalist who would truthfully report his proceedings, his aim to gain a " Free Parliament " might be defeated. So an officer of his Army was instructed to write an account of all that had taken place and to refute Nedham's falsehoods. Accordingly, the *Faithful Intelligencer from the Parliament's Army in Scotland* was printed at Edinburgh, and, as regards the first number at least, was reprinted in London, probably brought thither by Clarges, who had at the same time received instructions to find a journalist in London to represent Monck.

But, before Clarges returned, the " Committee of Safety " perpetrated its last and most fatal blunder. The City apprentices had circulated and signed a petition to the Lord Mayor, urging him to declare for a " Free Parliament." Three or four thousand apprentices had signed the petition, and the Lord Mayor had agreed to receive it on Dec. 5. The apprentices then rose in arms. Though the City was already full of soldiers, the " Committee of Safety " ordered four regiments to march into it in order to overawe the apprentices, and placed them under the command of the notorious Hewson, the hideous ruffian who spat in Charles I's face at the " trial," and who had carried out all the atrocities of Cromwell's massacre at Drogheda. Presumably the citizens anticipated that " Drogheda measure " might now be meted out to themselves, for, says Rugge, in his diary, " He had but one eye, but they called him ' Blind Cobbler,' ' Blind Hewson,'

---

[1] *Mercurius Politicus* for Nov. 17–24.

and did throw old shoes and slippers, turnip-tops, brick-bats, stones and tiles at him and his soldiers," as he was marching to the Royal Exchange. There he stayed a little space and then marched to the Guildhall, meeting with worse affronts on the way. Someone fired a pistol at them, and at last the soldiers fired in earnest, and " four or five of the apprentices, whereof one was a cobbler," were killed and others wounded, " some of the soldiers being also dangerously wounded. But the actions of the soldiers had been contrary to the orders of the Lord Mayor, who came out of the Guildhall and made a speech, begging them to desist." Hewson then marched back out of the City, taking down the gates of Temple Bar on his way home. The Lord Mayor and Common Council then received the apprentices' petition and promised to consider it, which was a distinct blow to the " Committee of Safety."

But the apprentices still considered a way " to clear the City of the Lobsters," as they called the troops of horse, and, until Monck's arrival in London, remained in a condition of open rebellion against the Army. The trade of the City in the meanwhile had vanished.

Events then moved rapidly. After his defeat by Lambert at the Houses of Parliament, Hesilrige had fled to Portsmouth, where the garrison declared for the Speaker as their General against the Army. Admiral Lawson, who was an anabaptist, also declared for the Rump and set sail for the Thames. The " Committee of Safety " sent as many troops as they could spare against Portsmouth, but when the men arrived there they mutinied and also declared for the Rump.

In the meantime, the " Committee of Safety " pressed forward with its arrangements for the meeting of yet another imposture to be called a Parliament. On Dec. 13 it published " Seven Principles and Unalterable Fundamentals of the General Council of Officers at Wallingford

House." [1] Stripped of the phraseology in which men of their class delighted, the gist of the whole of these was summed up in the third " principle " : " That an Army may be continued and maintained and be conducted, so far as may secure the peace of these nations, and *not be disbanded*, nor the conduct thereof altered, but by consent of the ' Conservators ' appointed."

A new set of twenty-one officials with the high-sounding title of " Conservators of Liberty " was then appointed—really with the object of enslaving the nation to the Army.

Nedham then again intervened with fresh falsehoods. " In the evening," wrote he, after setting out these " principles," " the committee of the City had a meeting here [at Wallingford House] with his Excellency [Fleetwood] and some of the officers; at which time the said Principles and Fundamentals being communicated to them, they seemed to receive contentment therein."

This was the last straw, for the very next day (Tuesday, Dec. 20) after Nedham's *Publick Intelligencer* (for Dec. 12–19) had appeared with these comments in it, the Lord Mayor and Aldermen met and denounced its " many false and scandalous aspersions upon the Lord Mayor and committee" appointed to confer with Fleetwood " as if they had betrayed their trust." This denunciation of Nedham's *Publick Intelligencer* was printed at once, as a broadside, and posted about the City, by the Cty printer, James Flesher.

Finally, Fleetwood's officers and men mutinied; Lawson and the fleet were at Tilbury; the common soldiers were unpaid and clamoured for the money which the City refused to supply. Lambert's Army in the north had dwindled away day by day for the same cause, until at last he could no longer face Monck and Lord Fairfax (who was also in arms). Fleetwood acknowledged to the Speaker, in asking him to send to the Rump to return,

[1] *Publick Intelligencer* for Dec. 12–19, 1659.

that " the Lord had blasted their counsels, and (to use his own words) spit in their faces." [1]   So, on Boxing Day 1659, the Rump, for the third and last time, recommenced its sittings as a " Parliament," dismissed Vane and Fleetwood and the other " nine worthies," and ordered them out of London to their own homes.

[1] Baker's *Chronicle*.

CHAPTER V

HENRY MUDDIMAN AND GENERAL MONCK—CLUBS, SONGS, AND BALLADS OF THE TIMES

A QUAINT expression of the times, used of writing, was that a pen " walked " upon paper,[1] and with the re-entry upon the scene of the Rump on Dec. 26, pens began to " walk " furiously. Scot was totally unable to control the printing presses, probably because City magistrates were unwilling to act and City juries unwilling to convict. So, henceforward, a vast number of unlicensed tracts and broadsides began to appear—the fact that they were unlicensed being demonstrated by the absence of any printer's or publisher's name upon them.

That great enemy of bishops in general and of Archbishop Laud in particular, the old Puritan Prynne, was now hard at work on behalf of his King. When he studied he used to " put on a long quilted cap which came down over his eyes, serving as an umbrella to defend them from too much light, and, seldom eating a dinner, would every three hours or so be munching a roll of bread, and now and then refresh his exhausted spirits with ale." [2] He is said to have written a page for every day in his life and, signing his name boldly to them all, now began to pour pamphlets from the Press.[3]

[1] Cf. The *Kingdom's Weekly Intelligencer* for Sept. 25–Oct. 2, 1649, in which the " author " remarked : " I have for the most part waived the Parliament news, and shall so continue till I am better satisfied with what safety in relation to their counsels this pen may walk upon this paper, which I conceive was never more uncertain than at this present."

[2] Anthony a Wood's Life of Prynne in *Athenæ Oxonienses*.

[3] The dates and titles of some of these are all that most readers will care to see :

He grew so outrageously and, indeed, so rancorously demonstrative against the King's enemies, that, a few weeks later on, General Monck had to send Mr. William Morice to stop him, by telling him that he was doing more harm than good.

The most ominous sign of all for the Rump was that London began to sing. Everywhere songs were written, parodying the old ballads, to the detriment of the Rump and the Army. Some circulated in manuscript, others were printed as broadsides (or posters) to be posted on the walls of taverns, and sung by their patrons. This was an old custom in London.

It was nearly twenty years since London had seen its King and his nobles in all the state of those days. The people wished to go to Whitehall as of yore, and from the galleries of the perfumed great Hall to witness the King and Queen dining in public, attended by the great officers of the Household, and with the waiters kneeling as they presented each dish.[1] And, above all, they had missed the gorgeous processions preceding all the great Court ceremonies.

The Presbyterians had never wished to diminish the state that surrounded the King; indeed, while diminishing his absolute powers, they would rather have increased the ceremony with which the Sovereign was surrounded. So

---

Nov. 4, 1659. " A short, legal, medicinal, useful, safe, easie prescription to recover our kingdom, church, nation from their present dangerous distractive, destructive confusion, and worse than Bedlam madnesse."

Nov. 7, 1659. " A brief necessary vindication of the old and new secluded members," etc.

Nov. 8, 1659. " Conscientious, serious, theological and legal queries propounded to the twice-dissipated, self-created, Anti-Parliamentary Westminster Juncto," etc.

Feb. 2, 1660. " A legal vindication of the liberties of England against illegal taxes and pretended acts of Parliament."

Feb. 13, 1660. " The signal loyalty and devotion of God's true saints and pious Christians towards their kings."

[1] The Stuart kings were the last to be served " on the knee " and habitually dined publicly. Henry Muddiman's MSS. supply many instances of this.

that even they heartily took part in the revival of Martin
Parker's, the famous old ballad-writer's song, " When
the King enjoys his own again."   Composed in 1643, when
the King's fortunes were falling, this song, in one form or
another (for there are many different versions), was
wedded to a catching tune and became the comfort of the
adherents of the House of Stuart right up to the end of the
Jacobite rebellions of the eighteenth century.   This was
now re-issued, to the intense exasperation of the Rump,
and undoubtedly served the cause of the Restoration :

> " Though for a time we see Whitehall
> With cobwebs hanging on the wall
>   Instead of gold and silver brave,
>   Which formerly 'twas wont to have
>   With rich perfume
>   In every room,
> Delightful to that Princely train
>   Which again shall be
>   When the time you see
> That the King enjoys his own again." [1]

Scot's first care when this deluge of literature began had
been to secure the " news-books," and in this respect only
was he successful.   At the end of the first week in December he suppressed all of them, with the exception of the
bi-weeklies written by Marchamont Nedham and by John
Canne.[2]

Canne's *Particular Advice from the Office of Intelligence*
was now re-named *An Exact accompt of the daily Proceedings in Parliament*, and with its supplement, entitled

[1] The notes to this song in Ritson's *Ancient Songs and Ballads* are
absurdly erroneous.   Booker was an astrologer and almanac-maker,
and so were " Pond," " Swallow," " Dove " and " Dade."   Their
almanacs still exist.   " Walker " was Henry Walker (alias Luke
Harruney), the author of *Perfect Occurrences*, and is nicknamed " Toby "
because of John Taylor's burlesque sermon by him on " Tobies dogges
Tayle."

[2] MS. notes by George Thomason in Volume E, 1013, of his tracts.
After Tract No. 1 in this volume he wrote, " No more weekly news, as
' Scout,' ' Intelligencer,' and all prohibited," and there is a similar note
on the title-page of Tract 23 in the same volume.   The suppressed
periodicals were, *The Loyall Scout*, the *Weekly Post*, the *Weekly Intelligencer* and the *Perfect Diurnall*.   No copy of the latter has survived
(for 1659).

Occurrences from Foreign Parts, became the organ of the restored Rump. Nedham's two periodicals, *Mercurius Politicus* and the *Publick Intelligencer*, remained as they were, and were the organ of the Army.

Thus, when Clarges returned from Scotland with orders to find a journalist to represent General Monck, the need for protection against the falsehoods of Nedham and Canne was more urgent than ever. Clarges was an apothecary in the Strand, on the north side, near Charing Cross, and his sister, Nan Clarges, was the widow of a milliner named Radford, in the New Exchange, when she married Monck. The New Exchange was an arcade, with upper and lower galleries, situated on the south side of the Strand, about fifty yards east of what is now Charing Cross Station. Thus it is quite clear that in selecting the son of another Strand tradesman, Edward Muddiman, who lived at the " Seven Stars," between the New Exchange and York House, for his journalist, George Monck followed the advice of his brother-in-law and wife, and chose someone who was well known to all three. Clarges, therefore, induced Henry, the son of Edward Muddiman, to abandon his career as a schoolmaster and to issue a news-book under his own direction.[1]

Thus, Monck's journalist was not brought into contact with Thomas Scot. Henry Muddiman was the son of Edward Muddiman, by his first wife, Alice, and was baptized at St. Martin's in the Fields on Feb. 5, 1629. Edward Muddiman came of ancient Warwickshire stock, from Wolfamcote, not far from Nuneaton, on the borders of Northamptonshire, and had settled in London with his brother William.[2] By the time when Charles II was

[1] On Dec. 26, 1659, the date of Muddiman's first number, Clarges wrote to Gumble : " The scene of affairs here is much altered in one week, as you may perceive by the enclosed diurnall, which is a book published by my directions, for I have been a great printer since I came hither." (Leyborne-Popham MSS. p. 137.)

[2] Maria, daughter of William and Elizabeth Muddiman, was baptized at St. Martin's-in-the-Fields on August 11, 1627. John Muddiman,

crowned, William Muddiman had been knighted, for, at
the coronation review in Hyde Park, on May 7, 1661, we
are told that " after the King was seated, there passed by
him only one regiment of foot and Sir Nicholas Crisp's
regiment of horse; then my Lord Mayor's troop of horse,
commanded by Sir William Muddiman, all citizens. For
state before him was led a goodlike horse, with bridle,
saddle and furniture after the Indian manner, and a tall
swarthy-complexioned man leading him, clad also in a
loose garment, cap and boots or buskins after the same
manner." [1] This, it would seem, was in compliment to
Catherine of Braganza's dowry of Bombay. Edward
Muddiman was a man of some substance, for at the commencement of the year 1646 he was appointed by Parliament one of the two collectors of the assessment for the
parish of St. Martin's-in-the-Fields, " for raising of money
for Sir Thos. Fairfaxes Army." [2] He died in July 1659,
and thus did not live to see the Restoration.[3]

The future journalist was educated at the choir school
of St. Clement Danes, Strand, under Mr. Burnap, and
on Sept. 24, 1647, was admitted a pensioner at St. John's
College, Cambridge,[4] where his tutor was Mr. Burnby.
Muddiman, however, does not seem to have graduated,
probably because the college later on was converted into
a prison. By 1659 he was a schoolmaster, probably at
St. Clement Danes.

On Monday, Dec. 26, " No. 1 " of Henry Muddiman's
news-book appeared under the full title of *The Parlia-*

---

son of Sir William Muddiman or Muddyman (as the name was sometimes spelt), was a friend of Rochester. There is a somewhat scandalous
letter from him to Rochester printed in the Calendars of MSS. of the
Marquess of Bath, Vol. ii, 152.
    [1] Historical Manuscripts Commission, Report V., Appendix, p. 203
(Duke of Sutherland's MSS.).
    [2] Cal. S.P. Dom., Charles I, 1645–47, pp. 327–8.
    [3] Nuncupative will, proved July 28, 1659.
    [4] *Admissions to the College of St. John the Evangelist, in the University
of Cambridge*, Part I, p. 86 : " Henry Muddiman, de Strand," London,
son of Edward Muddiman, " sutoris vestiarii."

mentary Intelligencer, comprising the Sum of Forraigne Intelligence, with the affairs now in agitation in England, Scotland and Ireland. To this was added the motto, probably taken from Erasmus's *Colloquies* (then much in repute with schoolmasters as a means of teaching Latin), "Nunquam sera est ad bonos mores via." This paraphrase of " It is never too late to mend " was perhaps intentionally ambiguous, but for the moment referred to the restoration of the Rump. Entire absence of a controversial tone and the adoption of all the cant political phrases of the times added further to the deceptive appearance of Muddiman's news-book, and in his second number he even wrote of Charles II as " the pretended King of England," and of his brothers as " the titular Dukes of York and Gloucester." [1] But Muddiman was extremely careful to do what Canne and Nedham did not do—that is, to chronicle Monck's proceedings in great detail. Ten days later (on Jan. 5) there appeared the Thursday's version of this news-book, entitled *Mercurius Publicus*, etc., with the different motto, taken from Virgil, of " Hic noster nuncius esto." [2]

This was written by Giles Dury, of whom nothing is known, save that in all probability he was a Scotsman, and that Anthony à Wood states that he " gave over " after the Restoration and left his collaborator Muddiman to write and control both periodicals. It seems certain that he then became Muddiman's chief clerk and managed his news-letter correspondence for him.[3]

[1] In the *Parliamentary Intelligencer* No. 2, for Dec. 26–Jan. 2. p. 14, when informing his readers that Charles II arrived at Brussels on Dec. 26. The first two or three numbers contained only eight pages. Muddiman had not had time to organize his correspondence, but later on the regulation size of two sheets, or sixteen pages, was adopted by him.
[2] The earlier numbers of *Mercurius Publicus* are only to be seen in Wood's collections at the Bodleian Library. No. 13, for March 22–29 1659–60, was the first " printed by order of the Council of State " and dropped the quotation from Virgil.
[3] When Sir John Trevor was appointed Secretary of State, in succession to Sir William Morice, in 1668, Hickes wrote to Williamson that

The ubiquitous Pepys, of course, made Muddiman's acquaintance and recorded the fact in his Diary on Jan. 9, 1660, as follows : " Met with W. Simons, Muddiman, and Jack Price, and went with them to Harper's, and in many sorts of talk stayed till two of the clock in the afternoon. I found Muddiman a good scholar, an arch rogue, and owns that though he writes new[s]books for the Parliament, yet he did declare that he did it only to get money and did talk very basely of many of them. . . . Thence I went with Muddiman to the coffee-house and gave 18*d.* to be entered of the club."

Had Pepys been better informed at this time, he would have known that General Monck's journalist was not likely to speak very cordially of the Rump, and that Scot was not his censor.   However, it was not long before Pepys was undeceived.

The origin of London clubs has been a matter of conjecture.   Most writers date their origin to the convivial evenings spent in taverns by Shakespeare and by Ben Jonson in the company of their friends, but nothing more can be said about either of these two coteries than that they were in the habit of frequenting a particular tavern, for the word " club " did not come into use until the times of the so-called Commonwealth.   Aubrey, who was a well-informed contemporary, states distinctly that the word " club " was introduced about this time and that it signified " a sodality meeting in a tavern."

---

he believed " J. D." and " H. M." would be " much to seek for their employments and intelligences " (Cal. S.P. Dom., 1667–1668, p. 549). By "J. D." Hickes almost certainly meant " G. D." or Giles Dury.   The original draft of Henry Muddiman's news-letters is almost entirely in the handwriting of one man—Muddiman himself and others of his clerks merely contributing occasional paragraphs.   The draft (which extends from 1667 to 1689) bears every appearance of having been dictated, and was probably taken down by Dury in the first instance in shorthand.   Muddiman himself wrote with numerous contractions, and his characteristic handwriting is easily identified by means of his letters to Williamson in the State Papers.

We first begin to hear of clubs shortly after Cromwell conferred upon himself the title of " Protector," and their origin seems to have been due to two different causes—the introduction of coffee into England,[1] and the cliques formed, probably limited to elected members, who met to discuss plans for Cromwell's overthrow.

One of these clubs, and I think it must have been the first, dated from 1657, was called the " Commonwealth Club," and met at a tavern called the " Nonsuch," in Bow Street, Covent Garden, a house in which one William Parker had been installed by Wildman, the Leveller. Wildman, it is needless to add, was in Cromwell's pay, as a spy, at the time. The " Commonwealth Club " numbered eighty members, amongst whom were Harry Marten, Okey, Hesilrige, Hacker and Wildman himself—all the discontented spirits of the time, as a matter of fact. Thanks to Wildman the plans of this Club were always defeated.[2]

The club to which Muddiman took Pepys was the " Rota Club," founded by James Harrington in 1659, in order to discuss his proposed constitution for the Commonwealth of England, on which subject he had published pamphlets.

Like everybody else, Harrington had a scheme for a Parliament in place of the Rump, and this scheme took the fantastic form of an assembly of a thousand and fifty members, one-third of whom were to be balloted out every year in rotation. Hence the name of " Rota " given to the club whose members met to discuss Harring-

---

[1] The first advertisement of coffee was printed in the *Publick Adviser* of 1657. A pamphlet entitled *Endless Queries; or, An End to Queries*, published on June 13, 1659, asks : " Whether the learned College of Physicians, if they be not too full of practice, should not do a good act to meet and examine whether coffee, sherbet, that came from Turkey, chocolate, much used by the Jews, Brosa, by the Muscovites, Ta and Tee, and such other new-fangled drinks, will agree with the constitution of our English bodies."

[2] The account of this club is given in Bilcliffe's evidence, in the State Papers, Domestic Series, Charles II, Vol. 41, Nos. 30 and 32.

ton's theories and plans at Miles's Coffee House in Palace
Yard, " where you take water." Aubrey says the speeches
in the Parliament House were but flat to those to be heard
at the Rota, and in any case many of the thinking men of
the times—whether attracted by the debates, or by the
novelty of the recently introduced beverage—were
members of the Rota Club. They sat round an oval table,
with a passage in the middle for Miles to deliver his coffee.
Milton, Marvell, Cyriac Skinner, Nevill and Sir William
Petty were all " disciples and virtuosi " of the Rota. At
one time, Aubrey tells us, " Mr. Stafford and his friends
came in drunk from the tavern and affronted the Junto."
Whereupon " the soldiers offered to kick them down
stayres, but Mr. Harrington's moderation and persuasion
hindered it."

The Rota came to an end with the Restoration, but
attracted a great deal of attention and some satires
during its brief period of existence.

Pepys's mistake in thinking Muddiman wrote for the
Rump had been aided by the new journalist's selection
of John Macock as his printer, for Macock was the actual
printer of the Rump, nearly all of whose documents in
1659 were subscribed " Printed by John Streater and John
Macock." Streater had been an officer in Cromwell's
Army, and when Cromwell assumed the title of " Protector," became one of his bitterest opponents.[1]

Cromwell arrested and imprisoned him repeatedly—on
one occasion for two periodicals which hinted at the ad-
visability of assassinating him [2]—and Streater was never

---

[1] Streater's career has never been traced, and it does not seem to have
been realized that he was the Colonel Streater who took part in arresting
Lambert, at Daventry, in 1660. His autobiography was printed on
May 23, 1659, and entitled *Secret Reasons of State*. On Nov. 21, 1653,
he published *Clavis ad aperiendum carceris ostia*. He republished
Killing no Murder in 1659, under the initials " J. S.," and made some
additions to this tract.

[2] The two periodicals were *Observations, Historical, Political and
Philosophical, upon Aristotle's first book of Political Government, together*

quite free until the Rump returned to power in 1659. Then he was rewarded by being promoted Colonel, and on Aug. 9 was appointed " Comptroller of The train of Artillery." About the same time he was appointed printer to the " Parliament," in lieu of Henry Hills,[1] Cromwell's printer, who, however, continued to print for the Army.

As Streater's more lucrative military occupation prevented him from following his calling, he farmed out his work to John Macock, and thus the Rump's official documents bear the imprint of " John Streater and John Macock." Macock's printing house was on " Addle Hill, near Baynards Castle." Streater, of course, had no business address at this time and lived at Highgate. A

---

with a narrative of State Affairs in England, Scotland and Ireland (No. 1, April 4–11, 1654, only to be seen in the Burney Collection), and a Politick Commentary upon the Life of Caius July Cæsar (No. 1, May 23, 1654).

[1] Henry Hills was the son of a ropemaker at Maidstone and postillion to Thomas Harrison, the regicide. He first printed for the Army in 1647, at Oxford, and afterwards at London. In 1651 Hills was sued for " crim. con." by Thomas Hams, a tailor, of Swan Alley, Blackfriars, and cast in damages for £260. He then addressed a letter from the Fleet Prison to Hams, imploring his forgiveness, and published his tract entitled The Prodigal's Return to his Father's House, to which Kiffen and King contributed prefaces. Next, in company with one Ives, he misappropriated the anabaptists' funds. On March 6, 1656, Cromwell ordered the copyright of the Bible to be entered in the Stationers' Registers as the joint property of Hills and John Field of Cambridge. (Cal. S.P. Dom., 1655–1656, p. 289, and Transcript of the Stationers' Registers, March 6, 1656.) The resulting Bibles were the most erroneous ever printed. One omitted the " not " in the Seventh Commandment. (W. Kilburne's Dangerous Errors in several late printed Bibles, 1659; and The Printers' Lamentation, or the Press opprest and overpressed, Sept. 3, 1660.) Hills then became printer to every form of Government up to and including that of James II, shortly before whose accession he had become a Catholic. Papists generally refused to believe in his conversion, and the result was that a full Life of H. Hills was printed in 1688 by an indignant " recusant." Hills's son Robert, by his second wife, Elizabeth, " a born Papist," was presented to a demyship at Magdalen College, Oxford (Bloxam's Magdalen College and James II). At the Revolution, Hills fled to St. Omer, where he died in 1691. ("Petition of Henry Hills, junior," his son by his first wife, in Cal. S.P. Dom., William and Mary, 1690–1691, p. 485, and Petition of his widow in ibid. 1694–1695, p. 206.) The life of Hills in the Dictionary of National Biography confuses him with his eldest son, and should be discarded in favour of the tracts it misdescribes as " scurrilous," and the records cited above.

curious piece of evidence, to be adduced later on, will prove that Macock lived at Hornsey.

Even before the Rump had resumed its sittings the apprentices of the City indicted Hewson for the murder of the apprentices killed by his orders on Dec. 5.[1] The "malice and hatred they bore him," says Rugge, " was testified during the heavy snows of January," for the young men in Fleet Street and St. Paul's Churchyard made an effigy in snow of Hewson " with one eye in the head and with an odd face, a halter or rope about his neck, a horn on his head and a writing on his breast, ' This is old Hewson the cobbler,' for he was but a cobbler by trade and had but one eye and an odd face." But the Rump, to the disgust of all, pardoned Hewson. On Jan. 6, 1660, he returned thanks to the House,[2] but was ordered to leave London for the country. He was at once celebrated in a song, of which three verses will bear quotation :

> " Listen awhile to what I shall say
> Of a blind cobbler that's gone astray
> Out of the Parliament's Highway :
> Good people, pity the blind.

> " Oliver made him a famous Lord
> That he forgot his cutting board,
> But now his thread's twisted to a cord :
> Good people, pity the blind.

> " Sing Hi, Ho, Hewson, the State ne'er went upright,
> Since cobblers could pray, preach, govern and fight ;
> We shall see what they'll do now you're out of sight :
> Good people, pity the blind."[3]

---

[1] " They have found by the coroner's inquest that they who killed the men the other day are guilty of murder, and have caused Hewson to be indicted of the murder."—Clarendon to Sir H. Bennet on Dec. 27, 1659 (*Clarendon's State Papers*, iii. 636).

[2] Commons Journals, Jan. 6.

[3] " *A Hymne to the Gentle Craft; or, Hewson's Lamentation. To the tune of the Blind Beggar.*" Published on Jan. 11, 1660. A satire entitled the *Outcry of the London Apprentices*, published on Jan. 16, began as follows :

" Sound Drums and Trumpets ! Will you buy any brooms ? Have you any boots and shoes to mend ? So cries the noble Lord Hewson, Baron of Bungle Hall, to his lasting honour and renown."

Hewson was thus enabled to escape from England into France when the King returned, and instead of being executed for high treason, died of starvation at Rouen in 1661 or 1662, a refugee among the very Papists hatred of whom was the overmastering passion of his life.[1]

Broadside after broadside ridiculing the Rump and the Army in verse now appeared. *England's Murthering Monsters, set out in their colours in a dialogue between Democritus and Heraclitus,* published on Jan. 5, can hardly have been regarded by the so-called " Parliament " or the Army with equanimity, more especially as it went on to add, "*Weeping Heraclitus laments to see Jack Anabaptist in such a state to be. Democritus hopes before the month of June that the birds will sing another tune,*" *A New Year's Gift for the Rump. The Rump roughly but righteously handled in a new ballad; to the tune of Cook Lorrel,* and a *Letany for the New Year* followed, and were abusive in the highest degree. And on Jan. 16 the writer of *A New Ballad to an Old Tune,* " *Tom of Bedlam,*" sang :

> " Make room for an honest red coat
> (And that you'll say is a wonder);
> The gun and the blade are his tools—and his trade
> Is—for pay—to kill and plunder."

On the same day *The Gang; or, The Nine Worthies* appeared as well as *The Hangman's Last Will and Testament,* with its threatening burden of " I and my gallows groan " :

> " I have lived to see such wretchedness
> Where none but honesty are crimes,
> That my ropes are turned into rimes.
> I and my gallows groan."

Vane had a special ballad devoted to him on Jan. 18 (after the Rump banished him) entitled *Vanity of Vanities; or, Sir Harry Vane's Picture; to the tune of the Jews' Corant.*

---

[1] Evidence of Richard Harby, who was arrested on suspicion of being Hewson in 1666. The document is inaccurately summarized on page 321 of the Calendar for 1665, all mention of Hewson's death from starvation being omitted, as well as other details tending to establish the truth of Harby's story.

> " Have you not seen a Bartholomew baby,
> A pageant of policy as fine as maybe,
> That's gone to be shown at the Manor of Raby,
>   Which nobody can deny."

One verse in this alluded to Vane's defeat of the Royalist rising, by the aid of Willys :

> " Of this State and Kingdom he is the Bane,
> He shall have the reward of Judas and Cain,
> And 'twas he that overthrew Charles, his wain,
>   Which nobody can deny."

Last of all, a song expressed the universal anxiety with which Monck's arrival in London was awaited :

> " Till it be understood
>   What is under Monck's hood,
>   The City dare not show its horns
>   Till ten days be out.
>   The Speaker's sick of the gout,
>   And the Rump doth sit upon thorns." [1]

On New Year's Day, 1660, General Monck's famous march from Scotland, the " Iter Boreale " of the poem of John Wild, the Presbyterian, began. Hobbes describes it as " the greatest stratagem that is known in history."

" 'Twas now the 1st of Jan. 1660, it was the Lord's Day too, and it was His doing," wrote John Price, Monck's chaplain. " The frost was great, and the snow greater, and I do not remember that ever we trod upon plain earth from Edinburgh to London. The air this day was so very clear too, that we could distinguish the very colours of the pebbles in the Tweed."

The Rump had suggested that Monck should come down with five hundred men. He came with four thousand foot and eighteen hundred horse, splendidly equipped in every way. And the provident Scots had furnished him with £70,000 with which to pay his men. Lambert's soldiers vanished before him, those of them who remained being disbanded and paid off. They had taken " free quarter " everywhere. Monck's men paid for everything.

---

[1] *The Rump dock't*, published on Jan. 21, 1660.

As Monck moved on in a semi-royal progress, petitions poured in, all, without exception, begging for a " Free Parliament " or for the restoration of the secluded members. To all he returned evasive answers or referred them to the " Parliament." The Rump, greatly alarmed at all they heard of what was going on, sent Scot and Robinson (member for Scarborough)[1] to meet him at Leicester, ostensibly to welcome him, but really to spy upon him and see and hear what was done. They did not scruple to bore holes in doors and partitions, the better to conduct their eavesdropping, but all in vain. " George was dark," chewed his tobacco, gave nods or frowns to importunate persons, and left Scot and Robinson to do the talking. One of Monck's own officers publicly accused Monck of an intention to restore the King, and was publicly caned by the General for his pains. At St. Albans, after a speech to Monck from a local magnate, Sir Richard Temple, Scot flew into a rage, " turned into Mars," and told Sir Richard " that he himself would first take up the sword, as old as he was" before the things that the Hertfordshire gentry were petitioning for should be granted.[2]

The Rump had filled London with eight thousand foot and two thousand horse, but when Monck reached

---

[1] Luke Robinson was expelled from the House of Commons in July 1660; and, " before his exit he made a recanting speech at the bar of nearly half-an-hour long, all bathed in tears " (Historical Manuscripts Commission, Report V., Appendix, p. 199).

[2] These petitions were all printed separately, but can most conveniently be seen in a collection entitled *A Happy Handfull; or, Green Hopes in the Blade*, etc., published on May 2, 1660. This contains the Declaration of Sir George Booth; the Declaration of Lord Mayor Alleyn and the Common Council of Dec. 20, 1659, against Nedham; the Petition of the Apprentices, read on Dec. 5; the Petition of the Apprentices to Monck at St. Albans of Feb. 2; the Declarations of the Nobility and Gentry of Kent, Westminster, Leicester, Northampton, Bucks, Gloucester, Suffolk, Norfolk, Devon, York, Lincoln, and of the Watermen (with the Hue and Cry after Colonel Whitton and his decoys). Also the " Remonstrances " (or declarations) of the Eastern, Southern and Western Associations, of Bedford, Essex, Nottingham, and of Coote and the officers in Dublin, with many more from Royalists.

St. Albans he demanded their withdrawal, on the ground that their quarters were needed for his own men.

The Rump complied, but was unable to pay the men they sent away, so the result was a mutiny. The men " fell upon their officers, beat them, took away their colours, broke the drums in pieces, and secured Somerset House, mounting seven pieces of ordnance by the doors." They then also cried out for a " Free Parliament " and " threatened to blow up the Rump." The same night the London Apprentices joined in and " beat up a drum for a Free Parliament," but were scattered by a regiment of horse.[1] When he heard of this at St. Albans, Scot rose out of his bed in the middle of the night and, attired only in his cap, nightshirt and slippers, went to Monck, and " by his authority required him to march into London at once and suppress the mutiny. But the General calmly answered, ' I will undertake for this night's disturbances and be early enough in the morning to prevent any mischief.' And thus this artifice to mingle the soldiers, so that they might be less at the General's devotion, was prevented." [2]

In the meantime, the Royalists were dangerous, as Clarendon's correspondence proves. A new rising was contemplated.

A second rising in arms would at once unite the Army and the Rump, and thus the cause of religion and liberty for which Monck stood might be imperilled or lost. No county had given Monck so much trouble by its exuberant loyalty as his native Devon, obviously because Devonshire men knew all about him and knew what his sentiments really were. At any rate, Mr. Rolle and the Devonshire gentry had sent a letter to Monck which seems to have demanded the restoration of the King. Monck answered with a letter, dated Jan. 23, read in the House of Commons

[1] Letter of Feb. 7 in Leyborne-Popham MSS., p. 144.
[2] Price's *Mystery and Method*, etc.

on Jan. 26, and printed and published, in which he repeated the stock arguments of the Rump. Monarchy could not possibly be admitted, wrote he, because of the forfeited estates of the King and the Church. Nor could the secluded members be readmitted, because such a thing would " immediately involve all these nations in most horrid and bloody war afresh." This was a set-back to the " ranting royalists," and had the beneficial effect of preventing any fresh attempt at a rising in arms like that of the previous August.

But these were not Monck's real sentiments and (no doubt by private arrangement) the only man whom he really trusted, William Morice, immediately answered him in a pamphlet published on Feb. 3. As Morice was in Devon at the time, this points to some arrangement between the two.[1]

The General's arguments, Morice replied, were supported on the " Harringtonian principle, that the support of monarchy being taken away that Government cannot be admitted, I must first remember him that the King's lands are not all the support of monarchy." Morice went on to quote Grotius and Aristotle to prove that monarchy was the best form of government, and that one king was better than many kings, typified by the Rump. The King thanked Morice in a letter from Brussels dated 17/27 March.[2]

In the meantime the Rump determined to get up some petitions to itself, requesting it to go on with its work and keep out the King, in order to counteract the effect

[1] *Animadversions upon General Monck's letter to the gentry of Devon ; Wherein his arguments for anarchy are considered, and the weakness of his Harringtonian principles detected. By M. W.* Thomason has filled in William Morice's name to these initials on his copy. Many others must have been equally well aware who " M. W." was, and thus the effect of the pamphlet would be the greater among Monck's personal friends.

[2] The letter is in the Thurloe State Papers, vii. p. 859. It does not mention the pamphlet, but there can have been no other reason for it at this date.

of the petitions to Monck. The watermen, as being the most illiterate class in the community, were selected for the first experiment. One Colonel Whitton obtained the marks of several thousands of them to a petition he had drawn up, informing them that it was to have hackney coachmen put down. The petition was presented nevertheless on Jan. 31, met with a most gracious reception, and was reported in full by Nedham and Canne in their news-books, but ignored by Muddiman. When the watermen were told of what they had really " signed " they were furious, and applied to old Prynne for relief. That worthy at once drew up a manifesto and a " Hue and Cry after Colonel Whitton and his decoys," which was said to have been " signed " by ten thousand watermen between London and Staines.

Early on Friday, Feb. 3, General Monck marched into London from Finchley Heath, down Chancery Lane and along the Strand to Whitehall and St. James's.

" The foot were the likeliest men I ever saw," wrote an eye-witness. " All the officers had red and white favours in their hats, and his trumpeters and foot-boys bore a red livery, laced with silver lace." Still, the soldiers of Somerset House would not budge, until a couple of hours later they were found ten shillings apiece. Then they parted quietly and marched off to Canterbury, according to their orders. The next day, Saturday, the 4th, the oath of abjuration of the House of Stuart was tendered to Monck. He refused to take it.

CHAPTER VI

MONCK RESTORES THE LONG PARLIAMENT—MUDDIMAN
AND DURY OFFICIAL JOURNALISTS—MEETING OF THE
CONVENTION PARLIAMENT AND RECALL OF THE KING

O N Monday, February 6, Monck attended in the House
of Commons. Refusing a chair, he stood whilst
he addressed the members present and made some
ominous remarks in his reply to Lenthall : " As I marched
from Scotland hither," said he, " I observed the people in
most counties in great and earnest expectations of settlement; and they made several applications to me, with
numerous inscriptions. The chiefest heads of their
desires were for a full and free Parliament." Here his
eyes must have roved round the rows of empty seats
before him. " And," he added, " for admittance of the
members secluded before 1649, without any previous
oath or engagement . . . I must say, with pardon to
you, that the less oaths and engagements are imposed
(with respect had to the security of the common cause)
your settlement will be sooner attained to." [1]

This speech really was an attack upon the " qualifications " discussed at intervals by the Rump throughout
the previous year, and the sole object of any " qualifications " at all was to prevent all but the supporters of the
Rump and the Army from voting for, or becoming

[1] As this speech was printed separately by Macock on the same day
it must have been previously prepared and handed to Muddiman to see
through the press. Orders from Monck to Muddiman about his
documents will be quoted later on. The speech also appeared in
Muddiman's *Parliamentary Intelligencer*, No. 8, for February 6–13,
without any comment.

members of, the House of Commons. In a satire, published two or three days previously, a pamphleteer neatly hit off the true state of this subject as follows :

" The Representative of the Parliament of England," said he, " had for many years employed their constant endeavour to impose freedom and liberty upon these nations, notwithstanding their obstinate reluctancy and opposition thereunto, who would take upon them, against all right and reason, to be their own judges." So that the " Representative," after " two scandalous ejections, found to their signal grief, that the red-coats, in whom they had always loyally acquiesced, failing of their pay, likewise of their trust," were changing sides and " adhered to the common enemy, that is to say, the Three Nations, in complying with their desires and addresses; which are to have this present Representative dissolved and a free Parliament speedily convened (which they tremble to think upon) or the secluded members admitted (which they equally abominate), or this present House supplied with new elections, which their bowels sigh to reflect upon." [1]

Angered by the plain hints in Monck's speech, Scot's first plot against Monck's life was now formed. He had made up his mind, directly he refused the oath of abjuration, that he would set him to work upon a task which Monck would refuse to undertake and thus give the Council of State the opportunity to send him to the Tower and try him for his life. Unfortunately for himself he had confided this plan to his son on the previous Saturday, and his son told his landlord, one Sturdy, in Russell Street. Sturdy went to Monck on Sunday the 5th, and the first result of the plan was that Monck took possession of the Tower on that day. Later on Sturdy was rewarded with a place in the Life-guards.

[1] *The Qualifications of Persons declared capable by the Rump Parliament to elect or be elected Members to supply their House*, published February 3, 1660 (Thomason tract E, 1015 (6)).

Scot's opportunity, however, came on Wednesday the 8th. The City, upon which the Rump had laid a tax of £100,000, " which nettled the citizens shrewdly," met in Common Council on that day, and resolved to adhere to a former vote not to pay any taxes. At a previous Council, of December 24, the Lord Mayor and Aldermen, mindful of the outrage by Hewson, had ordered chains and posts to be set up at the City gates and in principal places, in order to protect themselves against the soldiers. The Council of State, therefore, when it heard of this vote, ordered Monck to march into the City to destroy not only these chains and posts, but also the very gates and portcullises of the City. He was also to arrest a number of Common Councilmen who had been prominent in passing the vote hostile to the tax. If anything could put an end to Monck's popularity and render him odious to the City, it was thought, it would be for him to obey these orders. On the other hand, if he disobeyed, grounds for action against him would have been given.

Nevertheless Monck marched into the City the next day, Thursday the 9th. He removed the posts and chains, but before he destroyed the gates and portcullises he appealed from the Council of State to the Rump itself, sending a letter from the Guildhall to them that morning. In this he asked the Rump to remit the rest of the order and to be more lenient with the City, and to send out writs for a new Parliament. This letter was read in the afternoon, at the three o'clock sitting in the House of Commons, and the Rump, jubilant at the humiliation it was inflicting upon Monck, replied at once ordering him to proceed and to destroy the gates and portcullises. " Now, George, we have thee, body and soul," said Hesilrige in triumph, but Price wrote, " I took notice that he was more angry at the spies that were about him than at the work he was doing."

" Upon these further positive orders," wrote Muddiman,

" his Excellency suffered the soldiers to pull down the
Gates and Portcullisses; several are quite destroyed,
some yet stand; the ruines of the former bearing witness
of his obedience, whilest the latter remaine standing
monuments of his Love and Compassion to this great
City."

On the same day Praise-God Barebone, the anabaptist
leather-seller of Fleet Street, presented a petition to the
House. " Leanbone " (as he was nicknamed) asked: (1)
That no person should be allowed to sit or vote in this
or any other Parliament, or to hold any office in the Army
or Navy, or to be a public preacher, or instructor of youth,
unless he should abjure the whole line of the Stuarts, or
anyone else pretending to the Crown; and (2) that anyone
offering or taking any kind of step towards the introducing
of " Charles Stuart " should suffer the penalty for high
treason (that is, drawing, hanging and quartering); and
(3) that the same penalty should be awarded to anyone
who even ventured to propose the revocation of this law
when it was passed. He was thanked for this.

Nedham and Canne set out this truculent document in
full in their periodicals. Henry Muddiman ignored it
altogether, simply remarking that the House thanked
Barebone for proposing a new oath, but without telling
his readers of what nature it was.

General Monck slept at the Three Tuns Tavern in Guildhall Yard that night, and on Friday, the next day, which
was also the last day of his commission as one of the
Rump's Commissioners, marched out of the City back to
St. James's.

On February 13, Muddiman took care that all that had
been done should be known, by publishing a large broadside, printed by Macock, setting out the orders to Monck
and Monck's letter from the Guildhall asking for leniency
and for the filling up of the Parliament, together with
the Rump's reply.

The Portraiture of M[r] Praise God Barebone

(From the print in the Thomason tracts)

That Friday night Monck summoned his officers to him and drew up a lengthy letter to the Rump. This was sent to the House the next morning, Saturday, the 11th February. It was peremptory in tone, and in effect amounted to a command that " by Friday following they should send forth writs to fill up vacant places in the House, and when that was done fix a determinate time to their sitting and give place to another Parliament." [1]

By this time the City was, of course, literally infuriated with the Rump and did not in the least comprehend Monck. But the letter of the 11th made a large amends. Pepys went to see the Speaker read it, and says that after it was read Sir A. Hesilrige came out very angry, and Billing, a Quaker, standing at the door took him by the arm and cried, " Thou man, will thy beast carry thee no longer ? Thou must fall ! "

The blow was all the more severe, for on that day the Rump had made Monck one of five new Commissioners for the government of the Army. This Commission he never accepted. Three were to form a quorum and it was not necessary for Monck to be one of the three. Thus they were paving the way for more extreme measures against him.

Monck then marched back into the City on the same day, Saturday the 11th, and sent for the Lord Mayor and Aldermen to meet him at the Guildhall. Then, when they had sulkily obeyed, he made them a speech. He had noted, he said, " that the City had no representative in Parliament and that trade was suffering. And so he had written to the Commons telling them that their duty was to restore the secluded members and to issue writs

---

[1] The *Parliamentary Intelligencer*, February 6–13. Muddiman says that the letter of the 11th was too lengthy for him to set out in his newsbook, and refers his readers to the " true copy printed by his Excellencies own order, by John Macock." This also was published on February 13.

for a full and free Parliament, for which purpose he had
allowed them a week, and, until it was done, had informed
them that he had retired into the City." At this the
countenances of all changed and delight was the order of
the day. The news spread like wildfire and presently a
great demonstration took place.

All the bells of the City rang, the people thronged the
streets, shouting and cheering, and the citizens distributed money amongst Monck's soldiers. In the
evening, bonfires were lit everywhere and rumps of beef
roasted at them in derision of the mock Parliament.
The butchers in the Strand rang a peal with their knives
when they were going to sacrifice their Rump, and the
boys in Fleet Street broke Barebone's windows, noted
Pepys. Saturday night and Sunday night Monck passed
at the Glass House in Broad Street, attending St. Paul's
on Sunday with the Lord Mayor. On Monday, February
13, Monck removed to the house of Alderman Wale in
Throgmorton Street, next door to Drapers' Hall, and
during these three days Secretary Scot played his last
card, by plotting to assassinate him. There are several
witnesses to this fact, of whom Sir John Hinton, the
King's physician, is the most important.[1] The trap was
set by an invitation to dinner from some officers, and
the day before the dinner Hinton, having been called in
to attend a woman at the house where the dinner was to
have taken place, observed so many soldiers and arms
ready fixed that he took alarm and informed Monck, who
sent some people to investigate the matter and so did not
attend the dinner.

To the next number of his *Parliamentary Intelligencer*

---

[1] *Hinton's Memoirs.* A tract published on February 14, 1660, and
entitled *Peace to the Nation* (by Sir R. l'Estrange), also gives an account
of this plot. And see also the *Nicholas Papers*, iv. p. 197. On
December 26, 1662, Monck gave a certificate that William Carr was
instrumental in discovering a plot by Francis Scot, son of Thos. Scot,
to kill him. (*Clarke Papers*, IV. 273.)

Muddiman prefixed a fresh motto, taken by him from Plautus :

"non sic minantia pila
quam tutatur amor."

Finding that the Rump had not complied with his requests at the end of the week given them, that is, on Friday, February 17, Monck sent for the secluded members as well as for some members of the Rump to meet him at Alderman Wale's house on that day, where he heard all that both sides had to say.   Finally, after hearing everybody, he marched back to Whitehall on the 21st, mounted guards at the doors of the House of Commons, sent for all the members of the Long Parliament once more, and addressed them, telling them that he intended to readmit them, and stating that as regards any future settlement he placed himself " at their feet."   In order that he might not seem to adhere to any cause, or to dictate to them what he really wished them to do, he then proceeded to deliver himself of sentiments which were certainly not his own. He recommended to them a Commonwealth, without a King.   Thus, up to this moment, no party could claim that General Monck was its adherent.   He had entered into the secret councils of no party, he had effectually checked both the new Royalist rising and a projected massacre by the anabaptists.   He had not restored, did not restore, the King.   His great work, for which he deserves to be honoured by posterity, was that he restored the People, by giving them back their Parliament.   On the afternoon of that day, after more than ten years' interruption, the Long Parliament, so far as its House of Commons was concerned (for the House of Lords did not resume its sittings until Tuesday, April 25), commenced to sit once more, and the Rump, and all that it typified, was at an end for ever.

There was much hilarity as the secluded members resumed their places.   Prynne had armed himself with an old basket-hilted sword, which got between Sir William Waller's short legs and threw him down. Hesilrige stormed and raved outside and would not go in,[1] for, so Pepys tells us, he and his party knew nothing of what had taken place until they went to Westminster and found the secluded members in their seats.

The Rump's downfall was duly celebrated in a song representing its last lament :

> " Farewell
> False honours and usurped Power, farewell,
> For the great bell
> Of Justice rings in our affrighted ears.
> The Gripes
> Of wounded conscience far exceed all stripes,
> Yet are small types
> Of those sharp pains, Rebellion justly fears.
> See how
> Th' unmasked People hiss us out of doors
> And call us knaves,
> Because, though we their servants be,
> We made them but our slaves." [2]

Monck was at once appointed Lord General.

On the 23rd, Scot was ejected from his office of Secretary and a new Council of State of thirty-one appointed, chosen from all parties,[3] with Annesley as President. On Saturday, the 25th, Cromwell's old secretary, Thurloe, and Auditor-General Tompson were appointed Secretaries of State. John Rushworth was clerk. One sinister figure appeared on this council. It was Anthony Ashley Cooper, the future Earl of Shaftesbury, afterwards to be identified with the success of Titus Oates's " Popish Plot." This unscrupulous man was described by Butler as—

> " a politician
> With more heads than a beast in vision,
> And more intrigues in every one
> Than all the whores of Babylon."

---

[1] " Whether Sir Arthur did not act the raging Turk in Westminster Hall, when he saw the admission of the secluded members? " (*Free Parliament queries*, published on April 20, 1660. E, 1019 (23).)

[2] February 23, 1660. " *The Rump Ululant ; or, Penitence per force. Being the recantation of the old rust-roguy-rebellion-rampant, and now ruinous-rotten-rosted-Rump.* To the tune of Gerrard's Mistress."

[3] *Parliamentary Intelligencer*, February 20–27.

Butler added that, in the Council of State :

> " He, therefore, wisely cast about
> All ways he could, t' insure his throat,
> And hither came to observe and smoke
> What courses other riskers took,
> And to the utmost do his best
> To save himself and hang the rest." [1]

Finally, writs for a new Parliament, which ran in the " names of the keepers of the liberties of England by authority of Parliament," were issued.[2] This new Parliament, or Convention, was to assemble on April 25, 1660.

On Thursday, the 15th March, 1660, the Long Parliament sat for the last time. No one doubted what the new Parliament would do when it met. When all was over on that day, about six o'clock in the evening, a painter, Michael Darby by name, was passing by the Royal Exchange, on the outside of which was an empty niche where formerly stood the statue of King Charles the First. Over it the Rump had, in 1649, ordered the words to be painted, " Exit tyrannus, regum ultimus, anno libertatis Angliæ restitutæ primo, annoque Domini 1648." At the suggestion of some soldiers, Darby took his paint-pot, ascended his ladder, painted out the inscription, painted in " Vive le Roy," threw his cap into the air and called out with a loud voice, " God save King Charles the Second ! "

In August, 1660, Darby was appointed painter to the Mercers' Company in reward.[3]

In the meantime, Milton made a futile attempt to rehabilitate the Rump on March 3, by publishing his "Readie and Easie way to establish a free Commonwealth." This was published by the Fifth Monarchy bookseller,

[1] Butler, *Hudibras*, Part III. canto ii.
[2] *Parliamentary Intelligencer*, March 12–19, 1660.
[3] *Parliamentary Intelligencer*, March 12–19; *Mercurius Publicus*, August 16–23, 1660; Clarendon's *StatePapers*, iii. 725; and Pepys' *Diary* Guizot was the first writer to draw attention to this, but the man's name has hitherto been unknown.

Livewell Chapman, on March 3, and, put shortly, Milton's plan was to restore the Rump to unlimited power and to deprive the people of their rights in Parliament.

Needless to add, this advice fell quite flat. But the booklet elicited several answers, of which the most telling was by an anonymous writer, pretending to be Harrington, of the Rota Club.[1]

Milton's prose works, said this writer, were " printed for the Chandlers and Tobacco men," who used them to wrap up the candles and tobacco they sold, for nobody ever read them, though he had written his eyes out and they had cost the Rump £300 a year. " You have done your feeble endeavour to rob the Church," went on this satirist, " in your work against tithes. You have slandered the dead, worse than envy itself, and thrown your dirty outrage on the memory of a murthered Prince, as if the hangman were but your usher. These have been the attempts of your stiff, formal eloquence, which you arm accordingly with anything that lies in your way, right or wrong, not only begging but stealing questions and taking everything for granted that will serve your turn. For you are not ashamed to rob O. Cromwell himself and make use of his canting with ' signal assistance from Heaven ' and ' answering Condescensions.' The most impious Mahometan doctrine that was ever vented among Christians, and such as will serve as well to justifie any prosperous villainy amongst men."

Finally, Milton had " really proposed the most ready and easy way to establish downright slavery upon the nation that can possibly be contrived." For when the power of proposing and debating and the power of legislating were in one and the same hands, as he would have it, " that government was inevitably arbitrary and tyrannical."

[1] *The Censure of the Rota upon Mr. Milton's Readie and Easie way to establish a free Commonwealth.*

But Milton was outdone by Marchamont Nedham·
Nedham now forged a letter from Brussels, the " principal
drift " of which was " to personate a Royalist, charging
the Presbyterians with the murder of the King and
professing an implacable animosity against the whole
party," [1] in order to set Royalists and Presbyterians at
variance. This appealed to Praise-God Barebone, the
great medium of communication between disloyal writers
and printers, as a work of great value, and so he conveyed
it to Livewell Chapman, who published it on March 23,[2]
under the title of " Newes from Brussels, in a letter from
a neer attendant on his Majesties Person." This was
answered by John Evelyn, the Diarist. On the same day,
also through Chapman, Nedham issued another fraud.
" A Letter intercepted. . . . In which the different forms
of Monarchy and popular government are briefly con-
troverted." " By N. D. Gent." This was at once
answered by Roger l'Estrange, on March 29, in " Sir
Politique, uncased; or, a sober answer to a juggling
pamphlet." [3]

---

[1] *The Fanatique Powder Plot ; or, the design of the Rumpers and
their adherents to destroy both Parliament and People. With a caution
against forged intelligence.* Published on March 26, 1660.

[2] Anthony à Wood, *Athenæ Oxonienses*, iii. 1186.

[3] Sir Roger's tracts, issued at this time, were written with great
rapidity and have never been identified. He himself, however, gave a
list of some of them, in *l'Estrange, his Apologie*, as follows :

Dec.	6, 1659.	" Declaration of the City to the Men at Westminster."
Dec.	12, 1659.	" Engagement and Remonstrance of the City."
Dec.	19, 1659.	" Final Protest and Sense of the Citie."
Dec.	27, 1659.	" The Resolve of the Citie."
Jan.	1660.	" A Free Parliament proposed by the City."
Jan.	28, 1660.	" Letter to General Monck from Gentlemen of Devon " (in answer to his of 23 Jan.).
Feb.	2, 1660.	" The Citizen's Declaration for a Free Parliament."
Feb.	14, 1660.	" Peace to the Nation."
Feb.	18, 1660.	" A Word in Season to General Monck."
March	16, 1660.	" No Fool to the Old Fool."
March	24, 1660.	" A Necessary and Seasonable Caution."
April	4, 1660.	" Double your Guards."

Probably also " The Fanatique Powder Plot " and " A Rope for
Pol." These are all in the Thomason Tracts. Others have not been
traced.

On March 28 there was a great feast at Drapers' Hall in honour of Monck. It says much for his personal popularity and good-nature that a song was then sung styling him a " jolly lad," and bidding people look in his face :

" (*Tom*)   Now would I give my life to see
               This wondrous man of might.

(*Dick*)   Don't see that jolly lad ?   That's he.
               I'll warrant him he's right.
               There's a true Trojan in his face;
               Observe him o'er and o'er.

Chorus : (*Dick*) Come, Tom, if ever George be base
               Ne'er trust good fellow more."

and :

        " My lord : In us the Nation craves
             But what you're *bound* to do.

(*Tom*)   We have liv'd drudges :   (*Dick*)   And we slaves.

(*Both*)   We would not die so too.

(Chorus)   Restore us but our Laws again,
            Th' unborn shall thee adore.
            If George denies us his Amen,
            Ne'er trust Good fellow more." [1]

A Proclamation for Livewell Chapman's arrest was issued on March 28 by the Council of State, and for a few months his activities ceased.[2] Nedham, however, succeeded in making good his escape to Amsterdam, and his career as a journalist ended for ever. The Council of State had taken action and, on April 2, the following order was printed in Muddiman's *Parliamentary Intelligencer* :

" Whereas Marchemont Nedham, the author of the weekly newsbooks, called *Mercurius Politicus* and the

---

[1] " *A Dialogue between Tom and Dick.   The former a countryman, the other a citizen.   Presented to his Excellency and the Council of State at Drapers' Hall, London, March* 28, 1660.   To the tune of ' I'll never love thee more.' "   (March 30, 1660.)

[2] Alderman Robinson wrote to Clarendon on March 30, 1660 : " I have discovered the printer, who is imprisoned, and the author of it (*i. e.* Newes from Brussels) is fled " (Clarendon's *State Papers*, iii. 711). Chapman gave a great deal of trouble to Cromwell, and in 1655 Barkstead wrote to Thurloe that he was an owner or a sharer in the private press that did so much mischief (Thurloe, *State Papers*, iv. 379).

Publique Intelligencer, is, by order of the Council of State, discharged from writing or publishing any publique intelligence, the reader is desired to take notice that, by order of the said Council, Giles Dury and Henry Muddiman are henceforth to write and publish the said intelligence, the one upon the Thursday and the other upon the Monday, which they do intend to set out under the titles of the *Parliamentary Intelligencer* and of *Mercurius Publicus.*" [1] The mistake in the order of this paragraph, by which the *Parliamentary Intelligencer* appears to have been written by Dury upon Thursdays and *Mercurius Publicus* by Muddiman on Mondays, was corrected in the next and subsequent numbers of both periodicals, which placed the two journals in their proper places and corrected the days of publication. On April 16 an addition was made to the original order, as follows :

" That the Master and Wardens of the Stationers' Company, London, be and are hereby required to take care that no books of intelligence be printed and published on Mondays or Thursdays weekly, other than such as are put forth by Mr. Henry Muddiman or by Giles Dury, who have an allowance in that behalf from the Council of State. Signed by the Clerk of the Council."

Songs of triumph at Nedham's final downfall were numerous. A " Hue and Cry " after him was printed,[2] containing an extremely personal description :

> " But if at Amsterdam you meet
> With one that's purblind in the street,
> Hawk-nos'd—turn up his hair,
> And in his eares two holes you'll finde,
> And (if they are not pawned) behinde
> Two rings are hanging there.

---

[1] The *Parliamentary Intelligencer,* No. 14, for Mondays, March 26—April 2, 1660.

[2] In *O. Cromwells Thankes to the Lord General,* etc., published on May 20, 1660.

The *Downfall of Mercurius Britanicus, Pragmaticus Politicus, that three-headed Cerberus,* published on April 9, after noting his various employments, ended :

> " Thus with the times he turn'd. Next turn I hope
> Will up the ladder be, and down the rope."

> His visage meagre is and long—
> His body slender, but his tongue
>   If once you chance to hear,
> Observe it well, it has a grace
> Becoming no such traitor's face
>   Of English, that are there.
>
> Some forty years he is of age,
> In's prime to act on any stage
>   And fit for any plot.
> Had he not been of Oxfordshire,
> Because he writes so much for hire,
>   I'd swear he was a Scot."

Later on, Nedham obtained a pardon under the Great Seal, and (surely the strangest transmutation of all) became a physician. In 1665 he published *Medela Medicina : A plea for the free profession and renovation of the art of physick, out of the noblest writers.*

Nevertheless, the position of Muddiman and Dury, as official journalists, did not pass without challenge from the anabaptists. Probably the Council of State had not time to investigate Oliver Williams's patent and, therefore, did not mention Canne by name in their orders. So Canne and Williams now claimed, not only that the patent the latter had purchased from Innes's widow gave him the right to print news, but also that it conferred upon him the *sole* right to do this. On April 16, therefore, " No. 1 " of a new *Publick Intelligencer*, and on April 19, " No. 1 " of a new *Mercurius Politicus*, were written by Canne and issued from Williams's " Office of Intelligence," marked, " Published by Authority." Their printer was Redmayne, a quite innocuous publisher who appears to have treated the matter purely as a question of business, and was not himself interested in the plot now begun by the anabaptists. The only person who noticed their claims was Muddiman, who, on April 30, repeated the Council's orders to Dury and himself, and made the following addition :

" An Advertisement. The reader is desired to take notice that, since this order, a certain person hath presumed, under pretence of letters pattent, to publish two idle pamphlets, under the title of the *Publick Intelligencer*, on Mundaies, and *Mercurius Politicus*, on Thursdays," [1] and then went on to point out mistakes in their news. For the moment Canne and Williams thought prudence was the better part of valour and did not venture to answer him.

Mr. William Morice arrived in London in the second week in March,[2] and was installed at the General's lodgings as his sole confidant, but the General still refused to countenance the Royalists in any way. Price relates that " The General being at St. James's was besieged with business and visits," and near kinsman as Sir John Grenvile was, " he could not gain an opportunity of having any conference with him, for though he would often spin out his visits to an extraordinary length, in expectation of the rooms being cleared by the breaking up of the company, yet, so soon as ever it was, and a convenience offered of unfolding a part of his errand, the General (well knowing the reason of Grenvile's long attendance) would immediately rise from his chair and say, ' Good-night, cousin. 'Tis late,' or otherwise excuse himself by pretending business. But Sir John, having been so often frustrated, and being impatient till he could give the King his master some further assurance of the General's good intentions," asked Morice's assistance to arrange an interview. Morice at last consented, after the dissolution of the Long Parliament, for Monck had been approached by the Portuguese Ambassador, who pointed out to him the danger the King was in by remaining in Spanish Flanders, and offered the hand of Catherine of Braganza, together with Bombay and Tangier as a dowry, if the King was restored.[3] On this Monck took

---

[1] The *Parliamentary Intelligencer*, No. 18, April 23–30, 1660.

[2] *Nicholas Papers*, iv. p. 195.

[3] This is Eachard's account, and his statements have been accepted by Sir Julian S. Corbett. The story is corroborated by the warning to quit Spanish territory.

action at last, and consented to see his cousin in private. Grenvile came to Morice's chambers by appointment, in secret, whither Monck followed him. " Sir John Grenvile and the General being now alone and Morice doorkeeper to the Conference, Sir John said that ' he was infinitely obliged to his Excellency for giving him this opportunity of discharging himself of a trust of great importance both to himself and the whole kingdom, that had been long deposited in his hands, and that whatsoever became of him, he thought himself very happy to have this good occasion of performing his duty in obeying the commands of the King his master.' He then handed the General the King's letter, which had so long awaited delivery, and produced another one directed to himself, with a commission from the King to treat with Monck.

" The General stepped back, and holding the letter in his hand, with a frowning countenance demanded of him how he durst speak to him in such a matter without considering the danger he was to run into. But Sir John's answer was, ' that he had long since duly considered this matter, with all the danger that might attend it, which was not sufficient yet to deter him from the per- formance of his duty in this particular, any more than in all others which he had cheerfully undergone at his Majesty's command; but that he was the more en- couraged to undertake this, in regard his Excellency could not but remember the message he received in Scotland by his brother.'

" Whereupon the General, without any other reply, approached him with a pleasing aspect and embracing him in his arms said : ' Dear cousin, I thank you with all my heart for the prudence, care and constancy you have showed in this great affair. And I am much pleased also at your resolute secrecy in it, for, could I have understood that you had revealed it to anybody living since you first trusted my brother with it, I would never have treated

with you.   Which now I shall most willingly, and with
you the rather because you are of my nearest kinsmen
and of a family to which I owe many obligations.'   Then
he read the King's letter at last, saying of his Majesty :
' My heart was ever faithful to him, but I never was in a
condition to do him service till this present.' "   Mr. Morice
was called in, and as the General still refused to commit
anything to writing, Sir John had to write down his
instructions himself and commit them to memory in the
General's presence.   When he had done this, Monck
threw the paper into the fire, " with charge not to commit
his instructions again to paper " until he reached Brussels.

He asked the King to send a declaration containing a
general amnesty to everyone for the past, save only for
such as the Parliament themselves should except (among
whom it was certain would be King Charles the First's
murderers), and a promise to confirm all in the lands they
had obtained, whether by forfeit or otherwise; which
would bring many to his side.   Other than this there were
no stipulations and conditions whatever and the King
was to make none.   Lastly, he charged Sir John very
severely to refuse all promises the King might make of
honours or rewards to himself.

Grenvile set out for Brussels, on Monday, March 26,
and stayed with the King while the necessary documents
were being prepared for him to bring back to England.

Next a " Remonstrance [i. e. Declaration] and
Address " of the Army officers was presented to
Monck on April 9, in which they engaged themselves to
submit " to whatsoever the Lord should bring forth "
in the forthcoming Parliament.   This document was
drawn up by Clarges, sent immediately by Monck's special
order to Henry Muddiman,[1] to be seen through the Press,

---

[1] The " Remonstrance and Address of the Armies of England,
Scotland and Ireland to the Lord General Monck.   Presented to his
Excellency the 9th of April, 1660.   St. James's, April 9, 1660.   Ordered
by his Excellency the L. Gen. Monck : That the Remonstrance and

circulated throughout the three kingdoms, and was signed by all the principal officers everywhere. By its means all danger of conflict was warded off, and those officers who did not sign it became marked men, to be placed out of position to do any harm. The day following, nevertheless, a serious piece of news reached Monck. Lambert had been committed to the Tower in March, but escaped on April 10, and if he was not recaptured at once there would yet be a conflict. Fortune stood the General in good stead, and Lambert was retaken by Ingoldsby and Colonel Streater at Daventry in Northamptonshire on Sunday, April 22,[1] his forces dispersing without a blow, and in spite of his piteous appeal to Ingoldsby, " Pray, my lord, let me escape," he was recommitted to the Tower.

Like Henry Muddiman, Colonel Streater, therefore, was marked out for reward when the King returned, and this took the unprecedented form of exempting him by name from all its provisions, by the " Printing and Printers Act " of 1662. No printer before had ever received such a mark of distinction.[2] Later on Streater became a prominent publisher of law books.

Charles II acted at once on Monck's suggestion and quitted Spanish territory for Breda in Holland—not a

Address of the officers of the Army, presented this day to his Excellency, be forthwith printed and published by Mr. Henry Muddiman. William Clarke, Secretary. London. Printed for John Macock." (Title-page of original in the Thomason Tracts.)

[1] *Parliamentary Intelligencer*, No. 18, April 23–30, 1660, pp. 276–8.

[2] 13 and 14 Car. II, c. 33. The sixth proviso at the end of this Act states that it is " Not to extend to prohibit John Streater, Stationer, from printing books or papers, but that he may still follow the Art or Mystery of Printing, as if this Act had never been made."

Writers usually miscall this Act the " Licensing Act." Attention, therefore, should be directed to the Rump's Printing and Printers " Acts " of September 10, 1649, and January 7, 1653, and to Cromwell's " Ordinance " of August 28, 1655. All of these are to be seen in William Hughes's *Exact Abridgment of Public Acts of Parliament from 1640 to the year 1656* (published in 1657). These are the only legal enactments that ever appointed licensers. Licensing was a matter of prerogative.

day too soon: a warrant for his detention in Brussels
having actually been signed on the day during the night
of which he made his escape. When his Majesty asked
Sir John what he should do for him in reward for his
services, Grenvile demanded nothing for himself, imitating
his cousin Monck in this, but just before he left Breda,
with the King's letters and Declaration, his Majesty
slipped yet another letter into his pocket. It was
addressed to himself, and when he opened and read it,
he found that it conferred the earldom upon himself
formerly designed for his father, Sir Bevill, together with
the places of Groom of the Stole and First Gentleman
of the Bedchamber. With these honours were coupled
the promise to pay his own and Sir Bevill's debts and to
settle upon the new Earl (of Bath) land to the value of
£3000 a year, for ever.

Grenvile sailed from Ostend for England, on April 8,
bearing with him not only letters addressed to each
House of Parliament, the City, the Council of State, and
Monck himself, but also the famous " Declaration from
Breda " of April 4, a Commission for Monck as Captain-
General, and a blank appointment for a Secretary of
State, to be delivered to whomsoever the latter pleased.
Monck refused all these except the letter to himself, and
ordered Grenvile to keep out of the way with the rest
until he should be warned to present himself. This was
probably caused by Lambert's escape and his still being
at large.

Parliament, including the House of Lords, met on the
25th of April, after attending St. Margaret's, Westminster,
where Dr. Reynolds preached from the text, " But unto
you that fear my Name shall the sun of righteousness
arise with healing in his wings." Dr. Reynolds was a
moderate Presbyterian who afterwards conformed and
became Bishop of Norwich, where he was noted for his
considerate treatment of the Dissenters. The next day,

Thursday, the 26th, Parliament passed the following memorable resolution, ordering it to be printed and published everywhere :

" That this day fortnight be set apart for a day of Thanksgiving to the Lord, for raising up his Excellency the Lord General and other eminent persons, who have been instrumental in delivery of this Nation from Thraldom and Misery." [1]

On this Day of Thanksgiving Monck's chaplain, John Price, was ordered to preach.

The Speaker, when delivering the thanks of the House to Monck, took notice of his conquest of the enemy : " without expense of blood or treasure. That God's making him so instrumental to keep up the nation from sinking when no way appeared whence deliverance should arise, could not but be acknowledged by all, and looked upon as a miracle." [2]

On Friday, April 27, the House ordered, " that the great business touching the settlement of these nations be taken into consideration on Tuesday morning next." The Houses then adjourned to that day.

On Saturday, the 28th of April, Grenvile, according to the instructions given him, presented himself at the door of the Council of State and asked for Monck. When the General appeared, he presented him with a letter bearing the Royal superscription : " To Our Trusty and Well-beloved General Monck, to be by him communicated to the President and Council of State." Grenvile was arrested and detained while the letter was presented. It was then resolved that it should be read in Parliament on the following Tuesday, and Monck declared that he would be responsible for his cousin in the meantime.

---

[1] *Parliamentary Intelligencer*, No. 18, April 23–30, 1660.
[2] *Ibid.* The Preamble to Monck's patent, creating him Duke of Albemarle (to be seen in Francis Peck's *Desiderata Curiosa*, ii. 514–15), terms him " victor sine sanguine."

On the Tuesday Grenvile presented himself at the Bar of the House with the King's letter to the Commons, and the Declaration from Breda; and, wrote Monck's journalist :

" Our chroniclers make mention of an ' ill May-day.' [1] Let this of 1660 henceforward be called the ' Good ' one for ever, as having produced the most desired, the most universally satisfactory, and the most welcome news that ever came to these three nations since that twenty-ninth of May which was the birthday of our Sovereign Charles the Second, whom God preserve." [2]

When the letter to the Commons had been read, Mr. William Morice stood up in his place and moved that the constitutional government of this country was by King, Lords and Commons. The motion was carried unanimously, and Monck was at the same time granted permission to communicate the King's letter to the Army. Similar scenes took place in the House of Lords, and the two Houses voted a sum of £50,000 as a present to the King, directing Sir John Grenvile to convey it to him, with their invitation to return and rule over his kingdom of England.

On Tuesday, May 8, the King was proclaimed in the principal places of London and Westminster with unusual ceremony, the heralds and trumpeters being accompanied by both the Lords and the Commons in full state. A long proclamation was read at Westminster Hall Gate first of all, and afterwards at Whitehall. Then the glittering show, with trumpeters and the whole College

---

[1] On "Evil May Day," 1517, a riot took place, headed by the London apprentices, and had for its object the driving out of foreign competitors with the English craftsmen. The rioters rose on the night of April 30, to the number of 2000, and sacked the houses of French and Flemish artificers, etc. Thirteen were condemned to be drawn, hanged and quartered. Four hundred of the rest were reprieved at the intercession of Wolsey (J. S. Brewer, *The Reign of Henry VIII*, I. 244 et seq., and Rawdon Brown's translation of Sebastian Giustiniani, ii. 69-77).

[2] *Parliamentary Intelligencer*, No. 19, April 30–May 7, 1660.

of Heralds in their tabards at its head, moved on in procession to meet the Lord Mayor, who awaited them at Temple Bar, clad in scarlet velvet and with his collar of " Esses " about his neck; and the whole court of aldermen round him in sumptuous robes.

When the procession arrived at Temple Bar the City gates were shut. Henry Muddiman's description of all that followed deserves to be recorded :

" Upon this the King-at-Arms, with trumpets before him, went to the gate, knocked and demanded entrance. . . . The trumpets immediately sounded, after which silence being made, it was demanded of the King-at-Arms ' Who he was, and what was his message? ' To which he answered, on horseback with his hat on, ' We are the Heralds-at-Arms, appointed and commanded by the Lords and Commons in Parliament assembled, to demand entrance into the famous City of London to proclaim Charles the Second King of England, Scotland, France and Ireland.' "

The gates were then thrown open, the whole splendid cavalcade entered the City, and after some further ceremonies the King was proclaimed a third time at Chancery Lane end. " At the word ' *Charles* ' in the Proclamation the King-at-Arms, lifting himself up with more than ordinary cheerfulness, and expressing it with a very audible voice, the people presently took it " (up), " and on a sudden carried it to the Old Exchange, which was pursued with such shouts, that near a quarter of an hour was spent before silence could be made to read the rest of the Proclamation. After this they went to Cheapside, where his Majesty was proclaimed a fourth time, where the shouts of the people were so great that, though all the bells in the City rung, Bow bells could not be heard there. Thence to the Old Exchange, where his Majesty was again proclaimed. The shouts and acclamations of the people to this gallant and well-ordered procession are not easily to be expressed.   But then the doubling and redoubling of them when the ceremony of proclaiming was performed none but he that was an eye- and ear-witness can conceive. . . . Major Nichols of his Excellencies regiment, who then commanded in the Tower, ordered three several times thirty-five great guns to be shot off at each time, which were ushered in by several peals of small shot, to testifie how freely he will pay that duty which he owes his Majesty.   The foreign ambassadors were not wanting in declaring their satis- faction with the work of this great day, amongst whom the Swedish ministers were eminently forward, throwing out money at their bonfires, to raise the hearts of those whom want might otherwise have dejected." [1]

On Friday, May 25, the King arrived at Dover at three in the morning, and word having been sent to General Monck at Canterbury, the latter arrived about one in the afternoon.   The King landed about three in the afternoon, on the beach near the pier, with the Dukes of York and Gloucester and many of his nobles.   Muddiman goes on :

" Now did all put themselves in a posture for to observe the meeting of the best of Kings and most deserving of subjects.   The admirers of Majesty were jealous on the King's behalf of too low a condescension, and the lovers of duty fearful on the other side of an ostentation of merit.   But such an humble prostration was made by his Excellency, kneeling, and so fitting a reception by his Majesty, kissing and embracing him, that all parties were satisfied, and the General now taught by the sight of his Sovereign to make a perfect mixture of Hephæstion with Craterus.[2]   So that what hath hitherto been done out of bounden duty to his Liege Lord, will hereafter be

---

[1] *Parliamentary Intelligencer*, No. 20, May 7-14, 1660.

[2] Hephæstion was celebrated as the friend of Alexander the Great, with whom he had been brought up.   Craterus was one of Alexander's generals.   Alexander called Hephæstion his own private friend, but Craterus the friend of the King.

continued out of loyal affection to his gracious Sovereign. His Majesty walk'd up with the General, a canopy being carried over his head and a [sedan] chair of State by him, towards his coach." [1]

At Canterbury William Morice was knighted and appointed Secretary of State. He thus became the *first* " Principal Secretary of State " of Charles II. Later on, Sir Edward Nicholas, the veteran servant of the Crown, was also appointed, and two " Principal Secretaries of State " became the rule throughout the reign of Charles II.

On the same day, the King's letter to Monck, to be communicated by him to the Army, and sent by Monck to Muddiman to be printed, was issued with the order to Muddiman on the title-page.[2]

[1] *Parliamentary Intelligencer*, No. 22, for May 21–28.
[2] (May 28) 1660. " *His Majesty's letter to his Excellency the Lord General Monck. To be communicated to the officers of the Army. Brought to his Excellency from his Majesties Court at the Hague by Sir Thomas Clarges. Rochester, May 24, 1660. I do appoint Mr. Henry Muddiman to cause this letter to be forthwith printed and published. George Monck. Printed by John Macock.*" (Title-page of original in the Thomason Tracts.)

S[r] WILLIAM MORICE
Secretary of State to King Charles II.

(From an engraving in the British Museum)

CHAPTER VII

THE ANABAPTISTS AND THE KING'S JOURNALIST—VENNER'S REBELLION

THE "Restoration" is really an inaccurate term, for the restoration of Parliament, that is, of King, Lords and Commons, implied that the vast mass of legislation of the Interregnum and Civil Wars—comprising all the "ordinances" of the Long Parliament to which the Royal Assent had not been given, and all the so-called "Acts" and Ordinances of the Interregnum became inoperative. Charles II, therefore, returned in the eleventh year of his reign and Parliament had an immense task before it, its first duties being to punish the regicides and to disband and pay off the Army of 30,000 men. Muddiman's news-books are full of details of the latter process, in which Clarges, now a baronet, took a leading part. Such regiments as were retained were officered by the nobility and gentry, who, in these patriarchal times, were their natural leaders, and who were now properly commissioned by the King. Lord Belasyse, for instance, took over the command of Streater's regiment. The Royal Assent, nevertheless, had been given by Charles I to the abolition of the Courts of Star Chamber and of the High Commission, and with them went the "Decree" of the Star Chamber regulating printing, so that up to the month of June, 1662, when

the " Printing and Printers Act " was passed, there were
no statutory or other enactments in force to control
the printing presses.[1]

It was now not necessary to enter anything in the
Stationers' Registers, which, as they survive, are always
an unreliable guide to the output of literature at any
time. That did not mean that anyone was at liberty to
print news, for that had always been a matter of Royal
prerogative.[2] And, if only to protect copyright, some
process of licensing was necessary for books in general.
Sir John Berkenhead, therefore, the former writer of
Mercurius Aulicus, acted as licenser of the news-books,
henceforth written by Muddiman alone.

Muddiman then became involved in his first journalistic
battle. The Council of State's authority to him had
expired with the Council itself, and his own position as
the King's journalist had not yet been officially recognized, nor had Canne's and Williams's claim been inves-
tigated. Several *Mercurii* had reappeared, amongst
others a new *Aulicus* and a new *Democritus*, and on

---

[1] The statistics of the output of the Press during the Interregnum
and after the Restoration, given by Masson in his life of Milton, may
be summarily dismissed. They can be refuted simply by counting
the entries in the Thomason tracts, and do not even approximate to
the output of the presses.

[2] A Royal Proclamation reciting the unanimous opinion of the
judges on this subject was issued at the commencement of Oates's
plot, when Parliament had refused to renew the " Printing and Printers
Act " of 1662. See the *Times Hand-list of English and Welsh Newspapers,
etc.*, p. 29, where the opinion and proclamation are set out at length.
On the subject of the Royal prerogative in licensing all printed matter,
Richard Atkyns's *Original and Growth of Printing*, published in 1664,
is valuable, because it advocates a continuance of licensing under
the Royal prerogative.

It was frequently asserted that many pages had been torn from the
Stationers' Register, and there exists among the State Papers a curious
proof of this allegation. On November 5, 1677, John Lilly, Clerk of
the Company, furnished the Secretary of State with a transcript
of the Register from March 26, 1676, to November 2, 1677 (Calendar of
State Papers for 1677–1678, p. 444). Comparison of this document
with the recently printed transcript proves that a whole leaf has been
torn out of the existing books, and thus a complete series of Lilly's
entries is missing in the modern transcript.

June 12 David Maxwell commenced a new *Mercurius Veridicus*. This does not seem to have been a disloyal print, but it reported the proceedings in the House of Commons so incorrectly that on June 25 the House of Commons made an order which reversed the attitude of the Long Parliament towards the publication of its proceedings. It was, " That no person whatsoever do presume, at his peril, to print any votes or proceedings of this House, without the special leave and order of this House." [1] Evasions of this order, of course, were continuous, the great Dr. Johnson being one of the offenders, but it continued in force right down to modern times. It certainly must have decreased the sale of the printed news-books by depriving them of the great topics in which everyone was interested, but at the same time it gave a great impetus to the circulation of written news-letters; to which this prohibition did not apply, probably because it would have been impossible to enforce it. Here, then, is the reason why news-letters continued to exist and even to compete with the printed news for quite a century longer.

The profits of the printed news-books, so asserted Sir Roger l'Estrange five years later on, dropped at once to £200 a year. But l'Estrange at that time was an interested witness and his assertion was probably an exaggeration. There yet remains a statement of account of the profit realized by the official news-books under Cromwell's rule, between May 22, 1656, and August 26, 1658.[2] This amounted to £1280 13s., or about £569 a year. Probably, therefore, the sale of the printed news-books was very much diminished by the order of June 25, 1660, but even if their annual income was not less than £200, that would amount to nearly £1000 in our money.

---

[1] Commons Journals. The order was duly set out by Muddiman in *Mercurius Publicus* for June 21–28, 1660.

[2] At the end of Morland's undated letter to Thurloe in 1658. *Thurloe State Papers*, VII. pp. 470–471.

Samuel Morland had been granted the moiety of the income from Nedham's news-books,[1] but Muddiman remained in the undisturbed possession of the whole income from *Mercurius Publicus* and his *Intelligencer.* And as he also sent out the written news, his total income cannot have been a small one.

In the meantime, the mendacious claims put forward by John Canne and Oliver Williams were also injuring the official journals. So Muddiman lost no time in drawing attention to them.

On June 28 he wrote as follows : " Books from the Office of Intelligence having formerly given you an account that Mr. Scot, of the late pretended ' high court of Justice,' for the trial of his late Majesty, was brought to Westminster, I must confess, though enquired of by many, I could not give satisfaction therein, being tender to gainsay anything I did not well know, especially in a matter concerning Mr. Scot, with whom that Pamphleteer formerly kept such constant intelligence; till meeting with a near relation of his, I was informed that he was at Brussels, where he had rendered himself to Sir Henry de Vic, till his Majesty's pleasure should be further known concerning him, laying himself now at last at the feet of his Majesty's mercy as his only security." [2]

The " Office of Intelligence " carried on by Williams, Canne, and other supporters whose names do not appear, then actually made an attempt by legal proceedings to capture the whole newspaper press of the kingdom. The first step towards this was to try to silence Muddiman. On the next day Canne announced [3] that action at law was to be taken against the printer or author of *Mercurius Publicus* for some obscure statement supposed

---

[1] Morland's letter to Thurloe, dated August 31, 1658, in *Thurloe State Papers,* VII. p. 367.
[2] *Mercurius Publicus,* June 21–28, 1660. See also the *Parliamentary Intelligencer* of the following Monday.
[3] *An Exact Accompt,* June 22–29, 1660.

to have libelled Major Aberin, " lately Governor of
Edinburgh Castle." Aberin did not, however, comply
with the Fifth Monarchy men's desires, and whether a
mistake had been made or not, took no action. The
next step, appropriately enough, took the form of a
trumped-up accusation.

Muddiman announced that Captain Rolle, son of Sir
Francis Rolle of Devon, had been arrested in Westminster Hall " for traiterous words." Canne at once
published a denial of this fact, in a document signed by
Josias Calmady, one of the two members ordered to sit
for Okehampton until the question of which of the two
was the rightful member could be decided.[1]

This was a serious matter had the document signed by
Calmady been truthful, and would have brought Muddiman into conflict with the House of Commons had he
attacked Calmady. He, however, refused to print
Calmady's denial, a copy of which he admitted had been
received at his house, and, finally, saw Calmady himself,
when the whole affair was found to have been a trick of
the " Office of Intelligence." On July 5 Muddiman
wrote :

" I have, as I acquainted you in my last, made en-
quiries into the business of Capt. Rolle, which was con-
tradicted in some late pamphlets, but upon discourse
with Sir James Smith and Mr. Calmady, I find that
Mr. Rolle was seized for speaking words, and that
Mr. Calmady, giving too much credit to him that brought
the note, did in haste sign it." [2]

This was a very mild way of counteracting a pretty
little plot, but the failure of their scheme exasperated
Canne and Williams to such an extent that they lost all
caution and, in reply, attacked Muddiman in the most
offensive manner.

[1] *An Exact Accompt.* Return of Members of Parliament.
[2] *Mercurius Publicus* for June 28–July 5, 1660, pp. 430–1.

" The said *Parliamentary Intelligencer*," wrote Canne on June 29,[1] " in several of his pamphlets, was pleased to asperse divers persons of quality . . . this, though a great crime in itself, is yet but a peccability in comparison of the high affront he puts upon his Sacred Majestie and his two illustrious brothers, styling them in his 14th page [*i. e.* in the second number, published under the Rump's rule] the pretended King of England and the titular Dukes of York and Gloucester. Many other such stones hath he, like Shimei, cast at his Majesty and these high-born princes, all which to pick up is too great a labour, and would be nauseous to the reader; only this I shall hint, that these and many other such spurious products of his brain he presumes to publish in contempt of my patent, by virtue of his so often boasted order of the Council of State, which he wilfully deems to be still in force, and sticks not to prefer it before the grant which we have from the late King of happy memory, thinking belike to defraud us from our right due. Which is no better than taking a lease over a man's head, by which the world may judge how fitly qualified he is to be Nedham's usher in the school of juggling, having formerly professed to some of us that he would never meddle with intelligence if he thought it would be detrimental to us. But though it is evident that he can thus Nedhamize, we hope that in these better regulated times he will want a Thurlo to support him in his unjust usurpations. He taxes us for the compositor's misplacing Cheney for Chancery, which shows that he cannot yet forget his former pedantick whipping occupation, but in his fury jerks one for another. In our next (if he proceed to be contentious) we shall take notice of some more of his transgressions and exhibit him as a second part of ' Priscianus verberans et vapulans.' "

[1] *An Exact Accompt*, No. 103, June 22–29, 1660.

Muddiman's reply was very much to the point, and was to the following effect : [1]

" To those that know me I need make no apology; to those that do not, it will be enough to tell them that I never writ anything of this sort till entreated to it, for a just vindication of his Excellency and his Army, to give faithful intelligence of their transactions, which were at that time so basely and falsely represented by the pamphleteers then in being. His Excellency was pleased then to send me several of his papers to commit to the Press, which, when known to the world, any sober discreet man may judge with what cautiousness and design I must behave myself, with what reluctancy to myself I was forc'd sometimes to imitate this very fellow (I mean no farther though than in writing) to free myself from the inquisition of his prying master (Scot), who employed such busie instruments to entrap men.[2] How could I safely represent the numbers that desired a Free Parliament, if not in a disguise? Which, however, was necessary should be done to balance those things he so often foisted in and crowded week after week into his books; such as his Barebone's Petition and that pretended to be the Watermen's. Which suspicion might not a naked simplicity have cast upon the Master I wrote for? This, though his shallowness cannot reach, wise men have thought meritorious and, in consideration of my services, the late Council of State ordered me one day in the week to write the intelligence and none else on the same day. Which I must tell my gentleman I think of as a sufficient power for the writing of a gazet. I confess I have not seen his power, but because the gentleman in some of his former papers hath told me I knew

[1] *Parliamentary Intelligencer*, No. 27, June 25–July 2, 1660.
[2] Scot's " two bloodhounds, Rookwood and Leadsum, the one a Carthusian . . . the other a misshapen lump of roguery and treachery," are described in *The Private Debates, Conferences and Resolutions of the late Rump*, Thomason tract E, 1019 (10).

it, I'll tell him my opinion of it—that he may have power to keep a shop or stall, to give information of money to be laid out in Bomaria [Bottomry bonds], or where a man may with most security venture to have his corns cut, where the Rat-catcher lives, or what house is to be let on the Bank-side, where young men and old matrons may hire maid servants, and that bargains are to be made there. But how this entitles him to Press work, I leave it to himself to make out. . . . I will not trouble myself any more with his impertinences as to what he can say of me in relation to my writing."

The controversy was then summarily ended. The Government's attention had been drawn to the fact that a clique of Fifth Monarchy men was actually attempting to control the whole of the newspaper press of the nation, and was issuing four periodicals a week marked " Published by Authority " and insulting the Government journalist. Action was taken by the Privy Council on the 18th July, when orders were given for the suppression of all printed news whatever other than Muddiman's *Parliamentary Intelligencer* and *Mercurius Publicus*, and no doubt the Office of Intelligence itself was subjected to a close supervision.

The sequel will prove that such supervision was necessary. Muddiman's claims for reward and recognition were at the same time amply recognized. His journals, formerly marked " Published by Order of the late Council o:. State," were now marked " Published by Order," commencing with the *Parliamentary Intelligencer* for July 16–23, and he himself was attached to the office of the oldest Secretary of State, Sir Edward Nicholas, and given the task of organizing the correspondence of the Secretaries all over the kingdom. For this his office of official journalist peculiarly qualified him. A written order was sent by Sir Edward Nicholas to the Letter Office, directing James Hickes and the other clerks to pass Henry Muddiman's own letters free, including his news-letters, coupled with instructions that all letters addressed to Muddiman, whether at the Secretary of State's offices or at his own private address, were also to pass free of charge.[1] Thus ended the first battle over the Restoration newspaper press. James Hickes, later on, asserted that this privilege of free postage alone was worth £400 a year,[2] and in any case there can be no doubt that it placed Muddiman above competition from other journalists, quite apart from the advantages of his official position, by enabling him to charge less for his news-letters.

With the commencement of the year 1661, Muddiman gave his old *Parliamentary Intelligencer* the more appropriate title of the *Kingdoms' Intelligencer*, and thenceforward remained the sole journalist of the kingdoms of England and Ireland up to the month of September 1663. In Scotland, Thomas St. Serf, or Sydserf (the name is variously spelt), son of the Bishop of the Orkneys, issued *Mercurius Caledonius*, commencing with 1661, but his periodical was almost entirely taken from those published by Muddiman, and does not seem to have been an unqualified success. Under the title of *Nouvelles Ordinaires de Londres*, Muddiman's pamphlets were also translated into French by his neighbour Thomas Henshaw (cousin of the Major of the same names) of Kensington, printed by Brown, the foreign bookseller, and circulated in Holland and France. Even in these days French was the language of diplomacy.

But the suppression of John Canne had not put an end to the anabaptist conspiracy against the Government. " Holy, humble " Jessey at once succeeded to Canne, in carrying on the Fifth Monarchy cause.

---

[1] See Hickes's lengthy *Narrative*, set out in Appendix D.
[2] On January 20, 1666, Hickes wrote to Williamson : " Unless his (Muddiman's) services be very ample, it is not to the King's interest to pass his letters free to the value of £400 a year." (Cal. S.P. Dom., 1665–6, p. 213.)

On August 1 Jessey published a booklet which Anthony
à Wood terms " a seditious, lying and scurrilous pamphlet,
published while the Visitors of the University of Oxford
sat, reflecting upon them and other matters done about
that time in the University." This was said to have
been taken to the press by Barebone, was published by
Livewell Chapman and Francis Smith, and was entitled
" The Lords Loud Call to England. Being a true relation
of some late wonderful judgments or handyworks of God
by Earthquake, Lightening, Whirlwind, great multitudes
of toads and flies, and also the striking of divers persons
with sudden death in several places. For what causes let
the man of wisdom judge . . . Published by H. J."
[In order to understand the mental attitude of this writer
it is necessary to add his description :] " A servant of
Jesus the Christ and a lover of Peace and Holiness." [1]

This pamphlet contained forty-five pages and a preface
by its writer. At Oxford, persons who had taken part
in a play ridiculing Puritans, and the first man who read
the Common Prayer at Wadham College, had been " cut
off " by sudden death, averred Jessey. The clerk's
daughter of Brokingham in Gloucestershire, fell down
dead on June 3 after " reviling " the Fifth Monarchy
preachers — " gifted   bretheren,"   " pretious, humble,
tender-hearted men "—who wanted nothing but " execution " by ten thousand of the " Saints " upon the
" ungodly." But this was nothing to what had happened at Fairford in Gloucestershire on Midsummer's
Day, when a company of " Christians " went to a meeting
and were reviled by people who were countenanced by
the Lord of the Manor.

[1] As far as Oxford was concerned this was refuted seriatim by Wood
in his *History of the University of Oxford*, Vol. II, Part II. pp. 704–8.
Other falsehoods were refuted by Robert Clark in a pamphlet published
on September 20 and entitled *The Lying Wonders, or the Wonderful
Lyes*, etc., and in John Gadbury's *Britain's Royal Star*, issued in
November.

" In the evening of that same 24 day, there was seen coming up from the Mill Lane great multitudes of small toads. They that saw them said they might have taken up many bowls full of them, and as they were going they divided themselves into two bodies. First, one body or division of them went to the Lord of the Manors house (which was about one acres length from the place they were first seen). They came up through his Orchard, and went under his gate into the inward court, and some did endeavour to prevent their coming into his house, but could not, though they killed many of them." An " honest man," went on Jessey, saw many thousands of them there the next day. The other body of toads went to a neighbouring justice of the peace, who remarked that " it was a judgment upon them for suffering the boyes to abuse those honest men in the Town. And no man can tell whence these toads came." Further abuse of these " Christians " brought forth huge swarms of flies upon the Lord of the Manor a fortnight later. There had also been a great earthquake on the 11th of June. This conveniently took place in France. A whirlwind of a remarkable kind occurred in Leicestershire on June 2, declared Jessey, and then went on with a relation of the sufferings of the ministers of his very peculiar gospel since the King had come in. It is difficult to credit that he really believed in all the nonsense he had written, yet, undoubtedly, many people did, and thus began the " judgments " of the reign of Charles II, afterwards to become the " legenda nigra " of the anabaptists. For Jessey's booklet initiated a campaign of wilful and deliberate lying in print which continued throughout the reign. This culminated in the Popish plot of Oates, whose objects really were the same as those of the Fifth Monarchy men, amongst whom he had been born and bred, namely, the extermination of the Papists and the exclusion of the Stuarts from the throne.

In October the regicides were proceeded against with great lenity. Ten only were executed in 1660, and three in the following year. Of these, eight were hanged and quartered on the site of Charing Cross, marked at present by the statue of Charles I, in order that they might be within sight of Whitehall Gate, where the King had been beheaded. But the space was a narrow one, for Trafalgar Square was then covered by the Royal Mews, so that the inhabitants of the surrounding houses petitioned for the executions to take place elsewhere, in order that they might not be further annoyed by the horrible details incident to them. Thus Hacker and Axtell were executed at Tyburn on October 19.

A full official account of their trials was printed, and stated that owing to the restricted space at Charing Cross, no complete record of their dying speeches could be taken.

The first regicide executed was the Fifth Monarchy man, Thomas Harrison, on October 13, who explicitly asserted that he should return again in three days' time at the right hand of God, to judge his judges.[1] Pepys's remark about this was, " His wife do now expect him." Another Fifth Monarchy man, John Carew, followed on October 15, John Cooke and Hugh Peters on October 16, and others up to the 19th. In each case there were aggravating crimes to be laid to the charge of the condemned men. Cooke was known to have been a thief; Axtell, formerly Hewson's lieutenant-colonel, was excepted out of the Bill of Indemnity " for his murders and cruelties in Ireland," and the madman Peters was

---

[1] Historical Manuscripts Commission, 5th Report, Appendix, p. 157 (Letter of Andrew Newport), and the Letter of William Smith on page 174 of the same Appendix. These are the two most important documents in existence which describe the execution of the regicides. No historian has ever cited them. See also the *True and Perfect Relation of the Grand Traytors Execution* (Thomason tract 669, f. 26 (31)) for a corroboration of Harrison's " three days " prediction, noticed by Smith.

a notorious adulterer who had commanded a regiment in Ireland.[1]

In December, 1660, and not before, the first edition of a fraudulent book, purporting to be the " dying Speeches " of the ten regicides, appeared. Undue credence has been given to this book in modern times, but it proceeded upon the principle of contradicting facts described by every known witness, was but one of the anabaptist or

---

[1] As this characterization of Peters contradicts the modern eulogies of this fellow, I subjoin quotations substantiating facts known to all in his time :

(a) *Military Career*

On April 28, 1650, Endecote wrote to Winthrop : " Mr. Peters is Colonel of a foot regiment in Ireland " (*Collections of the Massachusetts Historical Society*, Series IV. vol. vi. p. 153). Again, " Col. Lockhart, after a victory Mr. Peters gained in Ireland, said he was a fit minister for soldiers " (*Ibid.* Series I. vol. vi. p. 254). Compare Cal. S.P. Dom. under date of October 19, 1649, the *Moderate Intelligencer* for September 13–20, 1649, and the *Man in the Moon* for November 14–20, 1649; also Christoph Arnold's Letter of 1651, in Georg Richter's *Epistolæ Selectiores*, pp. 482–94, published at Nuremberg in 1662.

(b) *Madness and Immorality*

May 5, 1655 (*i. e.* 1656) : " I am glad to hear that Mr. Peters shews his head again. It was reported here [at Amsterdam] that he was found with a whore a-bed and he grew madd and said nothing but, ' O Blood, blood ! that troubles me.' " (Letter in *Thurloe State Papers*, IV. 734.)

May 2, 1656. Thos. Smith to Daniel Fleming : " Hugh Peters, who lately fell into a ' premunire,' was so schooled for it by the protector that it put him into a high fever, which soon after turned to a downright frenzy. The physicians took about 30 ounces of blood from him, yet nothing would do until the protector sent to see how he did. He intends shortly to take the fresh air and to publish something in the nature of a recantation " (Hist. MSS. Comm. 12th Report, Appendix VII. p. 22). Compare with this Mabbot's letter of April 5, 1656, in the *Clarke Papers*, iii. p. 66. Hooke's letter from London of April 13, 1657, in the Collections of the Mass. Hist. Soc. Series III. vol. i. p. 183, and the full story as told by George Bate, in his *Lives, Actions and Execution* of the regicides, printed in 1661.

On September 28, 1659, the Rev. John Davenport, writing to Winthrop, stated that he had received a letter from London, from one Blinman, saying that " Mr. Hugh Peters is distracted and under sore horrors of conscience, crying out of himself as damned and confessing haynous actings. *He concludes for the truth thereof, Sit fides penes auctorem* " (Collections of the Massachusetts Historical Society, Series III. vol. x. pp. 25–6).

Fifth Monarchy series initiated by Jessey,[1] issued in preparation for the rising which took place a month later on, and should be read in conjunction with the manifesto then distributed and its sequel, *Mirabilis Annus*.

On the morning of Sunday, January 6, 1661, Venner, the wine-cooper, preached a sermon to his congregation in Swan Alley, Coleman Street, in which he stirred his people up to fight " for King Jesus," and assured them that they should be invincible, for " one should chase ten and ten should chase a thousand." The night of that day (the Feast of the Epiphany) was " Twelfth Night," the children's festival, upon which a pretty old custom sanctioned their choosing a king and queen from among themselves. All was quiet until darkness set in. In the meantime, someone came and told Lord Mayor Sir Richard Browne of the morning's sermon. The Lord Mayor thought little of the matter, but, as in duty bound, went out in the first instance accompanied only by four halberdiers and six persons with swords, to give warning about the City that a rising might take place. In the dead of the night, when the City was asleep, Venner and his followers, armed " with back, breast and head pieces," sallied forth to initiate their millennium. They carried with them quantities of a printed manifesto, entitled " A Door of Hope; or, a Call and Declaration for the gathering together of the first ripe fruits unto the Standard of our Lord, King Jesus." [2]

---

[1] The various editions of this book and the evidence about the real facts were discussed in a series of fourteen articles entitled, " The forged Speeches and Prayers of the Regicides," printed in *Notes and Queries*, Series XI. vols. vii. and viii.

[2] Original in the Thomason tracts. Thomason's note to his copy is : " This libell was scattered about the streets that night those bloody villains intended their massacre in London, which was upon Sunday ye 6th of January, 1660 (*i. e.* 1661), being twelfth night." This note, written upon a fly-leaf, was originally prefixed by Thomason to tract " 19 " in Vol. E, 764 of his tracts (that is, to the " Door of Hope "), and is also numbered " 19." In the process of rebinding the volumes

THOMAS VENNER,
ORATOR CONVENTICULORUM REGNI
MILLENARII ET LIBERTINORUM SEDUCTOR
et CAPITANEUS SEDITIOSOR. ANABAPTISTARUM
ET QVACKERORUM IN CIVITAT. LONDINENS.
Decollato in quatuor partes dissectus D. 19. Jan. Anno 1661.

(From a print at the British Museum)

" C. (harles) S. (tuart) the son of that Murtherer (Charles the First) is proclaimed King of England," said the author, " whose throne of iniquity is built on the blood of precious Saints and Martyrs (*i. e.* the regicides executed in October), and on the blood of all our brethren in the late wars."

The King was descended from Nimrod, the tract continued, whose " cursed seed and serpentine offspring " he was, and the " common enemy," " risen up in the spirit of that murtherer Cain." The pamphlet then went on to abuse the King with the titles of all the tyrants of antiquity, to condemn those who had restored him, and to assert that by " the sweet harmony and agreement of the prophecies," the executed regicides were the " witnesses " spoken of in the Scripture, who were about to rise again. Then, in horribly blasphemous terms, it claimed that the Fifth Monarchy men were the " chosen of God," the " Saints " " cut out for this work," for whom Heaven was prepared. After this the tract (somewhat unnecessarily) roundly abused Cromwell, as an " apostate " from their principles, and declared that the Fifth Monarchy men would never sheath their swords until they had subjugated not only England, but " France, Spain, Germany and Rome, to destroy the Beast and the Whore, to burn her flesh with fire," and " to bring not only these but all nations to the subjection of Christ " (by which they meant themselves). On page three, the following inducement was held out :

" We say when we consider these things we are so far from being dejected that we cannot refrain from singing and praise, knowing that this will make for God's honour, our good and this work's advantage. *And they shall not*

---

the note has been displaced and will now be found at the end of Vol. E, 763, to which it has been transferred by accident. The " Door of Hope " was at the same time renumbered " 7," but the original number " 19," marked on it in ink by Thomason, still remains.

be able to touch one hair of our heads ; nay, we were very much confirmed in our hopes by the sudden appearance of this work by the coming in of their poor wretched King, at whom (as the daughter of Zion did at that great boasting Assyrian) we laugh and have them in derision." To accomplish their ends, all the laws of England were to be " razed, destroyed and perpetually rooted out."

Finally, " We declare—

" (1) That we will not have one stone of Babylon for a corner or a foundation. We will not have anything to do with the anti-christian Magistracy, Ministry, Tithes, etc.

" (2) That all Civil liberty and rights of man . . . shall rise alone upon the foundation and grow upon the visible kingdom of our Lord. . . .

" (3) That the chief of the spoil which shall be taken in battle and all the estates which shall be forfeited through treason (!) and rebellion (!) shall be brought into one common treasury."

Sufficient of these mad ravings has been quoted to prove that what was contemplated was a renewal of John of Leyden's Kingdom of Münster.

In the meantime, the Lord Mayor called out the " train bands " and chased Venner's men from place to place until eleven at night, amid an uproar which, in the dimly lit narrow streets of the times, can well be imagined. At last, at midnight, forty or fifty of the Fifth Monarchy men were met and bidden to stand by two files of the train bands. The rebels asked the train bands who they were for, and received the reply, " For God and King Charles." They answered, " And we for King Jesus," fired upon the men, killing two, and ran away to Aldersgate, where they forced the watch upon the gate and went to Whitecross Street. Here they killed the constable and wounded the Bell-man (crier) and several others.   This party then disappeared.   About the same time another party appeared at Bishopsgate and fired upon the guard at the gate, killing one man and wounding others.   One rebel was captured at this place.   The rest, having overpowered the citizens, then escaped.

The next day, Monday, the Lord General (Monck, now Duke of Albemarle) sent Sir Thomas Sandys with a troop of horse and his own regiment of foot " to scour Canewood (Caen Wood, or Kenwood), betwixt Highgate and Hampstead, where these savage rebels, as many as were left, were said to be together."   At last, at nightfall once more, Sir Thomas found the rebels lining a hedge near a gravel-pit, charged them, and was fired upon somewhat ineffectually, for only one soldier was hurt. As there was no moon that night, the rebels then dispersed in the wood and made good their escape.

But all was not over yet.

On Wednesday, January 9, another party was discovered in arms " in a lane beyond Leaden Hall," where they made a stand between five and six in the morning. The Lord Mayor got out of bed and was up and on the rebels before they could do anything, and after some firing on both sides, the rebels retreated, made a second stand " in Little East cheape, and then retired to London Stone," where they were all dispersed.

When this was over the Lord Mayor went to encounter another party in Wood Street, who had been at his house in Maiden Lane in the hope of surprising him in bed, shouting, " Now for Browne !   Now for Browne ! " At the last place they were met by some of the train bands and part of the King's Life-guard, with whom they fought well until the arrival of the Lord Mayor.

Then, Major Henshaw made a fresh charge, in conjunction with the train bands and Life-guards, and killed five or six of the rebels, wounding others, including

Venner himself, whose wounds were supposed to be mortal.

The remnant, seven in number, were pursued " to the postern gate at London Wall," where they took refuge in a house and " stood out till five of the seven were killed, the other two crying for quarter, which was granted." But as soon as the officer entered " one of these desperate rebels stabbed at him, which falling upon his corslet, took no effect."

The Dukes of York and Albemarle, the Earls of Oxford and Northampton, Lord Fairfax and many others then came up amid the shouts and cheers of the citizens. The Lord Mayor commended Colonel Cox, Major Henshaw and Captain Clarke and others, to the Duke and Lord General.[1]

In the midst of this riot, on the night of Tuesday, the 8th, Sir Arthur Hesilrige died in the Tower of London.

Sixty-six prisoners were sent to the Gatehouse,[2] and others were sent to Newgate and the two " Compters." A false list of the prisoners in a pamphlet in praise of the Lord Mayor entitled *London's Glory* was denounced by Muddiman, and contained the name of Oliver Williams, who was not arrested. A Proclamation against the meetings of " Anabaptists, Quakers and Fifth Monarchy Men," dated January 10, was the sole practical result of all this madness. Venner did not die and, on January 16, was arraigned at the Sessions at the Old Bailey, for murder and high treason, with nineteen others, the trial of the dangerously wounded being put off for a time. Sixteen, including Venner, were found guilty and sentenced to be drawn, hanged and quartered, and four were acquitted.

[1] *Mercurius Publicus*, January 3–10, 1660–1.
[2] *Kingdomes Intelligencer*, January 7–14, 1661. A list of thirty-eight others in the other prisons was printed by Muddiman in *Mercurius Publicus*, January 10–17, 1661. Muddiman grimly remarked

The King commuted the sentences to hanging and beheading, except in the cases of the two ringleaders, Venner and Hodgkin, who accordingly were executed before their meeting-house in Swan Alley, Coleman Street.

On Saturday, January 19, the very day upon which, in 1649, Lord Mayor Browne was sent prisoner to Windsor for refusing to acknowledge the Rump, the rest were hanged at intervals in appropriate places of the City and their heads set up on poles on London Bridge.

The Fifth Monarchy men did not cease to preach their doctrines after the failure of Venner's mad attempt, but still continued to uphold their plans for rebellion in private conventicles. One of these was at Bulstake Alley, Whitechapel, and its preacher was one John James, a silk-weaver. On Saturday, October 19, 1661, the anniversary of Hacker and Axtell's execution, James preached a seditious sermon there, of which no reliable account remains, but the drift of it was to urge a fresh rising, because " the cup of iniquity was filled more fuller by the blood of the Saints at Charing Cross a twelvemonth last, and by the blood of the Saints in Scotland, to wit, the Covenanters." [1]

An example, therefore, was made of James. He was tried for high treason at the King's Bench Bar and executed at Tyburn on November 27, 1661. In the following year, 1662, the authors of the " Speeches and Prayers " of the regicides produced a " Narration " of his trial, also " with Passages and Speeches," and " An Account of the death of several persons since the execution of John James known to be active and diligent in that

---

that although the " Door of Hope " had promised that not a hair of the heads of the Fifth Monarchy men should be touched, they would find that their necks were not invulnerable.

[1] No official account was published of the trial of John James. *The Speech and Declaration of John James*, printed for George Horton in 1661, is merely a catchpenny affair.

matter." To this title the same text was appended as to the bogus " Speeches and Prayers " of the regicides. " By it he being dead yet speaketh." [1]

Livewell Chapman and four or five other Fifth Monarchy booksellers then initiated a campaign of seditious literature without a parallel in English history. The first two booksellers to come to Chapman's aid were Giles Calvert and Thomas Brewster. Both had repeatedly given trouble to Cromwell, and both had printed Fifth Monarchy literature in 1659.

Calvert was the son of the vicar of Meere, Somerset, and his sister was Martha Simmonds, the Quakeress, who took part with James Naylor in his entry into Bristol. Up to the Restoration, therefore, Calvert's imprint will be found attached to a large number of Quaker manifestoes as well as to Fifth Monarchy tracts. But when the Quakers saw the kind of literature Calvert and his friends were issuing in 1660, they withdrew their custom from him, and henceforward Calvert and his wife Elizabeth ceased to be connected with the Quakers. Thomas Brewster had published Anna Trapnell's tracts.

Directly the Solemn League and Covenant had been burnt by order of Parliament on May 22, 1661, the trio issued a little book. In 1650, for the (as it proved) temporary possession of the kingdom of Scotland, Charles II had been forced, mainly through the instrumentality of Argyle, to take the " Solemn League and Covenant," to stigmatize his mother as a Papist and " idolater," and generally to comply with the most extreme form of Presbyterianism. With that dry humour which ever characterised him, the King is said to have expressed his wonder

---

[1] This tract, which, of course, bore no imprint, is set out in that hopelessly uncritical collection of " State Trials " published by Cobbett. The gravest charge that can be made against this collection is that the documents reprinted in it, true or false, are all mutilated. As evidence, therefore, this collection of reprints is worthless, the original tracts should be consulted.

that he was not compelled to lament that he ever was born. It was the most discreditable episode of Charles II's career, as discreditable to himself as it was to the men who imposed these shameful conditions upon him. There was, therefore, a certain amount of unwitting humour about the little book compiled by Chapman and issued by himself and his co-conspirators directly the " Solemn League and Covenant " was burnt by order of Parliament. This was entitled *A Phenix ;* [sic] *or, the Solemn League and Covenant,* and bore the imprint, " Edinburgh. Printed in the year of Covenant breaking." The book must have been intensely annoying to the King, for, in addition to the Solemn League and Covenant itself, it set out the order of the King's Coronation in Scotland in 1650, with Robert Douglas's sermon on that occasion; reprinted the King's Declaration in 1650, by which he affirmed his own adhesion to the solemn League, and wound up by reprinting Edmund Calamy's sermon on the " great danger of Covenant breaking," preached by him before the Lord Mayor on January 14, 1645. To modern readers the book will appear a very telling comment upon the vote of the Houses of Parliament; but, of course, at this time, great indignation was caused by its publication and search made for its publishers. The printer was found to be one Creake, and at his examination on June 29 [1] he not only confessed that he had printed the *Phenix* and delivered 660 copies to each of its three publishers, Calvert, Chapman and Brewster, but also that he had in hand a book of *Prodigies and Apparitions.* This last book was a much more serious matter, and the description of it must be reserved for the next chapter.

[1] Cal. S.P. Dom., 1661–2, p. 23.

CHAPTER VIII

THE BOOKS OF THE PRODIGIES AND FRANCIS SMITH—THE
LONG PARLIAMENT OF 1661—ROGER L'ESTRANGE'S
SERVICES TO THE GOVERNMENT—MUDDIMAN SUPER-
SEDED BY L'ESTRANGE IN 1663—HIS COUNTRY HOUSE

SECRETARY Sir Edward Nicholas was superseded
on October 15, 1662, by Sir Henry Bennet, who was
created Baron Arlington in 1663 and Earl in 1672.
In the ordinary routine work of his office as Secretary
of State, Lord Arlington did not interfere. He left
all to his under-secretary, Joseph Williamson, who had
also been under-secretary to Nicholas. Like Nicholas,
Williamson was a graduate of Queen's College, Oxford,
and up to the Restoration was a fellow of that House.
An indefatigable worker, Williamson soon made use of
the opportunities furnished to him by Arlington's indiffer-
ence to the office affairs, exacting gratifications from
suitors and missing no opportunity that presented itself
of accumulating a fortune. In 1660 he obtained the
minor appointment of Keeper of the King's Library, with
a salary of £160 a year. Latin Secretary, with a salary
of £80 a year, was another office held by him. This,
however, he was compelled to resign to Nicholas Oudart
in July 1666. In 1664 Williamson also became one of
the contractors for the " Royal Oak " lottery, and this
also helped to fill his empty pockets. Knighted in 1672

SIR JOSEPH WILLIAMSON. SECRETARY OF STATE
(From the painting at the National Portrait Gallery)

at the end of a diplomatic mission, in which the King had not entrusted him with his confidence, Williamson had saved enough money by 1674 to attain the goal upon which he had set his heart, and, according to the reprehensible custom of the times, bought the Secretaryship from Lord Arlington for £6000. While the negotiations for this purchase were proceeding, Arlington, who seems to have held his factotum in some contempt, offered the Secretaryship to Sir William Temple. Temple, however, refused the offer, remarking privately that he considered it no great honour to be preferred before Sir Joseph Williamson.

Williamson's great virtue, for which generations of research workers will always gratefully remember him, was that he had a habit of treasuring every letter and scrap of paper received by him at the Secretary of State's offices. Thus the State Papers of the Restoration are very voluminous, and contain a complete record of Williamson's relations with Henry Muddiman and James Hickes of the Letter Office.

In character Williamson was greedy and grasping. His office correspondence repeatedly affords evidence of an incredible meanness in small matters. Evelyn says that Arlington " remitted all to his man, Williamson," and writes of his " subtlety, dexterity and insinuation." Pepys met him in 1663, and said, " a pretty knowing man and a scholar, but it may be thinks himself too much so."

Such was the man with whom Henry Muddiman arranged the correspondence of the Secretaries of State after the Restoration. Many of the letters to Muddiman among the State Papers are addressed to him at his private office—the " Seven Stars " near the New Exchange, in the Strand. From the " Seven Stars," where they were multiplied by his clerks, Muddiman sent out his newsletters, but invariably headed them " Whitehall," in order to show the privilege with which he wrote. Some of his correspondents, such as the postmasters, probably obtained their news-letters at reduced fees on condition of supplying intelligence of what was happening in the neighbourhood of their homes. But all of them seem to have been keen to supply Muddiman with information that might prove useful either to himself or to the Government. Thus, Thos. Swan wrote from Newcastle Post House on October 12, 1663, addressing his letter, " For Mr. Muddiman at the 7 Stars in the Strand near the Exchange," [1] as follows :

" Mr. Muddyman. I received your last paper and give you many thanks, and I hope it will continue and that I shall have a further correspondence. As for the Scotts affairs I shall now and then be hinting to you of it [sic], but especially what noblemen goes by post or on journey. My Lord Lorne, Argyle's eldest son, went post from me yesterday, but what welcome he shall have at London I leave it to your paper. I shall not fail to gratify your clerks, and if there be anything in these parts wherein I may serve you, none shall be more ready than he, who is your assured friend to serve you,—Tho. Swan."

Argyle had been executed in May 1661, so that the movements of his son and successor were of interest to the Government, and account for the transfer of this letter by Muddiman to Williamson. It should be noticed that Muddiman's news-letters were termed " papers," probably because he never signed them.

Others varied the address. Thus, Edward Phelipps, of Montacute, M.P. for Somerset, who was one of Muddi-

---

[1] This letter is summarized in the Calendar of State Papers, Domestic Series, under the date cited, but the address is omitted. Many other letters in the same Calendar are also addressed to Muddiman " at the 7 Stars," etc., but in each case the address has been omitted, e. g. Jo. Norman, from Exeter, November 1, 1662, and T. T.'s letter from Chester on October 5, 1663. One letter was sent to Muddiman's private house, with the address, " Leave it at the Post House at Brompton "; another followed him to the Heralds' College, for what reason does not appear.

man's principal correspondents, addressed his letter of
October 12, 1663, " For Mr. Henry Muddiman.   Leave
this at Mr. Joseph Williamson's, at Mr. Secretary Bennet's
office, to be conveyed as directed."   Some sent their
letters to Williamson, but wrote to Muddiman.[1]   One
interesting letter, dated October 14, 1663, and written
by William Duckett, M.P. for Calne, is addressed, " Leave
this at Mr. Secretary Bennet's office in Whitehall with
Joseph Williamson, Esquire, for Mr. Henery Muddyman."
It runs as follows :

" Sir.   In your last you desired me to acquaint you
what nonconformists, papists and others were indicted
at quarter sessions.   Which were many, but I cannot
inform of their names, because I was not then present.
But yet we have many meetings of the separatists.   I am
now attending our deputy lieutenants at Chippenham,
who are putting our county in condition, I hope, not to
fear any insurrection that may happen.   We hear that
many are secured in Bristoll and several other parts about
us.   Sir, I am earnestly desired by Mr. Charles Seymour,
son to my lord Seymour, that you would let him receive
a letter weekly from you, and he will satisfie you to your
own demand for it.   If you please to send to him, you
must direct your letter to be left at the Post House
Marlburrow [Marlborough] for Charles Seymour, Esq.
And so desiring God to grant us peace and a happy
meeting, I rest your assured friend to serve you.   Will
Duckett.   (P.S.) Sir Edward Hungerford remembers him
to you, and just now we hear that some seven score are
secured at Bristoll and 1000 arms taken, and many
more Westward."

[1] The letter of William Nowell of Norwich, dated October 12, 1663,
begins, " Mr. Muddiman," and ends, " Alderman Lawrence desires to
be remembered to you and returneth you many thanks for his news-
books.   Your servant to command, Wm. Nowell."   But the letter is
addressed " For Joseph Williamson, Esq., at Mr. Secretary Bennets
offices at Whitehall."   All this is omitted in the Calendar.

Colonel Slingsby, Deputy Governor of the Isle of Wight, addressed his letters in the same manner, but Lord Herbert of Cherbury, writing from Llyssin in Wales, demurred when Muddiman asked him to report to Arlington, and wrote to the "Seven Stars" as follows :

" Mr. Muddyman.   In the close of your last of the 22nd I find you have received [orders] to give me notice that if anything occurs worthy the consideration of King and Council, that I should write it and direct to Sir Henry Bennet, the principal secretary.   If the order be particular, it gives me matter of admiration, being I live within Wales and the President now in London.   I pray satisfie me by your next, whether it be general or particular and from whom you had it; if it be the latter I may acquaint the Earl of Carbery with it, and that I desire you to do so." [1]

The important news in this instance was a report that Ludlow the regicide had been seen in Wales.

These letters are typical, and many others could be quoted, but enough has been set out to show the manner in which Muddiman conducted his correspondence and its utility to the Secretaries of State.

The Convention Parliament was dissolved on December 29, 1660, and the Parliament that succeeded it, termed the " Long Parliament of Charles II," because it sat until the year 1679, was elected during the excitement caused by the Coronation.   This took place with unusual pomp on April 23, 1661, all the ancient rites being carried out to the least detail.   Even those attending the creation of a number of Knights of the Bath were performed

---

[1] The summary of this letter on p. 532 of the Calendar for 1663–64 incorrectly states : " Lord Herbert to Henry Muddiman.   Is surprised at an order to give Secretary Bennet *notice of anything of consequence* [sic] now that the president is in London.   If the order is particular requests that the *the Earl of Carbery may be acquainted with it* " [sic].   This obscures Muddiman's position as journalist.

with the mediæval ceremonies of bathing, prayer in Henry VII's chapel, etc.[1]

It was the last Coronation of this kind England was ever to see. The new Parliament met on May 8, 1661, and it was at once apparent that the Presbyterians of the Convention had been swept away and their places filled by pronounced Cavaliers. Whatever prospect there was of an agreement between " Prelatists" and Presbyterians over the future of the Church of England (and there were great hopes of such an agreement) was at once removed by this reactionary Parliament. Perhaps it was to be expected that the " Solemn League and Covenant " would be ordered to be publicly burnt by the hangman and oaths of allegiance and supremacy imposed, but the provision in the Corporation Act of December 20, 1661, by which every office-holder was to receive the Lord's Supper within a year of election, tended to profanation of the Sacrament, and the Act of Uniformity, passed on May 19, 1662, rendered an agreement between the two great religious parties impossible. By St. Bartholomew's Day (August 24), 1662, all incumbents of livings were obliged to receive ordination from a bishop and to declare their unqualified acceptance of the Prayer Book. On the same day the last of the Printing Acts was passed. This was a commonplace measure, substituted for the infinitely more repressive measures of Cromwell and the Rump. It did little more than repeat the Star Chamber " Decree." The immediate effect of this was to render private printing presses illegal, to reduce their number, and to render difficult the printing

---

[1] A special number of his *Kingdomes Intelligencer* (No. 16, for April 22–29, 1661) was devoted to the coronation by Henry Muddiman, who described all the ceremonies with an evident relish. The account was not repeated in *Mercurius Publicus*, and the run upon the other periodical was so great that all copies of it seem to have disappeared with the exception of the copy still preserved in the Record Office. The account of the Knights of the Bath is extremely curious, but too lengthy to be inserted here.

of seditious books of the kind to which attention has been drawn.[1]

Given the attitude of mind of all seventeenth-century Governments, English or foreign, towards the freedom of printing, nothing else was to be expected, particularly at this juncture.

Attention has already been called to the pamphlets and broadsides of Roger L'Estrange, the Cavalier, printed just before the Restoration. L'Estrange alone had received no reward for his campaign on behalf of the King, but had not ceased to keep his claims for recognition before the public, chiefly by his pamphlet war with Edward Bagshawe, the Presbyterian, which was creditable to neither of the two disputants.

Roger L'Estrange came of an ancient Norfolk family, seated at Hunstanton, and was a Cavalier whose record, though singularly unsuccessful, was quite blameless. In Pepys' opinion he was a man " of a fine conversation, most courtly and full of compliments." Evelyn thought that he was "a person of excellent parts, bating some affectations," and suspected that his " pretence of serving the Church of England " involved a still stronger suspicion of " gratifying another party," that is the Catholics. Be that as it may, it is quite certain that L'Estrange's attitude towards the Presbyterians was most vindictive and unfair. They had played no mean part in restoring the King to his rights, and continually to attack them and draw attention to their enmity to the " Prelatists " in days gone by tended to drive them into the arms of sectaries with whom they had nothing in common. L'Estrange, therefore, hailed the reactionary Parliament of 1661 with delight, and when the Act of Uniformity and Printing Act were passed, sought for the office of

[1] The title of the Act shows its objects : " For preventing the frequent abuses in printing seditious, treasonable and unlicensed books and pamphlets, and for regulating printing presses." " News-books " were not mentioned in it.

Surveyor of the Presses in order that he might suppress all seditious and nonconformist pamphlets. Accordingly, on February 24, 1662, just about three weeks before the Royal Assent was given to these two acts, L'Estrange was (by a warrant signed by Secretary Nicholas) [1] appointed Surveyor of the Presses. L'Estrange took in hand the task of suppressing nonconformist publications with some vigour, formulated a series of proposals for further repressive measures (which were never carried into effect), based upon Cromwell's Ordinance of 1655, and generally took up the attitude of a Tory High Churchman of an extreme type. It is not possible to defend his conduct in these respects. All that can be said is that, if he had not filled this office, there were plenty of others able and willing to do so, amongst whom Henry Muddiman cannot be numbered, partly because he was no controversialist, and partly because he indirectly showed his sympathy with the Presbyterians, amongst whom he had been brought up.[2]

But there was another and far more important side to L'Estrange's work as Surveyor of the Presses, and it is one which has not received attention. The Fifth Monarchy men's activities did not cease with the publication of the pamphlets already noticed, and it is to be suspected that many nonconformists, goaded into rebellion by the legislation of 1662, now joined these men, using them as the spear-head for their own attacks upon the Church of England. A great exodus took place on St. Bartholomew's Day, Some two thousand ministers then quitted the Church of England; among whom were numbered good men like Baxter, Manton and Bates,

---

[1] Calendar of State Papers under the above date.
[2] He carefully chronicled the fact that Dr. Manton restored the use of the Book of Common Prayer at St. Paul's, Covent Garden, directly the King returned. It has been asserted that Manton did *not* do this. See *The Kingdomes Intelligencer* for February 25 to March 4, 1661.

whom the Church of England could ill afford to spare.
Others, the Presbyterians themselves would have turned
out, amongst whom men like Jessey and Canne, and the
ministers of Leicestershire praised by the Rump, must
be numbered; and on the other side, when men like the
scandalous old anabaptist Samuel Oates and his infinitely
more infamous son Titus could conform and be given
benefices, it is evident that all was not well with the
Church of England.   It is noticeable that both these men
ultimately reverted to their original creed, with the result
that in Titus's case, the baptists (as they had then become)
excommunicated him as " a scandalous person and a
hypocrite." [1]

The first result of the Act of Uniformity was the plot to
murder the King, Lord Chancellor, Lord General and
other great officers of State, and to set up a republic.
The ramifications of this plot were numerous, as William
Duckett's letter proves, but, in the first instance, the
plot was checked by the execution of six of the ringleaders—Thomas Tonge and others.   A clergyman, the
Rev. William Hill, was walking one day in London, clad
in secular attire, and was accosted by one of the conspirators, who took him to be of his party.   From incautious
expressions let fall by this man Hill divined that there
was a plot on foot.   He therefore wormed himself into the
conspirators' confidence, associated with them for several
days, communicating with the Lord Mayor for instructions all the time, and concealing the fact that he was a
clergyman.   When all was ripe the six men were arrested,
tried for high treason and executed on December 22, 1662.
Hill's behaviour was similar to that of the Royalist
traitors of 1658.   It was scandalous for a clergyman to
undertake the task of a spy, and Hill's address to the King

[1] The somewhat amazing record of the two Oateses has been written
by Mr. Seccombe, in his *Twelve Bad Men*.   The misdeeds of the two
began directly they joined the Church of England.

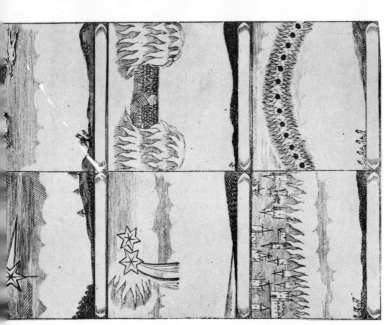

FRONTISPIECE TO "MIRABILIS ANNUS" (THE FIRST BOOK)

(From a copy in the British Museum)

plainly proves that the motive animating him in trepan-
ning these misguided men was to obtain preferment in the
Church. It is to be feared that he succeeded in obtaining
it.[1] The only interest in the trial itself was the revelation made that there were in existence two committees,
one in Holland and another in England, termed the
" Council of Six," [2] analogous to the " Sealed Knot "
in Cromwell's time, their objects, of course, being to
foment a fresh rebellion. It is from this Committee
that the Fifth Monarchy and other seditious writers and
printers now found support.

In June 1662, an anabaptist preacher, Francis Smith,
who carried on business as a bookseller at first at the sign
of the Elephant and Castle, near Temple Bar, but from
1670 at the Elephant and Castle in Cornhill, and thus
received the nickname of " Elephant Smith " (in order to
distinguish him from other booksellers of the same
surname), joined Chapman, Calvert, and Brewster.
Chapman and Smith had already published Jessey's
Lords Loud Call.

The four issued the first of the three books commonly
called the Book of the Prodigies, or Book of Wonders, or
Mirabilis Annus.[3] The work is of interest from a literary

[1] A Brief Narrative of that Stupendious Tragedie, etc., Hill's preface
of twelve pages to this is omitted in the reprint of this tract in " State
Trials "; the regicide Ludlow's untruthful account of the affair being
appended in its stead.

[2] The names of the " Council of Six " were mentioned in the
course of the trial, but differ from other lists to be found in the State
Papers. Probably the six varied from time to time.

[3] On September 11, 1662, Thresher, the binder, was examined, and
confessed that Francis Smith first printed the Prodigies in June, and
was partner with Brewster, Chapman and Calvert in the second printing (Cal. S.P. Dom., 1661–62, p. 87). There were three books of the
Prodigies. The commencement of the title of the first book of the
Prodigies was as follows : 'Ενιαυτος τερασгιος, Mirabilis Annus, or
the Year of Prodigies and Wonders, etc. These run from August 1,
1660, to the end of May 1661. The second book of Prodigies dropped
the Greek beginning, and was entitled Mirabilis Annus Secundus,
etc., extending from April 1661 to June 1662. The third book's title
was Mirabilis Annus Secundus ; or, the Second Part of the Second Years

point of view, for it suggested a title to the poet Dryden, and was the occasion of some discussion in clerical circles about omens and portents.

The first of the three books of " Prodigies " was undoubtedly edited by a man of some learning, and though Jessey's assertion that he did not write it may be true, for the astonishing series of lies contained in it was contributed by many inventors, yet everything points to Jessey as the author of the Preface.[1]

After a dissertation about the " Works of God," reinforced by texts from Scripture and St. Augustine, the writer proceeds : " We do make the same solemn protestation which Lycosthenes did in the like case, before God, Angels and Men, that we have not feigned any one of the particulars here inserted, not so much as a circumstance relating to any one of them, but have *faithfully* and *impartially* published them as they were

---

Prodigies, etc., and extended from June to September, 1662. The British Museum contains no less than fourteen copies of the three. See more of these in *A Protestant Monument, erected to the glory of the Whigs and Dutch* (1712), reprinted in the Somers Tracts, vol. vii. pp. 634–58.

[1] Jessey always assumed the rôle of Uriah Heep when imprisoned, and in 1661 wrote the following letter :

" Hon. S. Having sent this day to that party of whom I verily thought I had (upon my desire) obteined to get y⁰ book for me. The answer to the Party is to this effect. I know nothing of this. He *never Had* ye book from me. Or never desired me to procure it, etc. The trueth is I thought I had obtained it by this parties meanes, but now it appears I was mistaken. And now I cannot say from whom I had it.

" Sr. It being thus, yor best Advice and furtherance of the Enlargement of one of known Innocency in things charged, until a day be set to hear him and Accusers face to face (fro an Inne whereby many noyses till midnight, very early, hinders rest, have occasioned Aches in Head, eyes, teeth, Aguishness, symptoms of piles and if not helped may hasten death) is humbly desired by Sr. An Ancient servant of Jesus the Christ, though an unworthy one. H. Jessey, 10 of X 1661. from the Lamb Inne by St. Clement Danes."

" For Mr. William Howard, Esq. over against Dunstan's West." (S.P. Dom. Charles II, Vol. 45, No. 33.)

Jessey died in 1663, and the elegy printed by his followers in his honour was entitled " A Pillar erected to the memory of that Holy, Humble and faithful servant of Jesus Christ, Mr. H. Jessey," etc.

communicated to us from credible persons, whose proofs
also we scanned and weighed to the uttermost, and
received ample satisfaction in the validity thereof before
we made them publick, casting away many things which
we could not but judge probable, because not satisfied in
the certainty of them. . . . We shall go on to tell the
reader that the signs and prodigies contained in the
ensuing discourse are in themselves like the handwriting
upon the wall in *Belshazzars* Palace, which the *Sooth-
sayers, Astrologers* and *Chaldeans*, could neither understand nor read, but the *Saints* may with God's *Heifer*
come to know his riddles. *The wise shall understand.*"

An exposition of the significance of prodigies and
wonders followed, with lavish quotations from the Scrip-
tures, Fathers, and writers of antiquity, and, finally,
the Fifth Monarchy origin of the whole was revealed in
the last sentences :

" God is now making haste to *consummate* his *whole*
work in the earth, and to prepare the way for his *Son
to take upon him his great power and reign.* All these
prodigies being, according to our Saviour's own prediction, but præludiums to that signal and last revolution
which makes way for *the new Heavens and new earth wherein
dwells Righteousnesse. And if we look for such things,
let us be diligent that we may be found of him in Peace,
without spot and blamelesse.* Amen. July 25, 1661."

Fifty-four Prodigies and Apparitions, seen in the
Heavens from August 1, 1660, to the end of May 1661
followed; told in great detail, with names, dates and
places. These were interlarded with parallels and
quotations from Scripture, history and the Classics.

Then follow twenty-three more of Storms and Earthquakes from May 1660 to May 1661, ten prodigies in
the waters and twenty-seven remarkable " judgments
befalling divers persons from June 1660 to April 23,
1661." Finally, the perusal of a sermon by Luther was

recommended. A translation of this was also printed and entitled *Signs of Christ's coming and of the last Day*.

Among the Prodigies recorded were the following :

On October 17, 1660, when Scroop, Jones and other regicides were executed at Charing Cross, there was an apparition in the air at Shenley in Hertfordshire " of five naked men, exceeding bright and glorious, moving very swiftly." When their quarters were set up at Aldgate, there appeared over them a bright star " for two or three hours together, and continued so for four or five days." At Bishopsgate there appeared seven pillars of smoke ascending from the seven quarters there; " they reached up to the Heaven as high as the beholders could well discern."

One tale deserves quoting in full :

" Several passengers coming in a boat from Putney to London, about eight o'clock at night, March 14, 1660 [*i. e.* 1661], when they were near Westminster saw a dark and black cloud hanging over W(hite) H(all) which after a little space of time passed away, and in the room of it appeared a white bright cloud, which gave such a light that they could plainly discern the windows of the Parliament House and people walking to and fro upon Westminster bridge,[1] though before it was exceeding dark. Whilst they beheld this cloud they saw it drop down fire several times upon W.... H.... and then it removed and stood over the P.... H.... and did drop down fire upon that also several times; then it removed back again to W.... H.... and dropt down fire again and then went back again to the P.... H.... and did the like again there, and so it continued to do successively for 4 or five times together, to the very great affrighting of the passengers, but especially the Watermen. One of the Gentlemen that was in the boat came (as we have

[1] This cannot mean a bridge over the Thames. There is no record of such a bridge until 1739.

been informed) to W. . . . H. . . . and related this story to
several persons there; the same apparition was seen at the
same time and over the same places by divers travellers
that came from Kensington towards London that night."

The rest of the portents—blazing stars, double moons,
earthquakes, tales of hogs walking into Canterbury
Cathedral choir during Divine service and of people
"struck dead," etc., were all in the same vein. In an
age when even scholarly men believed in witchcraft, and
poor women were sent to death upon evidence which
nowadays provokes a pitying smile, the effect of this
book upon a credulous people can well be imagined.
The book and its two successors gave great alarm to the
Government.[1] Its influence was very great outside
London and tales of this kind extended even as far as
America. The celebrated New England minister, John
Davenport, educated at Oxford, whose brother, Chris-
topher, was a Franciscan and chaplain to Queen Henrietta
Maria, actually wrote as follows on " 2 of 9 mo. 1665 " :

"Most of the intelligence recd. by Mr. Russel was with
us before, but that miracle of the Dumbe boy I never
heard till his report. Did God ever speak so loud and shew
soe cleerly by multiplied signes, in Heaven, earth and sea,
and in the bodyes of men; giving speech to the dumbe
and hearing to the deafe, noe man knows how, & causing
an infant 18 weeks old, yea, an oxe to speake and fore-
tell calamities approaching, as He hath done to England
since the late change of Government. Noe history hath
recorded the like in soe few yeares and the next age will
wonder at the Dedolency and stupidity of this age, in
which so few discerne the signes of the times."[2]

___

[1] See the Calendar of State Papers for 1661–2, pp. 23, 54, 87,
104, 106, 107, 128, 184, and 207. Compare Henry Muddiman's
exposures in his *Kingdomes Intelligencer* for October 14–21, 1661, and
Mercurius Publicus for July 2–9, 1663.
[2] *Collections of the Massachusetts Historical Society*, Series IV., vol.
iii. p. 126.

When men like Davenport could express themselves in this manner, Roger L'Estrange's conduct in suppressing literature of this kind, and in hunting out its publishers and destroying the presses that printed it, needs no defence.

The books of the Prodigies were sold at sixteen pence each. Nathan Brookes, bookseller in Moorfields, dispersed them in Leicestershire for that sum,[1] and no doubt the Rump's Leicestershire ministers, inspired by a " Gospel spirit of Meekness, Sincerity and Holiness," helped him in his task.

" Elephant " Smith, Brewster, Chapman and Calvert, all went to gaol for the first book of the Prodigies, and when it was found that notwithstanding this, Calvert's wife Elizabeth still continued to print and sell the book, she also was sent to the Gatehouse, on October 4, the warrant stating that the book was " a forgery of false and feigned prodigies, prognosticating mischievous events to the King and instilling into the hearts of subjects a superstitious belief thereof and a dislike and hatred of his Majesty's person and government, and preparing them to effect a damnable design for his destruction and a change of government." [2]

The career of Francis Smith is of very great importance for the history of the reign of Charles II, and I shall have to recur to this man's proceedings in a later chapter. He had commenced business in the middle of the year 1659 or earlier, but except for a tract attacking the Quakers, and a few unimportant pamphlets in support of the Rump, he published nothing worth notice until March 15, 1660, when he issued *A Brief Confession ; or Declaration of Faith set forth by many of us, who are falsely called Ana-Baptists*. Signed by himself and thirty-nine other " elders, brothers and deacons " in " the first month,

[1] Cal. S.P. Dom., 1661-2, p. 104.
[2] *Ibid.*, p. 106.

called March," this confession of faith would need no notice but for the statement at the end of the reasons which called it forth :

" We do utterly, and from our very hearts, in the Lords fear, declare against all those wicked and divillish reports and reproaches falsely cast upon us, as though some in and about the city of London, had lately *gotten knives, hooked knives,* & the like and great store of arms besides what was given forth by order of Parliament, intending to cut the throats of such as were contrary minded to us in matters of religion, and that many such knives and arms, for the carrying on some secret design, hath been found in some of our houses by search," etc.

Yet Smith himself, as we have seen, was associated with Chapman, Calvert and Brewster.

That Jessey, as Antony à Wood asserts, was the editor of the first book of " Prodigies," issued (as to its first impression) by Smith alone, can be inferred from the fact that he, with Henry Denne and John Gosnell, contributed a preface to a religious treatise written by Smith and first published by him in May 1660. This was entitled *Symptoms of decay and growth to Godlinesse,* and, to an uncritical reader, would seem to be the work of a pious but eccentric nonconformist. This book, however, was remarkable for containing an anabaptist " imprimatur," signed by William Jeffery, Thomas Munck, Benjamin Morley and Thomas Wright.

But when Francis Smith was arrested for publishing the first book of the " Prodigies," and was examined on December 19, 1661, he denied all knowledge of its composers, asserted that he himself had had nothing to do with its compilation, and averred that he " never received any copies of that book, after printed, from any person." [1]

[1] Smith's examination, noted on p. 184 of the Calendar, S.P. Dom. for 1661–2, is as follows :

The Government seems to have been at a loss what to do with this man, for if he had been indicted he would have certainly suffered the penalty for high treason. No doubt the King was unwilling that this penalty should be inflicted. Smith, astutely conscious of this, anticipated a trial for misdemeanour only, with a heavy fine as the result. So he sold the lease of his house, the " Elephant and Castle " in the Strand, near Temple Bar, and submitted to a (collusive) judgment on his goods for money raised by him. Thus, had he been fined, he would have evaded payment.[1] Some months later on he was released and then promptly returned to the " Elephant and Castle " in the Strand and from that

---

" The examination of Francis Smith, Printer, taken before ye Rt. Honble Mr. Secretary Nicholas att Whitehall, ye 19th day of Decemb. 1661.

" This Examint saith,

" That he never sent into ye country to have any account of Accidents or Prodigys (such as were of late printed in a Book called ' Annus Mirabilis ') nor did ever disperse any copyes of ye said Booke.   That he did never meet wth any persons about ye compiling ye said Booke.

" *That he never did heare* [original italics] of a book that was about to be printed containing severall prodigies and accidents.   Mute.

" That he never contributed any sum towards ye printing of yt book.

" That he never received any copyes of that booke, after printed, from any person.

" Being asked whether he did not deliver and give out copyes of yt booke to some person & persons—to this Mute."

The first question to which he was " mute " was whether he had not contributed the sum of £20 towards printing the book, and the last question was, " Had you not divers of their copies in your house and some of them about you under your cloak at the time when the messenger served you with a warrant to appear before Mr. Secretary Nicholas ? "

The seven interrogatories precede the paper containing this examination.

[1] A long letter was sent by Smith to Nicholas, after he had been twenty weeks in confinement, and is undated, but noted in the Calendar for 1661-2, on p. 235, with the erroneous date of February 4, taken from a note on the back.   In this Smith told Nicholas he had sold his house and submitted to a judgment on his goods in order to satisfy the extortions of a cruel gaoler.   He said that he had appeared before the judges but had not been tried, and that he was kept " close prisoner for treacherously and seditiously compiling and printing *a book which I never so much as read*."   He had a wife and three small children and begged for his release.

address issued another seditious book, entitled, " A True and Faithful Account of the several Informations exhibited to the honourable Committee appointed by the Parliament to inquire into the late dreadful burning of the City of London. Together with other informations touching the insolency of Popish priests and Jesuits and increase of Popery, brought to the honourable Committee appointed by the Parliament for that purpose."[1] This was anything but a " true and faithful account," nor did the Committee find that the fire was the work of the Papists. While still living in the Strand, Smith was " teacher " of a congregation of 400 or 500 anabaptists, who met in Goswell Street;[2] but this congregation does not seem to have had any connexion with the historic congregation of baptists in this street. By 1672 Francis Smith had removed to Cornhill, where he retained his sign of the " Elephant and Castle." Under the King's declaration of indulgence he was licensed " teacher " of a congregation meeting in a former malt-house at Croydon.[3] In 1673 he was arrested for printing notes of the proceedings of Parliament without leave, and (as usual) denied that he had done this.[4]

Giles Calvert died in August 1663, so that there is nothing more to record about him.[5]

L'Estrange's services up to 1663 in suppressing *Mirabilis Annus* and other dangerous pamphlets, had been very great; for a fresh rebellion was brewing, as the Government well knew. Hitherto L'Estrange had received only

---

[1] See Cal. S.P. Dom., 1667, p. 330. This worthless tract had many reprints and another title, *London's Flames*. Ultimately the Perjurer Bedloe reissued it as his own. It is reprinted in "State Trials," but mutilated.

[2] *Ibid.*, 1666–7, p. 430.

[3] *Ibid.*, 1671–2, pp. 348 and 356; *Ibid.*, 1672–3, p. 94.

[4] *Ibid.*, 1673–5, pp. 42, 46, 54 and 146.

[5] His will, dated August 11, was proved by his widow, Elizabeth, on August 28, 1663 (P.C.C. Juxon, 106). This date is important, because he has recently been asserted to have been " persecuted " after he was dead.

a grant of money and was without a fixed salary, nor had his Office of Surveyor of the Press been formally sanctioned by the King. Lord Arlington, therefore, decided to obtain Letters Patent from the King, creating this Office for the benefit of L'Estrange, who at the same time and by the same instrument was appointed Licenser of the Press. For his remuneration L'Estrange received the sole privilege of writing " all narratives not exceeding two sheets of paper " [*i. e.* pamphlets of sixteen pages quarto], " Mercuries, Diurnals, Play-bills, etc." [1]

At the end of the month of August 1663, therefore, Roger L'Estrange not only supplanted Muddiman as writer of the printed news, but was also armed with additional powers against seditious writers and printers. Before the end of the year he was to justify his appointment.

According to his own account L'Estrange foresaw difficulties in this arrangement, and thought that he himself, in turn might be removed from the post of writer of the printed news. " I told your lordship," wrote he to Arlington in 1665,[2] " that to fit myself for this duty [of Surveyor of the Press] I must be at a very great expense to furnish myself with a house, a family and assistants, besides the very great charge of spies for discoveries and the infinite trouble of personal attendance upon the press. And I then put the case, to your honour, what a ruinous and ridiculous disorder I should find in my little affairs if, after the drudgery done of purging the press and engaging myself in a further debt to effect it, I should then come to be stripped of those benefits which his Majesty had granted me in consideration of

---

[1] The warrant for the grant is summarized on p. 240 of the Calendar for 1663–4, and is dated August 15. The grant itself followed rapidly, for Henry Muddiman's news-books ceased at the end of the month.

[2] Letter to Lord Arlington of October 19 (Thursday), 1665, dated from " Canfield House, London." This is very inadequately summarized on p. 22 of the Calendar of State Papers for 1665–6.

the service." In reply, Lord Arlington, he says, told him to "quit those scruples" and to rely upon his kindness, and he had received "innumerable expressions of the same quality since."

Thus a pamphleteer, without any experience in journalism, succeeded the best journalist of his times as the sole dispenser of the printed news. The result, as L'Estrange had foreseen, was to be disastrous.

Henry Muddiman's *Mercurius Publicus* and *Kingdomes* (or *Kingdoms*) *Intelligencer* therefore ended upon August 20 and August 24, 1663, respectively, the two news-books issued by L'Estrange being entitled *The Intelligencer, published for the satisfaction and Information of the People. With privilege ;* and *The Newes* (with the same addition). No. 1 of the former was issued on Monday, August 31, and No. 1 of the latter on Thursday, September 3. It is invariably asserted by modern writers that L'Estrange's periodicals were termed the *Public Intelligencer*, and a misreading of Anthony à Wood's MSS. has aided this error; but the *Public Intelligencer* died for ever in 1660, and was never connected with L'Estrange.

In his first number of the *Intelligencer* L'Estrange recited his patent and expressed his views on the subject of the publication of "printed Intelligence." He remarked, "A Publick Mercury should never have my vote, because I think it makes the multitude too familiar with the actions and counsels of their superiors, too pragmatical and censorious, and gives them not only an itch, but a kind of colourable right and licence to be meddling with the Government." Nevertheless, he thought that at this juncture "a paper of that quality" might be "both safe and expedient."

Indeed, perhaps it might even be "necessary," for the "humours of the Common people" were "much more capable of being tuned and wrought upon by convenient hints and touches in the shape and air of a pamphlet than by the strongest reasons and best notions imaginable under any other and more sober form whatsoever."

There spoke a pamphleteer and not a journalist. And then L'Estrange announced, " Once a week may do the business, for I intend to utter my news by weight, not by measure." But he would leave himself free " to double at pleasure." He added, " One book a week may be expected, however, to be published every Thursday and finished upon the Tuesday night, leaving Wednesday entire for the printing it off."

And this was in a pamphlet of one sheet only, or eight pages, half the size of Muddiman's sixteen-page pamphlets, and sold at the same price—twopence. After this address, six short paragraphs of news followed, carefully spaced out, and some advertisements. That was all. " Methinks but a simple beginning," commented Pepys.

The outcry at the idea of " one book a week " was so great that L'Estrange was compelled to abandon this part of his programme, but he still continued the smaller-sized pamphlets, printing them in larger type and giving very little news in them. Commencing with Monday, January 4, 1664, he numbered and paged the *Intelligencer* and the *Newes* consecutively. Thus they no longer repeated one another. Still the people evidently thought they were being cheated of their money's worth. War with the Dutch was formally declared on March 4, 1665, but not even then did L'Estrange increase his news, and still he employed larger type and spaced out his paragraphs. Even his " narratives " or " relations," separately published, failed to please. " All are dissatisfied with it," wrote James Hickes to Williamson of one of them on June 10, 1665. " There is no account of the Duke of York's singular encounter with Opdam. . . . Nor is a word said of Prince Rupert." [1]

---

[1] " *Second narration of the signal victory which it pleased Almighty God to bestow upon His Majesty, May 3* " (June 1665). (Copy with the news-books in the Burney Collection.)

At last, on June 1, 1665, L'Estrange finally doubled the size of his journal, increasing it to two sheets (*i. e.* sixteen pages). Thus he could plead a little later on, " In doubling the sheet, I doubled also the value." [1] But all that he had done was to give his readers the same amount of printed paper as Muddiman, with about half the news.

Before narrating the inevitable consequences of the outcry against L'Estrange's journalism, we must return to Henry Muddiman. When the news-books were taken from him for the benefit of L'Estrange, Muddiman does not seem to have openly resented the transfer. Indeed, L'Estrange had so long intrigued for the office that something of the sort was to be anticipated. And as his privilege as " intelligencer," with the right of free postage, was continued, Muddiman, no doubt, felt that he could write L'Estrange out of the field by means of his news-letters. So when a request was made to him to help L'Estrange, Muddiman complied, but exacted a salary of £3 a week, more than half the profit of the news-books, then asserted by L'Estrange to have been worth only £200 a year. He does not seem to have placed the whole of his resources at L'Estrange's disposal, and, naturally, this arrangement soon came to an end.

L'Estrange asked that part of Muddiman's privilege of free postage, namely, that of free postage of letters from his correspondents, should be extended to himself, but Sir Philip Frowde, who was Deputy Postmaster, would not permit this.[2] At the same time, Muddiman, who had

---

[1] Letter to Lord Arlington of October 21, 1665, calendared on page 22 of the Calendar of 1665-6 as, " Has doubled the size and price of the book." This incorrect rendering, as usual, has misled many writers. The price remained the same, twopence. Previous to this L'Estrange had been charging twopence for one sheet only.

[2] Calendar S.P. Dom., 1665-6, p. 106. Letter of Hickes to Williamson dated December 18, 1665 : " Some time ago Mr. L'Estrange wanted to have his letters free, as Mr. Muddiman had, but Sir Phil. Frowde refused it and would not allow him, through one of his creatures

always been in the habit of enclosing the news-books with his news-letters, sent out L'Estrange's news-books in company with his news-letters, and thus the printed news actually became subsidiary to the written news. As he had the privilege of sending all his communications post free, he, therefore, probably was L'Estrange's best customer.   When the clerks at the " Letter Office " saw that Muddiman's news-letters were accompanied by the news-books, they, too, began to send out the news-books and some news-letters—notably James Hickes, to whom Muddiman was in the habit of presenting four copies of his news-letters every week " to write after."   Though the clerks had the privilege of " free postage," this was an abuse, for their privilege was intended to be for official correspondence, and not for their own private benefit. Thus, of the two journalists, Muddiman was still by far the most prosperous.   He had some hundreds of correspondents, and as he invariably refused a less fee than £5 a year for his news-letters, his income was a large one. Evidence on this subject will be quoted later on.   So he married and bought a country house at Earl's Court. As the name and actual site of this house can be traced to-day in " Coleherne Court," the history of the house will be of interest.   " Coldhern," as it was termed in Muddiman's time, was the property of Sir William Lister, whose daughter the quondam " Major-General," John Lambert, married.   Sir Willliam Lister died at Coldhern in 1648 and Lambert, whose wife had inherited the house, then resided in it before his removal to Wimbledon.[1]

Coldhern had thirteen acres of land attached to it, and thus Muddiman was enabled to gratify the taste for horses

at the Post Office, to receive his letters before the King's were given out.   During the plague, however, he got his letters free through Mr. Browne by favour of the Countess of Chesterfield.   Asks if this is to continue," etc.

[1] Lysons' *Environs of London* (1795), vol. iii. p. 205.

to which personal paragraphs occasionally added by him to his news-letters testify.[1]

A remarkable contrast to a modern editor journeying to his daily work by the Underground railway was presented by the bewigged seventeenth-century news-writer, mounted on horseback and travelling to White-hall or the " Seven Stars " in the Strand, armed with a sword, and a brace of pistols in his holsters, " because of the footpads at Knightsbridge." Here, at Coldhern, Muddiman lived quietly for the rest of his life,[2] mixed up in none of the follies of his time, and content to entertain his country correspondents when they came up to town.

[1] In Thomas Faulkner's *History of Kensington*, p. 432, there is the transcript of a contemporary document giving the contents " of every Person's land in the parish of Kensington and Manor of Earl's Court." Mr. Arnold, who lived at Earl's Court House, is entered here as the chief landowner, and Mr. Henry " Middleton " (a common misreading for Muddiman) as the owner of thirteen acres freehold. Mr. Arnold is stated in the parish register of Kensington parish church to have been present at Henry Muddiman's death " at Coldhern " in 1692.

[2] His name appears regularly in the " Hearth Tax " lists, imposed by 13 and 14 Car. II, c. 10 at the rate of 2s. a hearth. The first payment was made at Michaelmas 1662. The most perfect list at the Record Office is, " A true view of all the fire hearths and stones within the County of Middlesex, taken by Roger Higgs, Esq., Receiver-General for the said duty, for one year ended at Lady Day 1676, and presented to his Majesty's Justices of the general Quarter Sessions of the Peace held for the said County, April 12, 1678 " (Record Office, Chas. II, Subsidies, 143/340). " Earls Court, in Kensington. Math. Child 5 (hearths); Rich Awberry, 3; Wm. Arnold, 13; Edw. Clarke, 2; Kath. Terrell, 2; Wm. Fox, 2; (Empty, mr. Arnold, owner, 2;) Mr. Muddiman, 8; Dr. Hubert, 6." So there were only nine houses in Earl's Court in those times—a strange contrast to the present day.

CHAPTER IX

THE FARNLEY WOOD CONSPIRACY—TWYN AND THE PRINTERS OF THE "SPEECHES AND PRAYERS" CONVICTED—WILLIAMSON'S DESIGN AGAINST L'ESTRANGE AND MUDDIMAN—MUDDIMAN FOUNDS THE *LONDON GAZETTE*—L'ESTRANGE APPEALS TO THE KING AND IS PENSIONED—DEFEAT OF THE PLOT OF WILLIAMSON AND JAMES HICKES—SIR WILLIAM MORICE PROTECTS MUDDIMAN

IN 1663 the rising temporarily checked by the execution of Tonge and the others came to a head. " In June the agitators were sent from Scotland, to reconcile the sectaries, and these were entertained at one Oldroyd's house at Dewsbury, better known by the name of ' Divil of Dewsbury.' " Afterwards meetings were held at a place called " Stank House," in the same county, " whence Marsden and Palmer were sent to London as agitators to the Council of Six.' On their return to Yorkshire they brought orders to rise on the 12th of October, " with assurance that the insurrection should be general and Whitehall attempted. Nottingham, Gloucester and Newcastle were to be seized for passes over the Tyne, Trent and Severn, and Boston in Lincolnshire for a port, to receive succours and ammunition from Holland and other foreign parts. York they aimed at, but of Hull they despaired." All " the gentry " were to be secured, and officers and soldiers listed all over England. The objects were " to re-establish a gospel magistracy and ministry and to restore the Long Parliament, as the only basis they could build upon. And lastly to curb the clergy, gentry and lawyers. This is the sum of the whole matter." [1]

Whilst all the preparations were being made in the north of England, Roger L'Estrange had got upon the track of the conspiracy in London. Chapman was in gaol for writing the *Phenix*, fortunately for himself, and was not discharged until May 8, 1664,[2] when he gave a bond with two sureties in £300 for his good behaviour. " Elephant " Smith, too, was in hold, and Calvert was dead before the end of August. So the Council of Six gave orders to John Twyn, of Smithfield, to print their manifesto, to be circulated in London at the rising on October 12.   Like Venner's *Door of Hope*, this document appears to have been composed by a Fifth Monarchy man, but it is not possible to be quite sure about this, as no complete copy is in existence.   Twyn was arrested in the act of printing the book and was examined on October 9, three days before the rising was appointed to take place.[3]

The book printed by Twyn was sent to him by Elizabeth Calvert, the widow of Giles, by her maid Elizabeth Evans. It was entitled, " A Treatise of the Execution of Justice; wherein is clearly proved that the Execution of Judgment and Justice, is as well the Peoples as the Magistrates duty, and if the Magistrates pervert Judgment, the people are bound by the Law of God to execute judgment without them and upon them." Twyn had already printed, corrected and read over the first two sheets. For 1000 copies of these he had received 40s.   A sheet seized by

[1] *An Exact Account of the daily proceedings of the Commissioners of Oyer and Terminer at York.   Against the late horrid and bloody conspirators* (1664).   There is a copy of this tract in the Library of Lincoln's Inn.
[2] Cal. S.P. Dom., 1663–4, p. 582.
[3] *Ibid.*, p. 292.   The name is misspelt " Twinne."

L'Estrange (pp. 25 to 32) still remains among the State Papers.[1]

The tract ordered the " Saints " to sell their garments and buy swords with which to " execute justice " upon the judges and magistrates, and to exterminate the King and the House of Stuart in revenge for the regicides and traitors executed since 1660. The necessary precautions were taken in London, therefore, and no rising took place. It was otherwise in the north of England, where a rendezvous took place at Farnley Wood, three miles from the then small town of Leeds. Here, thirty or forty men in arms were captured and tried at York Assizes, commencing on January 9 in the following year. One of the conspirators was named Oates (who turned King's evidence), and among the twenty condemned and executed at various places in the county was Peregrine Corney, a preaching anabaptist, who, " from the text ' Faithful and true are those which follow the Lamb,' inferred the lawfulnesse of the design so it were carried on for love of the cause and not for by-ends." [2]

When the judges returned, in the following month, John Twyn and the surviving printers and publishers of the *Phenix* and the " Speeches and Prayers " of the ten regicides executed in 1660 were tried. Twyn was indicted for high treason. He could have saved his life by disclosing the names of the Council of Six or of the writers of the book he had printed. He refused to do so and was executed in Smithfield on February 24. The wretched old woman, Elizabeth Calvert, escaped scot free. Continually imprisoned for printing seditious and fraudulent

[1] Inadequately described on p. 407 of the Calendar of State Papers for 1663-4. A long quotation from this sheet is set out in *Notes and Queries*, Series 11, viii. pp. 122-4.
[2] In addition to the tract cited, *The Newes*, No. 4 for January 14, 1663/4, and *Intelligencer*, No. 5 for January 18, 1663/4, contain a great deal of information. See also the 1662 edition of the " Panther Prophecy " for the prediction at the end of the rising in October 1663.

books, she survived until October 1674, when she died, bequeathing her body " to be decently buried among the baptists." [1] Thomas Brewster, the publisher, Simon Dover, the printer, and Nathan Brooks, the bookbinder, of the " Speeches and Prayers " of the ten regicides executed in 1660 were, by the King's clemency, indicted and convicted for misdemeanour only and were heavily fined and imprisoned. " Be it known to the Reader," said the official account of the trial of the four,[2] " that this book was not, as it pretends to be, a true account of the words (written or spoken) of dying men, but a meer forgery and imposture, fathered upon those who were executed, but contrived by the traytors that 'scaped; as deeming it their safest way to publish the designs of the living in the words of the dead and the most conducing to their project of destroying the present King, to persuade the multitude into a good opinion of the murder of the last. To conclude. Notorious it is that the whole libel is a cheat, the letters and speeches a counterfeit and framed only by recommending one rebellion to stir up another."

Brewster and Dover both died in prison two months later on.[3] Roger L'Estrange had justified his appointment and had broken up the knot of dishonest booksellers. No more books of " Prodigies " were issued. Conspiracies there were, but no more serious attempts at rebellion for fourteen years, and then the gravest crisis of all was to break out, under very different auspices than those of the mean men whose fate has been chronicled. The Press was " in order," so far as it is possible for the Press to be " in order " under repression.

[1] Will of Eliz. Calvert. P.C.C. Dycer, 12.
[2] " An Exact Narrative of the Tryal and Condemnation of John Twyn . . . with the tryals of Thomas Brewster . . . Simon Dover . . . Nathan Brooks," etc. " Published by authority. Printed by Thomas Mabb for Henry Brome, 1664." The reprint of this in " State Trials " is mutilated and worthless.
[3] *The Newes* for April 28, 1664.

In the meantime Williamson had watched Muddiman's prosperity with a greedy eye. Marchamont Nedham had never sent out news-letters, and the precedent had been set by Thurloe of allotting one-half of the profits of the news-books written by Nedham to the under-secretary, who presumably acted as Thurloe's deputy in revising them. But Muddiman, although he had lost the news-books, was subject to no supervision. Prudence, of course, prevented him from making comments in his news-letters which might be unacceptable to the Government, and he did not correspond with disloyal subscribers. Williamson did not even know to whom his news-letters were sent. He " several times asked for a list of his correspondents, but was refused." Muddiman did not trust him. So the cunning under-secretary formed the plan of getting the whole of the intelligence of the kingdom into his own hands. To get rid of L'Estrange would not be a difficult matter, for his failure to satisfy the public was notorious. And as the press was now " in order," the seditious publishers suppressed, and little work left for L'Estrange to do beyond keeping the press within the limits to which he had reduced it, Williamson waited for an opportunity to pension off the " Surveyor of the Press " with a small sum and place Muddiman in the same relationship to himself as Nedham had been to Thurloe. Whether he proposed to pay Muddiman a similar salary to that he eventually offered to L'Estrange, viz. £100 a year, there is nothing to show, but probably some arrangement of this kind was contemplated, for Muddiman was to write the " news-books " once more, and a certain number of Muddiman's correspondents were allotted by Williamson to his fellow-conspirator, James Hickes of the " Letter Office," as his share of the spoils.

It is important to bear in mind that there were no other news-books in existence at this time than those written by L'Estrange, and no other news-letters other than those sent out by Muddiman. The latter's privilege and " free postage " rendered all outside competition impossible up to the year 1679, when Oates's plot was in full swing.[1]

One circumstance, and one only, rendered this scheme possible, and it was that Williamson knew Arlington was about to receive a grant for ten years of the office of Post-master-General, the grant to the then lessee, O'Neal, expiring in 1667.

The warrant for the grant to Lord Arlington in succession to O'Neale was signed and dated on October 5, 1665,[2] and thus Williamson thought that he himself would be the real Postmaster-General, and that if Muddiman did not yield to his terms, he would be able to withdraw his privilege of free postage and forbid him access to the Secretary of State's offices. L'Estrange, however, had first to be disposed of, and the outcry against his journalism, coupled with the presence of the Court at Oxford on account of the plague in London, gave a plausible excuse for the printing of an official journal there. During the first part of the Court's absence from London, Muddiman had remained in charge of Lord Arlington's office, opening letters and sending them on to Williamson at Oxford.[3]

[1] There were no other news-letters until Williamson, through his clerks, Francis, Ball and Yard, also sent out news-letters, commencing with the year 1666. Nevertheless written news was to be found in London coffee-houses in 1674, so that it was proposed to suppress not only the coffee-houses, but also the sale of coffee itself (see the " Proclamations " on this subject). The dealers in coffee, however, pointed out that they would lose money if they were prohibited from disposing of their stock, and thus the Proclamation was not acted upon, a further Proclamation granting a respite. But, owing to the heavy postage rates, the news found in London coffee-houses did not circulate in the country, and Williamson's competition with Muddiman was of the feeblest kind.

[2] Cal. S.P. Dom., 1665-6, p. 5.

[3] There are a number of letters from Muddiman to Williamson at this time which prove this. On p. 521 of the Calendar for 1665-6 is summarized a letter in which he says that he sends on the foreign letters, " not knowing how it would be taken at Court were he to open them." On the same day, August 17, Hickes complained to Williamson that Muddiman's taking abstracts of the Secretaries' letters delayed his sending them off to Oxford.

After the warrant for Lord Arlington's grant of the Postmastership was signed, therefore, Muddiman was summoned by Arlington to Oxford and instructed to write the new official journal. But before this periodical appeared Williamson opened his campaign, by composing a letter for Lord Arlington to sign and by sending this to L'Estrange in London. He himself remained in the background and did not write to L'Estrange.[1] Arlington's letter was as follows :

"*Oxon*, y' 15 *Oct*. 1665.

" SIR,

" I am sorry the distance in which we are from you deprives me of the occasion of helping and directing you in the composing of the public news, as would be better for his Majesty's service and your own reputation. I have often advised you to agree with Mr. Muddiman in this matter, who, having had the good luck and opportunity of falling into the channel of these things, would have been very useful to you. And, in despair of seeing this effected in the future, I take the freedom to propose to you that, if you will relinquish to me your whole right in the composing and profit of the news-book, I will procure for you in recompense of it a salary from his Majesty of £100 per an. which shall be paid through my hands, being put to (account?) for it. If I tax it too low you

---

[1] The draft or copy of this letter, in Williamson's handwriting, is insufficiently and incorrectly summarized on p. 15 of the Calendar for 1665–6 and wrongly attributed to Williamson. Mrs. Green, in the first page of the Preface to this Calendar, makes the following assertions :

" Joseph Williamson, afterwards Sir Joseph Williamson and Secretary of State, took upon himself the editorship of the *London Gazette*, supplanting in that office Roger L'Estrange, surveyor of the Press. On October 15, 1665, he wrote to L'Estrange declining an application for assistance in collecting news, but offering to procure him a salary of £100 a year if he were willing to give up his right in the news-book." This, of course, is absurdly untrue. L'Estrange made no application at all, and the letter Mrs. Green supposed to have been written by Williamson, because the draft was in his handwriting, was signed by Arlington. The first sentence of L'Estrange's reply to Arlington proves this.

HENRY BENNET, K.G., EARL OF ARLINGTON
By permission of the Duke of Grafton, Sir Almeric Fitzroy and Messrs. Christophers
(From the portrait by Sir Peter Lely, at Euston)

must blame yourself for having told me several times
that the duty of it is very burthensome to you and the
profit inconsiderable. I pray you let me have your answer
to this by the first, and to assure yourself in the meantime
that I have the same desire and inclination to serve you
in all things in my power that I have ever professed, and
that even this proposition proceeds from that root.

"Mr. L'ESTRANGE." [1]

In the greatest alarm at this threatened loss of the news-
book L'Estrange wrote to Lord Arlington by each post
the following week. On Tuesday, Oct. 17, he wrote :—

"MY LORD,

"I have passed many a thought upon your letter
of the 15th instant, which I had the honour to receive
yesterday; wherein, upon the whole matter I find only
fresh and abundant instances of your exceeding generosity
and goodness, which I shall ever acknowledge with an
eternal submission and respect.

"Your lordship is pleased to charge mee with some mis-
carriages in the publique intelligence since I was out of
distance of your express direction. Wherein I dare not
justify myselfe, although upon a strict reflection I cannot
pitch upon the particular. But I hope the services I have
rendered his Majesty otherwise during the time of liberty
and contagion and the hazzards I have undergone upon
that account weigh down those failings.

"As to Mr. Muddyman, I did once make use of him.
I found him very short of intelligence, but it was during
Mr. Williamson's sickness and that perchance might be the
reason of it. Now if Mr. Williamson would be pleased
to engage him to deal more openly with me, I should take
the same agreement over again for an obligation and
immediately put that wheele again in motion.

"Touching your lordship's proposal of my relinquishing

---

[1] Calendar S.P. Dom. Charles II, 1665–6, p. 15. The above is a
transcript of the whole of the draft in Williamson's handwriting.

my right in the Newes book, upon a consideration exprest, it is certaine that both in gratitude and justice your power over me is without limits. But this let me offer withall, that it would utterly ruin me, the book being come now to above £400 a year. And I did ill explain myself if I was understood to complayn of the newesbook, for my trouble was the exclusive charge of entertaining spyes and instruments for the reducing of the press, which cost me about £500 out of my pocket the first year, and if your lordship had not most charitably provided me £200 from his Majesty, for my supply, I had found a greater obstruction in the work.

" I shall give you, my lord, no further trouble at present than to present you with the wishes of all imaginable comforts.

" My lord, your most obliged and ever obedient servant
" ROGER L'ESTRANGE." [1]

By the next post, of Thursday, the 19th, L'Estrange wrote again at very great length, repeated and increased his arguments and acknowledged that an " overture " had been made to Nedham, " when you were again pleased to repeat your bounty, in assuring me that you would make it your interest to see me otherwise well provided for, before I should be dispossessed of what I had."

He added that he had incurred a debt " of nigh £3000 " in the King's service and had never gained from his office. " And yet (however my writing be denied) even according to Mr. Muddyman's own calculation the newes book is now worth treble to what I found it, and the first brunt of my business as Surveyor of the Press being over, I was in hope to draw from it a comfortable subsistence." This increase of income, of course, was the real cause of the complaints against him. He charged the same as Muddiman, and gave little for the money.

[1] Cal. S.P. Don., 1665–6, p. 17 (original letter).

Moreover, he added that the " quality of my employment was to teaze and persecute the whole rabble of the faction, which I have done to such a degree that I have drawn upon my head all the malice imaginable. And can it be that now I am to be delivered up to those very people for a sacrifice, and with the brand of a fool upon me into the bargain? " And, " the newes book was given me to balance my service about the press, and in doing my work be judge, my lord, if I do not deserve my wages."

Finally, his services during the pestilence deserved recognition. For he had worked—

" till the plague came into my own family and, in truth, into most of the houses where I had to do, there being near 80 of the printing trade already dead of the sickness, besides that Mr. Lye (as by your lordships order) told me that your honour was resolved to recommend my diligence and perseverance to his Majesty upon that very account. Now after all this (if I may credit what I hear) I am marked out for beggary, infamy and contempt; and, briefly, for the worst that can befall an honest man and (to deal plainly) without being informed of any offence. But God's will and his Majesty's be done, I hope the best and I fortify myself for the worst and dare cast the whole upon this issue, that if then I fall it is beyond all precedent.

" I have served his Majesty and his blessed father almost thirty years with as great a passion and constancy (through all hazards and extremities) as human nature is capable of. Much of my fortune, my lord, is in your hand. If you think me worthy of your favour it will become me to endeavour that you never repent it. And I hope that his Majesty's interest will not be the less for rewarding a faith so inviolable and so unlimited an obedience. I doubt not but your lordship has received mine of Tuesday last, so that I may now close this with the protestation that you have not anyone more (faithful) in the world than, my lord, your honour's most obedient servant—ROGER L'ESTRANGE."

This letter seems to have remained unanswered, and on the following Saturday, October 21, L'Estrange made his last appeal, in which he stated that " by doubling the sheet " of the news-book " I doubled also the value," and repeated his offer to agree with Muddiman as before for " three pound a week." For, said he, " most certain it is that of £200 p. annum as I found it (the news-book) at the beginning, I have brought it up to above £500, and even at this instant it is worth £400, when the sale is at the worst."

It is very doubtful whether Lord Arlington ever saw either of these three letters, and in this case the reason why they still remain among Williamson's correspondence is explained. Arlington " left all to his man Williamson."

In spite of L'Estrange's protests, the projected new paper appeared, was styled the *Oxford Gazette. Published by Authority*, and was issued twice a week. The first number was undated, but appeared on November 16, 1665,[1] and was printed by the University printer, Leonard Lichfield.

The success of the *Gazette* was instantaneous, and Williamson claimed all the credit for it. He seems to have encouraged the belief that he himself was its writer. When it was reprinted in London by Thomas Newcombe, Pepys wrote, " This day (November 22, 1665) the first of the *Oxford Gazettes* came out, which is very pretty, full of newes and no folly in it. Wrote by Williamson." It is sad to be compelled to point out that the absence of folly referred to the absence of anything in the shape of a leading article. Muddiman knew his business and that

---

[1] There have been many mistakes about the exact date. The first number was not dated at all, though the news contained in it began with November 7, but the second number was dated for "16–20 Nov.," so that the first appeared for November 7–16, and thus should be cited as from the 16th—not the 7th.

the public wanted news, not disquisitions about the iniquities of the dissenters and seditious printers. Hickes wrote to Williamson on November 18, 1665, that he had disposed of all the " gazetts " sent him (five quires) " to our clerks and by my book woman to the Exchange yesterday; and in few words, no publick intelligence to this day ever received so general an applause. And I hope you have ordered it so as that they may be printed here in London for the general content of all." [1] No others would be sent for, he added.

The *Oxford Gazette* was only "half a sheet in folio," 11 inches by 6½, but it was closely printed in two columns on both sides and contained no advertisements. For many years to come this size and style was maintained, advertisements being added after Muddiman's editorship had ceased. Thus the *Gazette* was exactly the same size and shape as Muddiman's news-letters (a whole sheet folded once), more easily folded up with them than the preceding pamphlets; and, it must be admitted, was entirely supplementary to the news-letters, which contained parliamentary proceedings and other news not allowed to be printed. Only the well-to-do classes or coffee-houses could afford the luxury of a news-letter, for £5 a year was by no means a small sum in those days, and as the *Gazettes* (Anthony à Wood tells us) were sold for a penny each, the " people," as L'Estrange terms them, had to content themselves with the printed news for an annual expenditure of about 9s.

Thus the age of quarto pamphlets had passed for ever. The " paper," later on to be termed " newes paper," was in being.[2]

---

[1] Original letter of November 18, 1665.

[2] The first instance of the term " paper " applied to printed news is, I think, in a letter from Lord Arlington to Sir William Temple, on June 11, 1666, in which he says : " I must refer you to the printed Papers to supply what was wanting of the relation you had by the last " (Arlington's letters to Temple, Ed. Thos. Bebington, 1701). Again, writing to Temple on October 18, 1667, Arlington said : " I must refer

At first, Roger L'Estrange made an attempt to compete with the new *Gazette* by imitating its form and size. He also issued a first number of a "paper," entitling it *Publick Intelligence*. *With Sole Privilege*, on November 29, 1665,[1] but was compelled to discontinue it, on finding that he had no news-letters to send out with it, and insufficient news with which to fill it. He at once reverted to his pamphlets, and decided to adopt a better means of obtaining satisfaction, by an appeal to the King. As a result, Charles II came to a very just decision. He ordered that the £100 a year Arlington had offered should be paid to L'Estrange out of the profits of the news-books, but that the news-books should be "taken into the offices of the Secretaries of State." In addition, L'Estrange was to be paid another £200 by Arlington out of the secret service money, as well as "extraordinary expenses in the discovery of libels according to bills made out by him." Charles II, it is added, had appreciated very much L'Estrange's services as " Overseer of the Press, which he had reduced to that degree that his Majesty said several times he wondered how it could be done." [2]

The first part of Williamson's plot, therefore, was defeated. Neither he himself nor Lord Arlington received any assignment or grant of the " news-book," which was " taken into the Secretaries offices." Both Secretaries of State, therefore, proposed to issue a " news-book " or " paper "—a fact which Muddiman was swift to note—

---

you to our newes papers, for a further account of the proceedings of Parliament." Here the reference is to the " news-letters " sent out by Williamson's clerks, and by Muddiman, for Sir William Morice.

[1] This contained the following preface : " By this time you may perceive, my masters, that your intelligencer has changed his title, his form and his day, for which I could give you twenty shrewd reasons if I were not obliged to gratifie a point of prudence in myself [rather] than a curiosity in others; and I do assure you there is both discretion and modesty in the case. This short accompt will serve to satisfie the wise, and I shall leave the rest to content themselves at leisure."

[2] MSS. of the Marquess of Ormonde, N.S. vol. iii. pp. 351–2. A long statement, accompanied by a certificate from Arlington.

and the *Gazette* had been saddled with the charge of £100
a year, while L'Estrange himself had been pensioned with
£300 a year and was to be allowed all his expenses in
addition. According to Anthony à Wood, L'Estrange
ceased journalism on January 29, 1666.[1]

The assertions made in the Preface to the Calendar of
State Papers (p. viii) that "the editorship" (of the
Gazette) "was handed over to Williamson, whose official
position, combined with his laborious business habits
well fitted him for the post," are incorrect. Business
habits do not qualify anyone to be an editor, and Williamson's official position prohibited his writing the *Gazette*.
Two Gazettes, therefore, were to be issued, one from
the offices of Sir William Morice, the senior Secretary, as
well as that from the offices of Lord Arlington.

Before giving the proofs of this I must describe Williamson's attack upon Muddiman, carried out by Hickes; for
Williamson, as usual, remained in the background, and left
Hickes to take all the risks. James Hickes was probably
a native of Nantwich, and had been employed in the
management of the Posts ever since the year 1637, when the
"Letter Office" was first set up, and he had then taken
part in the formation of the "Chester road." His antecedents can be traced, partly in the Journals of the Houses
of Lords and Commons for 1642, and partly in his own
petition to the King, in 1660, for the continuance of his
clerkship in the Letter Office.[2] His strongest claim for
re-employment then lay in the fact that his father, aged

---

[1] Anthony à Wood's life of Marchamont Nedham in *Athenæ Oxonienses*,
iii. 1185. The final numbers of L'Estrange's *Intelligencer* and *Newes*
are only to be seen in Wood's collections at the Bodleian. (Wood, 392.)
Wood's note at the end is, "Roger L'Estrange desisted from writing
his news. Because the gazets which were out twice a week took up
all."

[2] Hickes's petition is set out in Appendix A. Mr. J. C. Hemmeon's
History of the British Post Office" (Harvard, 1912) contains an account
of Hickes and is the best book yet published on the subject, but this
writer has failed to notice the distinction between the "Posts," or means
of transport, and the "Letter Office."

seventy-four, had been killed at Edgehill, to his own "great loss and damage," and that he himself had been imprisoned in the course of the disputes over the ownership of the Posts in the year 1642; the gist of the whole matter really being that Hickes sided with Prideaux, who was afterwards a member of Cromwell's Council of State, and against the Earl of Warwick, the House of Lords claimant to the office of Postmaster. He had been rewarded for his support of Prideaux by a clerkship in the "Letter Office" in London, at a salary of £100 a year under Cromwell, and this post and salary were confirmed to him at the Restoration in 1660. The whole course of the plot between Williamson and Hickes against Muddiman can be traced in great detail in Hickes's voluminous correspondence with the under-secretary, though the whole story told by him is that of a declared enemy. On Muddiman's side there is no other evidence than his circular to his clients in 1666, a copy of which was taken by Hickes.

Other clerks in the Letter Office, notably Edmund Sawtell, and Mr. Hall, who was at the time in charge of a branch establishment (probably for the Government's service) at the "Round House," at the end of St. Martin's Lane, warned Muddiman in August 1665 of the plot between Hickes and Williamson, and that the former was trying to take lists of his correspondents, and had written to some of them. Muddiman was asserted to have said that he only remained in Lord Arlington's office because he knew that if he migrated to the office of the other Secretary of State, Williamson would then have been able to obtain a list of his correspondents from the other under-secretary. Muddiman thereupon became "very strange and jelious in all his deportments" towards Hickes, who then accused him of sending out little but the common news-books, to the prejudice of the post-office clerks. Muddiman thereupon snubbed Hickes, telling him that his news-letters went out upon the King's account.

When, therefore, he was summoned to Oxford to write the *Gazette*, Muddiman knew very well what would happen with regard to his news-letters, and made arrangements with Sawtell to send the bulk of his news-letters to him under cover and thus frustrate the plans of the conspirators to obtain a complete list.   At the same time, a number were sent in the ordinary way, to be initialled by Hickes. During the week ending December 1, 1665, Hickes copied the addresses of all the news-letters passing through his own hands, making two copies of the list, and sent one of them to Williamson at Oxford.[1]

To this list he appended the note, " I owne 28.   For his own accompt at least 76."   Twenty-eight corre- pondents, at £5 a year each, would have very much more than doubled Hickes's salary of £100 a year.   The motive for him to join in Williamson's little scheme was therefore very clear.   The lists betray the furtive manner in which they were taken by their spelling, which is unusually bad, even for Hickes.   On December 3 he wrote to Williamson : " For your own correspondents, you know best how now to order and direct, I having sent you a list of all Mr. Muddiman corresponds with, by which you may know your management by him.   And they rec^d for himselfe, which I suppose signifies more of profit to him than of advice to you, and the more advantageous to him by their freedom in passing free without postage."

Sawtell told Muddiman of what Hickes had done, and the latter then sent no more of his letters to Hickes, stopped the presents of his news-letters to him, and transmitted all his news-letters from Oxford to Hall or to Sawtell.

Hickes's true character then came out at once, in a venomous attempt to get Sawtell into trouble.   Writing to Williamson on January 10, 1666, Hickes, after saying

---

[1] The lists, which add the postage, and give the different " roads," are of very great interest in Post Office history.   I have therefore set the principal list out in full in Appendix B.

that the City was discontented at a report that Parliament was to meet at Oxford, went on : " The Lord in mercie give us contented hearts to fit us for Himself, if it be His blessed will. And while we live that we may live to His glory. Thus commending you to protection and keeping of the Almighty I take leave and respectfully am, Sir, your most humble servant, James Hickes." To this pious exordium he added a postscript : " I do pray you to write two or three smart words to the purpose that my lord (Arlington) understands that I keep the King's letters longer in my hands than I ought . . . the reason, I hint this much, is that Mr. Muddiman's agent [sic] Mr. Sawtell when I am going suddenly to make up [the letter bag] gallops to the tavern, whence I must send for him to make up Mr. Muddiman's. . . . And, as I am informed he (Muddiman) threatens me, as yet I dare not send away my letters without his, if I do I shall hear of it to some purpose, but I take no notice of anything of this nature, but if I stray a hair's breadth beyond my lords orders and yours, hang me." [1]

Among Williamson's friends was numbered Sir George Downing, and if the maxim " noscitur a sociis " held good, then Williamson's character cannot have been a good one, for it is not possible to say a favourable word of Sir George Downing. As far back as 1659 Mr. Broderick had written to Lord Clarendon that Downing was " as arrant a rascal as lives among men," [2] and since then he had proved the truth of the remark by betraying his old friends and associates, the regicides Barksted, Okey, and Corbet, who had taken refuge in Holland, and who, thanks to Downing, were captured, extradited and executed. The

[1] Untruthfully summarized on p. 198 of the Calendar for 1665-6 as follows : " Mr. Muddiman's agent Mr. Sawtell gallops up when the writer is making up Lord Arlington's letters to send by express, and threatens him if he will not at once make up Muddiman's letters and send them at the same time. Begs directions." This utterly obscures the whole meaning of the letter.

[2] December 16, 1659. Clarendon's State Papers, iii. 630.

service he rendered was no doubt a valuable one to the Government, but common decency should have forbidden Downing from effecting it.   Downing heard a good deal of what was going on in London, and wrote from Westminster to Williamson on January 13, 1666 : " A friend of mine and yours desired me to give you a hint that Mr. Mudiford [sic], your instrument, is somewhat discontented and would have had him carry him to Secretary Morice to have engaged there, but he persuaded him to desist and stopped him for that time.   You will make the use of it to keep him to you." [1]

Obviously alarmed at this, Williamson wrote twice to Downing (there was a daily post from the Court to London) and on the 16th Downing reiterated his warning :

" I have yours of the 14th and 15th instant. . . . My friend told me," wrote he, " that Muddiman in downright earnest desired him to carry him to the party mentioned in my last, and the account upon which he said it was to carry him his intelligence as he had done to you, and so also by consequence help the other Gazette. I know not Muddiman if I see him, and you are best judge of the consequences of the thing; keep this information to yourself." [2]

Williamson then ordered Hickes to stop Muddiman's letters, thinking, no doubt, that this would bring Muddiman to his knees.   On January 17 Hickes wrote to Williamson that he had done so, and was returning the packets of letters as they came in.[3]   On January 20 Hickes wrote to Williamson that he always treated Muddiman with respect, but thought that he kept most of his news to make up his news-letters (instead of inserting it in the Gazette).   But, he wound up, " Mr. Sawtell cries him up as the ' author ' of the Gazette." [4]

---

[1] Original letter.   S.P. Dom. Chas. II, Vol. 145, No. 8.
[2] Ibid., No. 52.
[3] Cal. S.P. Dom., 1665–6, p. 208.
[4] Ibid.

The Court removed from Oxford to Hampton Court on January 27, and to Whitehall during the following week, so that No. 23 of the *Oxford Gazette*, published on February 1, was the last to bear that title.   With No. 24, issued for February 1–5, 1666, the title was changed to that of *The London Gazette*, retained by it to the present day. This number and number 25, published on February 8, were the last written by Henry Muddiman,[1] who was now back in London and thus was enabled better to defend himself.   Directly he returned to London he saw William-son, and failing to agree with him, offered his services to Secretary Sir William Morice, who engaged him to write another official journal under the censorship of his own under-secretary, John Cook.   With John Cook Muddiman remained for years to come.   Cook was appointed Latin Secretary in December 1681, in succession to Nicholas Oudart.[2]   Williamson then wrote at once to Charles Perrot of Gray's Inn and engaged him to write the *Gazette* [3] in Muddiman's place.   Muddiman had countered the stop placed upon his news-letters by handing Hickes Secretary Morice's order, and in order to prevent Hickes's designs upon his news-letters, abandoned the miscellaneous crests with which he had been in the habit of sealing his letters, and adopted a new seal, a curiously intricate device of crosses and circles.[4]   He also gave notice to all

[1] " Narrative " of Hickes, paragraph 7.   The date of the last number written by Muddiman is fixed by his circular of February 24.
[2] Muddiman's news-letter of December 24, 1681.
[3] Perrot's reply to Williamson was dated February 4, 1666, and is to be found on p. 232 of the Calendar.   Charles Perrot graduated M.A. from Oriel College, Oxford, in 1653, and died in 1677.   According to Anthony à Wood (*Athenæ Oxonienses*, iii. 1185) he wrote the *Gazette*, though not constantly, until 1671.   This is corroborated by the notices of him in the State Papers.   Perrot was succeeded by Williamson's clerk Robert Yard, whose news-letters are to be found in the Le Fleming Calendar.   On May 11, 1670, W. Chetwynd wrote to Williamson, " I hope I may hear your Parrot talk once a week."
[4] To counterfeit the new seal would have been forgery.   Richard Watts, writing to Williamson on March 5, informed him of Muddiman's new seal and said that it was devised to prevent Hickes's " designs." This seal was in use up to 1670, when Muddiman changed it for the crest

his correspondents to send their letters to John Cook, secretary to Sir William Morice, his Majesty's first (*i. e.* earliest) Principal Secretary, and terminated Hickes's objections to the first order for free postage handed to him, by giving him Sir William Morice's general order.

But the two conspirators had already decided not to let the valuable news-letter correspondence slip out of their hands without another effort; so Hickes drew up a circular, to be sent round to Muddiman's correspondents, whose names he had succeeded in taking. The circular was secretly sent out in Hickes's own name, not Williamson's, and runs as follows:

" S_R,

" You have seene (untill of late) my Name upon Mr. Muddiman's letters, by which they have come franck to your hands. Now please to give me leave to acquaint you that Mr. Muddiman is dismissed from the Management of that correspondance hee formerly was intrusted with By the Right Honble the Lord Arlington his Ma^{ts} principall secretarie of State. And the honor'd Joseph Williamson Esqr his hon^{rs} Secret^y, for that hee hath contrived and managed that correspondance to his owne particular advantage. And not for the service of his Matie and those persons of hon^r as hee ought and they expected hee should have done. And being dismissed from that trust, and from the sight of any of their letters of correspondance much cannot be expected to be communicated by him unto you. And for as much as formerly I was by Order Comanded to take care of the Conveyance of his letters & franck them to whom directed, I am by the *same person* [this was untrue] comanded the contrary. Which I thought

---

and coat of arms of the Paulets, " differenced " by a crescent. He was the only news-letter writer ever permitted to head his letters " Whitehall," and by this heading and the seals in question his news-letters are easily identified. For a list of unidentified or wrongly identified letters by him to be found in the State Papers (stolen in transit by Hickes for Williamson's use), see Appendix G.

fit to make known unto you and to assure you that
respect upon your commands soe farr as in the power of
him that is
<blockquote>
" Sr,
<blockquote>
" yor most humble servant,
<blockquote>
" JAMES HICKES.
<blockquote>
" Ja. Hickes his Lr.
</blockquote>
</blockquote>
</blockquote>
</blockquote>

> " Letter Office Lond. february ye 13 to 15.   65.
>   Endorsed—' 1665. feb. ye 13 to 15.' "

The principal falsehood in this circular was that Muddiman's letters had been ordered to go free by Williamson
and Arlington, when as a matter of fact Hickes was
thoroughly well aware, and admitted to the Secretaries
in his " Narrative," that they were ordered to go free by
Secretary Nicholas.   Apart from this, one Secretary of
State had no right to " dismiss " the clerks of the other,
and this circular had not been sent out until *after* Muddiman had gone to Secretary Morice.   The veiled offer of
his own services, as news-letter writer, at the end of the
letter, discloses Hickes's object.

When Muddiman heard of this circular he was furious.
He went to Hickes " in a great huff and heat," ordered him
to recall his circular, and, on his refusal, sent out a circular
of his own, dated February 24, as follows :

" In answer to a little note from Hickes, a little fellow
of the Post Office, which I suppose among other my
correspondance may be come to y^r hands, I shall justly
inform you, that upon a misunderstanding betwixt Mr.
Williamson and myself about the Gazette, which I wrote
at Oxon and till the last weeke at London, I thought
it most advisable to quit that office wholly, and turne my
correspondents to Sir William Morice, his Maties first
principal Secretary of State.   I shall write as fully and
constantly as formerly and with the same priviledge and
post free.   Which if you find not, pray you signifie.   That

which chiefly thrust Hickes upon that device is that upon
detecting him of some practices I have not of late entrusted
him with putting his name to my letters. Which you may
perceive by comparing those of some late weekes. Nor
given him, as formerly, a coppy of my letters to write after
But as he is disowned in it by those he pretends orders
from, soe I shall make him sensible of the forgery."

(Copy—Endorsed by Hickes, " Mr. Muddiman's scandalous replye to Ja. Hickes his letters of ye 13 and 15 Feby.
65 " [*i. e.* 1666.].)

Objection was at once made by Hickes to the description
of Sir William Morice as " first " principal Secretary by
Muddiman in his notice to his clients, and he endeavoured
to represent this as a claim that Morice was Arlington's
superior. Muddiman's meaning was quite clear, and there
is no ground for supposing that he wished to do more than
draw attention to the fact that Morice was the senior in
point of time of appointment. Nevertheless, in his letter
of April 9, 1666, Hickes was able to give Williamson five
instances of Muddiman's correspondents unthinkingly
directing their letters to " John Cook, Secretary to his
Majesty's first principal Secretary." [1] This charge was
too absurd to be maintained and was dropped.

Hickes then played his last card, and petitioned both
Secretaries of State. It is probable that Lord Arlington
now, for the first time, heard of all that had been going
on. The petition is a remarkable document. Hickes
protests in it that he had always performed his duties

---

[1] This letter is the sole warrant for Mrs. Green's untruthful assertion
in the Preface to the Calendar of 1665–6, p. lx., that Muddiman " got
possession of much official information and insinuated everywhere that
Morice was the principal [*sic ;* both secretaries were " Principal "]
secretary, the one most trusted by the King." This falsehood has
misled some modern writers, who were not aware of the danger of trusting
to Mrs. Green's Calendars, and has led to a depreciation of Sir William
Morice himself. According to their seniority, the Secretaries of State
changed their offices at Whitehall; one set of chambers being more
commodious than the other. These changes of offices were notified
by Muddiman, in his news-letters, at each new appointment.

" as in the presence of Almighty God," and therefore
asks that Muddiman may be ordered to " repayre " him
for the charge of forgery, which meant nothing more than
that Hickes was endeavouring to substitute his own letters
for the official news-letters. He seems to have been
ordered to say precisely what he meant by this, and thus
his " Narrative " was drawn up.

New accusations were then made by Hickes in his
" Narrative " He asserted that Muddiman had sent out
letters of other business, in which neither the King nor
himself were concerned, in order to defraud the Post Office,
pointing out the large number of letters he despatched,
and adding that he sent out nothing but the common
news-books. This practically meant that Muddiman did
not send out news-letters at all. Hickes then proceeded
to make the most injudicious claim that the Letter Office
clerks alone were entitled to send out the news-books post
free, and ought not to be injured by Muddiman's habit
of sending them with his news-letters. Finally, he
asserted that Muddiman received " not one letter in answer
to most of the letters he sent, receiving yearly stipends of
40s. to above £40 per person," admitted his own intention
of preventing Muddiman from despatching his news-
letters before the *Gazette*, and said that it was the latter's
" scandalous circular " which had occasioned his " humble
petitioning."

This document fell quite flat. Up to March 25, 1666,
no decision had been taken by the two Secretaries of
State.[1]

By May Day he knew that he had failed, for he then
wrote to tell Williamson that " Mr. Cook orders Muddiman's letters to go free, as formerly."

---

[1] Hickes's letter of March 25, 1666 (New Year's Day of the times)
was dated by him in mistake " 1665," and has thus been calendared on
p. 273 of the Calendar for 1664–5. In it he expressed his longing to
hear the results of his petition.

A month later on Hickes and Williamson's defeat was signalized to the whole world.   On Monday, June 4, 1666, there appeared the first number of Secretary Morice's " paper," entitled *Current Intelligence*, published by John Macock, who had published Monck's documents in 1660.

The position of the *Gazette*, saddled with L'Estrange's £100 and opposed by its own founder, the ablest journalist of the day, became desperate.   Nor was this all; the issue of the opposition Journal entitled *Current Intelligence*, written by Muddiman,[1] and the fact that Muddiman had directed all his correspondents to send their letters to Secretary Morice's offices, placed Sir William Morice, who was known to have Presbyterian sympathies, in the foreground and seriously affected Lord Arlington's reputation.   A correspondent, writing to Williamson from Ipswich on September 1, 1666, said :

" I am now to tell you a tale in your eare in obedience to your commands.   I have endeavoured to fix you a correspondent here.   Upon my address to a sober person, in order thereunto, he told me he could not believe it worth his trouble, all business of concernment being intrusted with Secretary Morice.   I with much ado convinc'd him of his error upon mine own knowledge and desired to know (for he is a confidant of mine) by whom and what meanes he was drawn into that opinion.   His answer was, as being the discourse of all the gentry and people of intelligence in the whole Country (which indeed

[1] There is a complete collection of *Current Intelligence* in the Burney Collection at the British Museum.   Muddiman's authorship was stated as follows : " J. H." writing to Thomas Le Gros at Norwich on June 6, 1666, says that " the stories of each days action [with the Dutch] is now given at large in the diurnalls, of which there are now two, the *Gazette* written by order of Mr. Williamson, Lord Arlington's Secretary, and the *Current Intelligence*, by Muddiman, written by order of Mr. Cooke, Sir William Morice's Secretary " (Historical Manuscripts Commission, Tenth Report, Part IV. p. 449).   On July 2, 1666, Dr. T. Smith wrote to Daniel Le Fleming that, " The weekly print called the *Current Intelligence* is said to be done by Muddiman, and is looked upon as Secretary Morice's intelligence, the *Gazette* being Lord Arlington's." —(Calendar of the MSS. of Mr. Le Fleming, at Rydal Hall, p. 40.)

are those he most converseth with), and how that the
Generals sent all their dispatches to Mr. Secretary Morice,
by whom they having been communicated to his Majesty
(pray mark the extravagance), they were constantly
burnt without further communication to any.   And that
this mischief might be extensible and set all together by
the ears, they date the knowledge of all this for certain
truth from the Earl of Suffolk's [1] being in this county,
insinuating thereby as though he was the author of it.
Add to which a certain gentleman here who has formerly
complied with the presbyterians had repented himself
several times he had relinquished that party, it being trump
at last and would so continue.   And by this you may guess
at the production of the whole farce.   The very same discourses I have had even from some parliament men,
much of which has been levelled at my lord Arlington.
Sir, I am no novice to calumniations of those who are
intrusted by Princes, but these proceeding from some of
the biggest men I have presumed to give you these hints."

He concludes that " this being a story of John an Oakes
and John a Styles I am sure your kindness will pardon
it." [2]

Already, on August 8, Hickes had taken alarm at the
business-like manner in which Muddiman and his publisher Macock were pushing the sale of *Current Intelligence.*

" Yesterday my book woman [*i. e.* hawker] tould me
Mr. Macock and Mr. Muddiman gave the book women 20s.
a piece," wrote he to Williamson, " and hath invited them
all upon ffryday next to his [Macock's] house at Hornsey
to dinner and provided them coaches at his owne charge

[1] James Howard, 3rd Earl of Suffolk.
[2] Calendar of State Papers, Domestic Series, Letter of September 1,
1666, asserted to be from " J. Knight," but the endorsement is " R.
2. Sept. 66. Jo. Knight." The signature to the letter (unfortunately
quite illegible) is certainly not Knight.   The seal, quite intact, bears
the intitials R. M. R.   The letter was probably about Williamson's
wish to obtain Knight as a correspondent.

to carry them thither and home. Mr. L'Estrange gave
them all every month a quire of bookes, being double
sheets & every quarter 5s. a piece to encourige them in
his service, &c. Mr. Macock and Mr. Muddiman now
grow very kind and all to promote their intelligence. I
find Mr. Newcombe (publisher of the *Gazette*) gave amongst
them the last quarter 10s. according to account hee gave
you. They hope you will be as good a master to them
them as Mr. L'Estrange was, they knowing your single
Gazett in profit farr exceeds Mr. L'Estrange his dubble
sheets."

Then the unexpected happened and the famous old
newspaper was saved. The great Fire of London broke
out on September 2, lasting for four days [1] and every
printing house in London was destroyed by it. The
Letter Office was burnt down, posts were disorganized
and the *Gazette* could not be published for a week. When
publication of the *Gazette* was resumed, Newcombe was
compelled to print it in the open air, in the evil-smelling
churchyard of the Savoy, choked with the bodies of the
dead from the plague. Williamson probably seized the
opportunity to make terms, for *Current Intelligence* never
appeared again, and Henry Muddiman henceforth remained
in undisturbed and undisputed possession of his privilege
as the chief official supplier of the written news.

---

[1] A very interesting description of the fire was published in 1920 by
Mr. W. G. Bell in his *The Great Fire of London.*

CHAPTER X

MUDDIMAN'S conflict with Williamson, whether he
knew it or not, was really a campaign for the
freedom of journalism, and it is noteworthy that
after he had gained the victory in 1666, the solitary
printed newspaper in existence at once declined in popular
favour. Muddiman steadily wrote down the *Gazette*, in
spite of the fact that Williamson now began to send out
news-letters with it, composed by his clerks Robert
Francis, or, later, Henry Ball or Robert Yard. On
October 22, 1666, Ralph Hope wrote to Williamson from
Coventry that " Muddiman's letters to Mr. Throck-
morton were very much noticed there, chiefly as communicating the diurnal debates of Parliament," and
Hickes himself wrote to Williamson, on November 23,
that two gentlemen had written to decline taking the
Gazette, as they heard that Mr. Muddiman's letters were
more satisfactory. Next year, in 1667, the complaints
increased. One Summers wrote from Northampton that
since Mr. Muddiman's letter was received by Mr. Ives of
the " Swan " there, " the *Gazette*, which was looked upon
considerably before, was never asked for." Silas Taylor,
writing to Williamson from Harwich on June 15, 1667,
told him that " Mr. Muddiman's intelligence was very
large, and that persons of the greatest quality were then

constrained to betake themselves to it." On June 30, Taylor wrote again, begging Williamson to " enlarge his news, Muddiman's being very large." John Cooper of Thurgarton, writing to Williamson on August 24, 1667, suggested that he should suppress all Muddiman's papers to the postmasters, as the itch of news was grown to a disease.[1] That, however, it was out of Williamson's power to do. Finally, on December 27, 1667, Hickes himself was fain to confess that there was " a general complaint of the *Gazette* wanting domestic intelligence." He said that some in the (Letter) office who sent fourteen or sixteen dozen *Gazettes* weekly, then sent only half the number. Twenty dozen less than formerly were sent.[2] Hickes went on to give the reason for this :

" The people so much slight them, they having nothing in them of the proceedings of Parliament, which Mr. Muddiman writes at large. Were there but as much printed as he writes it would keep up the *Gazette* far beyond what it now is. Mr. Muddiman gives far larger accounts to his correspondents than you do, which makes them much desired."

Williamson and his editor Perrot were unable to remedy all this. The *Gazette* declined, and in the end contained little domestic news other than Royal Proclamations and a number of advertisements. The bulk of the reading matter contained in it was foreign news extracted from the Gazettes of Paris and Haarlem. Right up to the time of the Revolution the *Gazette* will be found, by those consulting its files, to be almost valueless for domestic news. Henry Muddiman's news-letters took its place.

It has already been pointed out that Lord Arlington received a warrant for his grant of the Post Office for a period of ten years in 1665, and that the subsequent grant dated from 1667. The most unexpected develop-

[1] Cal. 1667–8, p. 191.
[2] *Ibid.*, p. 102.

ment from this took place for James Hickes. Lord
Arlington superseded Sir Philip Frowde, the old deputy
Postmaster, by his own brother, Sir John Bennet, and
Hickes at once anticipated that the hour had struck for
his own reward for his services to Williamson in the
conflict with Muddiman. Sir Philip Frowde had been
transferred to Whitehall, apparently to manage the
King's Letters.

"I am infinitely obliged to you for your particular
letter by which (you tell me) you have had some conference with my lord concerning me," wrote Hickes to
Williamson, on April 2, 1667, "and your intimation of
my lord's good opinion and intention to have me advised
with in the concerns of this office." And he added, with
the greatest delight, that Sir John Bennet had taken
him to the "Shipp Tavern" in order to talk to him
privately and discuss the affairs of the Letter Office,
winding up by telling Williamson he was going to call
upon him and by desiring God to bless him.

Hickes could not forbear adding in a postscript the
reason for his delight:

"Sir. What Sir John Bennet hinted was to concern
me with Sir Philip and advised me to secrecy, but knowing
you the original cause of it I could not omit to intimate
what I have done and said, as in order to what you have
and may do in it further."

This meant that Williamson had tried to promote him
and to send him to Whitehall itself, with Sir Philip
Frowde, with whom he was to work. Piety and the
aged father slain at Edgehill were about to bear fruit at
last. Hickes would be able to afford to despise the
news-letter connexion he had failed to steal from
Muddiman.

But, alas! a bitter disillusionment was in store for
Hickes. Lord Arlington had not forgotten the petition
and "Narrative," and had no more taken Williamson

into his confidence than the King himself had done. Sir John Bennet issued new rules for the government of the Letter Office and posts, and part of these were aimed directly at the abuse of free postage by Hickes and others sending out the *Gazettes*. Arlington evidently thought with Hickes that the State journalist and the Letter Office clerks ought not to compete in this matter; only he drew the opposite conclusion to Hickes, by deciding that of the two the journalist was the proper person to circulate news-letters and newspapers and not the Letter Office clerks.

" Sir. I beseech you accomplish my desires sent you on Thursday," wrote Hickes to Williamson on June 20. His malpractices had evidently been found out by Sir John Bennet and himself taken to task, for he goes on to add, " Sir John stayed here till 2 this morning and will be here again this morning, that I cannot shift if you stand not firm to me. Notwithstanding all service and diligence, which I am sure none can say I have been backward to express, there will be little compassion. I hope to wait upon you to-morrow morning. . . . God keep you."

Hickes had not objected to the country postmasters being tuned up to the highest degree of efficiency and to reductions in their pay, but when the new broom began to sweep out the Letter Office in London he was loud in his protests. Encouraged by Williamson, now that the prospect of advancement to be Sir Philip Frowde's colleague had vanished, he seems to have behaved to Sir John Bennet, brother of Lord Arlington though he was, with unalloyed impudence, and cast aside his mask of servility.

On June 30 he wrote to Williamson that the deputy postmaster had told him and the other clerks that they were to pay for all the letters they sent out, and that they were not to send out the *Gazettes* without doing so.

Hickes confessed that he himself was the chief culprit in the matter and wrote twice a week thirty or forty news-letters to correspondents assigned him by William-son (of whom presumably Muddiman had been robbed), and that rather than have his salary reduced by the loss of them he would " withdraw himself and live with salt and water." [1] He then lectured Sir John on the adminis-tration of the office, and generally, according to his own account, behaved with such unrestrained insolence that it is rather wonderful that he was not discharged on the spot. But he acknowledged that Sir John heard him " patiently and kindly," and afterwards told him that he would not reduce his salary and would do nothing without his advice, " But for the news-books, he would not suffer to pass."   In conclusion he besought Williamson to help him and to move for his " settlement and favour."

It was all to no purpose; Williamson could not, per-haps dared not, interfere, and another immensely lengthy letter of complaint followed on July 2. [2] Reading between the lines of this, the only conclusion that can be drawn from it, is that Sir Philip Frowde's administration had been very lax, and that Hickes had been allowed by him to do very much as he pleased in the management of the posts. Sir John Bennet intended to be master and was not to be deterred from his purpose.

A " boye," Hickes indignantly protested, " had been put into the office to receive letters at the window," over the heads of the accountant and himself, and Sir John and the " boye " had actually unfastened and gone through Hickes's mail-bag after he had made it up, in order to see whether he was sending out the *Gazettes*.

---

[1] The letter is a Post Office curiosity, and is so lengthy that I have transcribed it in Appendix E.

[2] Transcribed in Appendix F.   This and the preceding letter contain a great amount of detailed information about the Post Office of the times.

The postscript, as usual, betrayed the real cause of Hickes's complaint. His salary was £100 a year, and he had sent out over fifteen dozen *Gazettes* on Tuesdays and seventeen dozen on Thursdays, some of which were to friends who did not pay, and others to people who paid twopence each, " and the most but threepence." Even on his own showing, therefore, he made a huge profit, for the *Gazette* sold in London for a penny. Finally, he asked that he should be allowed to continue to do this, and demanded a " letter under Lord Arlington's hand to that purpose." He did not get it.

Last of all, Hickes threatened to throw up his post, not apparently to Sir John, but to Williamson. He wrote on September 23 that if " no more kindness " was shown to him, " I shall say little but take my leave and rest upon God only, without the least expectation of comfort from any soul living, though all men that really know me and the services done by me cannot but judge I am but hardly dealt with. For let what cares and pains be taken to secure so much advantage, it contains not a candle, nor a cup of beer, as formerly granted, and with much freedom to me. The taking away of these poor petty things are the present rewards for the most considerable and advantagious services done."

Williamson must have found Hickes a great nuisance at this time, for two days later he took up his pen to abuse Sir John Bennet once more for *not* going to the Letter Office more than two or three times since the previous Thursday. "And when he comes, it is with such a port and carriage no King can exceed. God preserve you and us all, *though you may enquire of him when you see him how the letters came so late* " (!). " Yet take no notice of what I write of them. I am afraid a short time will make all now of this kind, by the miserable screws and hardships put upon all he hath contracted with in point of salary." The postscript added that

Sir John's design was, "God knows, to impose misery instead of comfort."

Things had not improved in 1668; for, finding that Hickes had monopolized the cellars at the Letter Office for his own use, Sir John turned him out of them, although they would "only hold but 3 chaldrons of coal, and 3 or 4 kilderkins of beer." Hickes remarked that he "had a bout" with Sir John over the cellars, and was told that it was not for him to dispute Sir John's interest in the house. He then concluded, as usual, "to lose my candles and pitiful letters" was but a "blind and dark recompense" from Lord Arlington for thirty years' service.

Muddiman does not appear in all this, but he must have watched this conspirator being blown up by his own mine with some satisfaction. And in the meantime, Williamson's own attempts to set up a news-letter correspondence were also unsuccessful, in spite of his position of Under-secretary of State. His clerks Francis and Ball were unable to compete with Muddiman, and at the last Williamson, in conjunction with James Hickes, actually stole his adversaries' news-letters in order to provide his own clerks with news. Every week Hickes intercepted one or more of Muddiman's news-letters in transit through the post, and handed them on to Williamson for the use of his own news-letter clerks. Mute witnesses of a series of petty thefts without a parallel, nearly all still remain among the State Papers to give evidence against Hickes and Williamson. All are dated, all are headed "Whitehall," all are sealed with one or other of Muddiman's two seals, and all are addressed to persons who never received them.[1] These thefts continued

---

[1] They, of course, were also unsigned, and Mrs. Green has committed an unpardonable series of errors in ascribing these news-letters to "Francis" and "Yard." The heading "Whitehall" alone should have warned her of her error, quite apart from the seals and the addresses, for she had noticed that Hickes was stealing Muddiman's

right up to the end of 1671, when Williamson was
sent abroad, but were not resumed when he returned.
Proof is not lacking of Williamson's complicity, for, on
August 20, 1668, when Williamson was at Billing, near
Northampton, Hickes wrote to him :
" I am glad I suit with your opinion and sense concerning the particular letters now and then sent you, of
which I shall say no more," [1] and enclosed in this Muddiman's news-letter of the same date, addressed to Mr.
Warner of Winchester.[2] He was not quite so guarded
in his reference on September 7, and commenced his letter
of that date by remarking, " I sent yesterday a letter for
you with two of H. M. and desired Mr. Francis to send it
to you without opening it." [3] Williamson and Hickes,
therefore, trusted no one with the knowledge of what
they were doing. But what can be said of a future
Secretary of State who could thus behave like a mean thief ?

Despite all his efforts and all his thefts, Williamson's
news-letter correspondence did not pay. His clerk, Ball,
wrote a full report to him on October 23, 1674, when he
was at Cologne upon a diplomatic mission, and appended
a list of those to whom news-letters were sent, together
with the sums paid by them. Those of Williamson's
correspondents who paid, contributed from £2 a year to
£4 or £5. Four clerks, amongst whom the writing of
the letters was divided, were kept besides Ball himself;
Ball adding, " I always helped them to do a share, or as
many as I could."

---

letters. A complete list is given in Appendix G, and the documents
have been conclusively identified by comparison with Muddiman's
drafts of them all.

[1] These words are omitted in the summary of the letter in the
Calendar for 1667–8, p. 543.

[2] Set out on p. 544 of the same Calendar and wrongly asserted to
be by Francis. Throughout this Calendar the stolen letters, in direct
conflict with all the evidence, are ascribed to Francis.

[3] These opening words are omitted in the summary of this letter on
p. 573 of the Calendar for 1667–8.

Two of these clerks had other duties to perform at the Rolls Office, on Wednesdays and Fridays, whilst the other two attended to the extracting news from the foreign packets (news-letters). On Tuesdays, Thursdays and Saturdays, the post days, all were at work on the news-letters. The number that each clerk wrote was on Tuesdays sixteen letters, viz. four long letters containing a whole week's news and twelve short ones containing two days' news. On Thursday each wrote thirteen, of which three were long and ten short, and on Saturday seven long letters, four of four days' news and eight short letters. The whole profit for a year was £174, of which the four " young men " were paid £120. The rest Ball himself retained for his pains and for petty disbursements amounting to £9 12s. He said that payments were uncertain, for the clerks took nothing from Williamson's friends, or from correspondents at the ports, and added that he had spared no pains in making the letters longer than they had been.[1]

L'Estrange had great difficulty in making Williamson pay the £100 per annum due to him from the *Gazette*. On April 22, 1668, he wrote a letter of complaint to Lord Arlington about it,[2] and eventually was compelled to appeal to the King through the Duke of Ormonde.[3]

Sir William Morice resigned his secretaryship at Michaelmas 1668, and retired to his estates in Devon for the rest of his life. There he lived, surrounded by his books, and is said to have cherished some resentment against the King for the corrupt manners of his Court. His son was created a baronet, but the line is now extinct. Morice was succeeded by Sir John Trevor, and although

---

[1] This report is printed in the Appendix to vol. ii. of the " William-son Correspondence " (Camden Society). The only collection of Williamson's news-letters is apparently that calendared among the MSS. of Mr. Le Fleming at Rydal Hall, and it is very incomplete.

[2] Calendar for 1668, April 22.

[3] MSS. of the Marquess of Ormonde, N.S., vol. iii. pp. 351–2.

Hickes anticipated that Muddiman would not get on so well with him, the latter remained with Trevor until his death on May 28, 1672. Henry Coventry was appointed Trevor's successor, and when he retired in 1680, was succeeded by Sir Leoline Jenkins. With both these last two secretaries Muddiman was on excellent terms, and wrote with high praise of both when they died.

Macaulay has written a description of the news-letter writer's calling, in which he assumes that there were numerous news-letter writers throughout the reign of Charles II. This is quite wrong, and it should be pointed out that, up to the year 1679, Muddiman was without any competitor other than Williamson's clerks.[1] His privilege of free postage and the hostile attitude assumed by the Government to all news not sent out from the Offices of the Secretaries of State rendered competition impossible until that year.

Before narrating the history of that competition Muddiman's growing prosperity must be noticed. He had removed his office from the " Seven Stars " to the " Peacock," also near the New Exchange, by 1670. Thus, he added a personal postscript to his news-letter of April 28, 1670, to the Hon. Edward Noell of Titchfield, afterwards created Baron Noell of Titchfield and Earl of Gainsborough, telling him that his fee for news-letters was £5 a year, and asking him to reply to the " Peacock." [2]

---

[1] Only one attempt to set up an outside news-letter correspondence has been recorded. This was by Thomas Bromhall, who kept a registry office for advertisements at the " Peahen " Tavern (not " Peacock " as the document calendared states) in the Strand. See the Calendar for 1666–7, pp. 433 and 535. The " booke " issued by Bromhall was a *City Mercury*, of which No. 34 for October 24–31, 1667, is to be seen at the Record Office. *City Mercuries* contained advertisements only, and were distributed gratis.

[2] Cal. S. P. Dom., 1670, p. 188 :

Hickes's assertion that Muddiman charged from 40s. to £40 per person was pure guesswork. He did not know what sum Muddiman was in the habit of charging. On June 27, 1666, Charles Duckworth,

In 1667 the war with the Dutch was in progress, and just before the enemy broke the boom at the mouth of the Medway and destroyed the ships at Chatham dock-yard, Sir William Coventry wrote to Williamson (on June 4, 1667) stating that no mention was to be made either of the King's ships coming into port or plying to and fro, or of those who took prizes—only of the prizes taken, and that these orders applied not only to the printed news, but also to the " written intelligences, which are weekly spread through the kingdom."

These orders put Muddiman on his guard. It was certain that sooner or later there would be trouble over some item of news in a news-letter, and in that case he did not intend to be made the scapegoat for mistakes made by Williamson's clerks. So from this time onward he kept the draft of every news-letter sent out by him. All were entered, with their dates, into a continuous journal extending from 1667 to October 1689, when he ceased writing. This journal is the only complete record extant of the events of the reigns of the last two Stuart kings, and though naturally it lacks the piquancy and personal note of Pepys' Diary, ending in 1669, yet this " editor's file," so to term it, clears up many disputed points about the reigns in question. That Muddiman was considered to be an almost infallible authority in

---

agent to Lord Leigh of Stoneleigh, one of Muddiman's clients alienated by Hickes's circular, wrote to Hickes as follows :

" Sir. The first letter of intelligence come from Mr. Williamson's clerks [*sic*, Hickes himself], bears date March the 3rd, and as soon as the time it runs out halfe a yeare I shall returne them the same gratuitie from my lord I usually sent Mr. Muddiman, which is fifty shillings half yearly, and that I signified to you before any letters came, (and have) here again intimated to you in answer to yours of the 21st and directed to my lord, which is all at present from yours to serve you, Charles Duckworth."

Lord Leigh appears to have been one of the thirty or forty (in Hickes's list) allotted to him by Williamson, as his share of the spoils. Lord Leigh, on hearing the truth about the " dismission," like many others, returned to Muddiman.

his own day there can be no question. Anthony à
Wood's diary contains abundant evidence of this.
Muddiman's name became a household word.[1]

In 1676 Sir George Etherege's famous comedy, the
Man of Mode ; or, Sir Fopling Flutter, was first produced
and in Act III. scene ii. Muddiman was referred to as
follows :—

Emilia. You are a living libel, a breathing lampoon,
I wonder you are not torn in pieces.

Medley. What think you of setting up an office of intelligence for these matters? The project may get money.

Lady Towneley. You will have great dealings with
country ladies.

Medley. More than Muddiman has with their husbands.

In the same year, 1676, Muddiman inflicted a somewhat severe rebuff to Sir Joseph Williamson, then Secretary of State. Sir Richard Haddock gave Pepys an
extract from a news-letter he had seen in Elford's coffee-
house[2] and had attributed to Muddiman, and a tre-
mendous fuss was the result, the King being particularly
annoyed. On October 7, Sir William Coventry wrote to

---

[1] See Wood's "Life and Times" (ed. A. Clark). The following
extracts from the Historical Manuscripts Commissions Report refer to
Muddiman :

"1676, April 2. Will Fall to Sir R. Verney : ' I have here enclosed
Muddiman's letter, which is very short, it being his Tuesday letter.
It seems he has altered his way and days of writing, for it's only
Saturdays and Tuesdays, so that this letter is one day staler than I
thought it would have been.' " (Sixth Report, p. 468.)
In 1678 the Marquess of Worcester wrote to the Marchioness :
" Thursday. Newbury. Being very inquisitive after news at this
time, enquired if there was no Muddyman's letter in the house, and at
last we heard there was a man in the house that had the liberty to
peruse a parson's letters that lives at Hamsted, who uses to have news.
I sent to him and he sent me Muddyman's letter." (Cal. MSS. of the
Duke of Beaufort, p. 77.)
On June 10, 1679, Windesor wrote to H. Thynne that he had " so
little intelligence, either Muddiman's letter or any other," that he
could not tell what the rebels in Scotland had declared for. (Fourth
Report, p. 250.)
[2] Set out on pp. 353–4 of the Calendar for 1676–7. The extract in
question does not appear in Muddiman's Journal.

Williamson that complaints had been made by several of the Council to the King that Muddiman had said in his letter that the King had resolved in Council that twenty men-of-war should set out against " Argier," and that, particularly, the Duke of Monmouth was to go in the *Resolution*. The King was very much offended at the presumption of making resolutions for him in Council which he never made, and, therefore, had commanded him to write to Williamson to speak to Pepys " to find out any such letter, and then to send for Mr. Muddiman to bring him before the Council and proceed to such reproof and correction as they should think fit, but to order the matter so that he and all others should understand that his Majesty would not suffer either Muddiman or any other person to divulge anything agitated in Council till his Majesty think fit to declare it." [1]

On October 13 Williamson was forced to reply to Sir William Coventry, that " on Wednesday last Mr. Muddiman was examined before the Council and absolutely denied having written anything of the kind, but offered to do his best to find out who had sent the letters to the coffee-houses," and that therefore he hoped the mystery would be discovered. But, he went on, it " already appeared that the substance of that very news and, for the most part, in the very words," was written by a clerk in his own office on the 2nd or 3rd.

This clerk was Robert Yard, then editing the *Gazette* as well as writing Williamson's news-letters, and Williamson had been aware of the fact that Yard was the culprit directly he received Sir William's letter.[2] But it is easy

[1] Cal. S. P. Dom., 1676–7, p. 356.
[2] See Williamson's note on p. 360 of the same Calendar. On September 6, 1677, John Rushworth wrote to the Hon. Thomas Thynne, M.P., at Drayton : " Muddiman is in custody for writing so confidently that the Spaniard intends war against us, and yet the merchants will not credit the contrary " (Fifth Report, p. 318). This also was a mistake. Muddiman had written nothing of the kind. Probably Williamson's clerk was again the culprit.

to see by comparison of the dates that what Williamson did not tell Sir William Coventry was that he had waited for Muddiman to appear before the Privy Council, and that if he had not then succeeded in exculpating himself, Muddiman would have been made the scapegoat. No doubt also that Muddiman cleared himself by producing his Journal to the Council. No wonder that he kept his Journal with great care.

In 1677 Sir Richard Newdigate, of Arbury, Warwickshire, from which district Muddiman's family came, approached Muddiman, through Royston the publisher, to seek his aid in enabling him to refuse a baronetcy the King had decided to confer upon him, so that by that time Muddiman was known to possess influence at Court.[1] This was probably through the Duke of York, afterwards James II, who received a grant of the Post Office this year, in succession to Lord Arlington, whose ten years' tenure of the Post Office then expired.

[1] Cal. S. P. Dom., 1677–8, p. 300. (Sir Richard's letter is dated August 11, 1677.)

CHAPTER XI

OATES'S AND SHAFTESBURY'S PLOTS—BENJAMIN HARRIS, FRANCIS SMITH AND OTHERS—NEWS-LETTER WRITERS AND THE PENNY POST

I DO not propose to attempt to describe the plot concocted by Titus Oates and Ezerel Tonge in 1678. Suffice it to call attention to the fact that this plot was really a revival of the Fifth Monarchy plots of the earlier part of the reign. No one can fail to be struck by the fact that the same objects, viz. to murder the King, fire London, and massacre its inhabitants, were now credited to the Papists. But the actual model of the plot Ezerel Tonge instructed Oates to discover was " Habernfeld's plot," communicated by Sir William Boswell, the British envoy at the Hague, to Archbishop Laud, just before the Great Rebellion. The narrative of the so-called " Andreas ab Habernfeld " was found by Prynne amongst the Archbishop's papers and was published by him on May 31, 1643, under the title of " Rome's Masterpeece." To the narrative of " Habern-feld," written in Latin, the Archbishop contributed the acute observation that nobody but an Englishman could have written such Latin. The whole subject of Habern-feld's plot still needs investigation, but it seems possible that the so-called " Habernfeld " was really an English anabaptist settled in Holland, and that his object was to make trouble between the Archbishop and the King.

On this tale, therefore, Oates modelled his story.[1]   Oates's tale of a Popish plot would have fallen quite as flat as the real plots for the same purposes had done had it not been for the discovery of the body of Sir Edmund Berry Godfrey, the magistrate who had taken Oates's and Tonge's depositions, in a ditch on the south side of Primrose Hill.   No notice whatever had been taken of Oates by Muddiman in his news-letters until October 1, when he noticed that a " dangerous conspiracy " against the life of the King had been made out upon oath and certain specified " Papists " secured.   But, on Tuesday, October 15, he wrote as follows : " The Town is full of discourse about the absence of Sir Edmund Berry God-frey, who, being the Justice of the Peace before whom Mr. Oates made deposition upon his discovery, and having now been wanting since Saturday morning, without any notice given (in which he was always observed to have been punctual) to his servant or relations, they entertain hard thoughts of the Roman party.   A little time may better inform us."   On the following Satur-day, October 19, Muddiman wrote as follows :   " On Thursday last, about 6 at night, the body of Sir Edmund Berry Godfrey was found with his own sword through it, in a field near Maribone, his money, etc., in his pocket, but upon inquisition it is believed murder and by a cravat about his neck he was strangled."

[1] " I went [abroad], says Oates, of my own proper motion, and out of a certain natural curiosity that I had, to be peeping among the casuists of the Society [of Jesus] to enquire about the growth of Popery. Now, says Tonge, on the other hand, I gave Oates the draught of the old plot of Con and Habernfeld in my ' Royal Martyr ' and sent him abroad among the Jesuites to try if he could match it.   And this was in 76 and 77."   (*The Observator*, vol. ii. No. 71, for May 30, 1684.)

According to Wood, L'Estrange refused to license the " Royal Martyr."   (See Wood's life of Tonge.)   It does not seem to have been printed.

Oates's claim to the title of Doctor of Divinity of the University of Salamanca was exposed in the *Loyal Protestant*, No. 223, for October 31, 1682, which printed the Latin original and translation of the denial by the Rector of the University.

I have quoted these passages because from them the news of the " plot " was started on its journey throughout the three kingdoms.   There is no good object to be served by discussing whether Godfrey committed suicide or was murdered by Oates's friends.   The point of which sight must not be lost is that the whole nation at once concluded that he had been murdered by Papists, and that there was a new plot on foot, similar to that of Guy Fawkes, still fresh in their minds.   Everyone then went mad with fear and horror of Popery.   Sixteen innocent men, priests and laymen, were executed as the result of Oates's lying tale and Godfrey's death, and in the persecution of Catholics which followed from this plot eight priests more were executed, only for being priests.   The last victim of all was the gentle and blameless Oliver Plunket, the Irish Archbishop, who was drawn, hanged and quartered on July 1, 1681.   Lord Essex, who later on committed suicide in the Tower, told the King that he knew the Archbishop was innocent.   " Then, my lord," answered the King, " his blood be on your head.   You might have saved him.   I dare not pardon him."   " God knows, I sign with tears in my eyes," the King was reported to have said when warrants for the execution of condemned Papists were tendered to him.

In the end, thanks to the King and to Roger L'Estrange, the nation paused and realized that the plot was a fraud, carried on by Anthony Ashley Cooper, first Earl of Shaftesbury, and the Whigs, for the purpose of excluding the " Papist " James the Second from the throne. Shaftesbury's machinations were dark and devious and have never been thoroughly brought to light.   A question of paramount importance in considering his relations with Oates, is that of the time when he began to support the latter.   Was he a co-conspirator from the very beginning?   The answer must be in the affirmative, for in the list of " Worthy men " and " Men Worthy " (to be hanged) found in his study in 1681, the name of Andrew Marvell occurs among the former. And Marvell died on August 18, 1678, whilst Oates and Tonge were concocting their " Articles." [1] That Shaftesbury conducted the whole of the Press campaign there can be no doubt. In the height of the plot he retired into the City to his own house—Thanet House, in Aldersgate Street, and, states an anonymous pamphleteer :

" All the applications of the Party, all informations, all councils and Cabals were at Thanet House. There the Protestant joiner, College, and fourteen of the jury who brought him in ' ignoramus,' who were of his lordship's neighbourhood; the anabaptist booksellers, Smith and Harris, Jack Starkey, etc.; the libellers of the Government, Care, Fergusson, etc., found warm entertainment. . . . Whole shoals of lewd and seditious pamphlets—' Letters to Friends,' ' Appeals to the City,' ' Dialogues between Tutors and Pupils,' were written, printed and dispersed by his direction and approbation . . . and the late abominable pamphlet of the ' Second part of the Growth of Popery,' etc." [2]

The arrests even of uncompromising Protestants, thanks to the Parliamentary Committees ruled by Shaftesbury, pass belief. Pepys and other Government servants were imprisoned and Sir Joseph Williamson was soon attacked. He was supposed to have countersigned commissions granted by the King to Papists. On the 18th November, 1678, the Commons sent him to the Tower. On the next day the King ordered the Commons to attend in the Banqueting House at Whitehall, and when they arrived informed them " that he would be civiller to them

---

[1] *The Observator*, No. 13, for February 6, 1683–4, and No. 14, for February 9, 1683–4.

[2] *Memoires of the life of Anthony, late Earl of Shaftesbury*, 1682/3. The " second part of the growth of Popery " was written by " Ferguson, the Plotter "—the first part was by Andrew Marvell, and is not nearly so untruthful or offensive.

than they had been to him, for though they had sent one
of his Secretaries to the Tower without acquainting him
of it, he would acquaint them that he intended to send
for him out again. Which he immediately did." [1]

Nevertheless, the wretch Oates had the effrontery to
appear at the bar on November 23 and impeach the Queen.
" I will not see an innocent woman wronged," said Charles
II, adding, " They think I have a mind to a new wife,
but they are mistaken." The days of the Long Parliament of Charles II were numbered when it also began to
attack the Duke of York.

Up to the end of 1678 little or no unlicensed matter
had been published in support of the plot. A weekly
pamphlet entitled, *A Pacquet of Advice from Rome ; or,
The History of Popery*, commenced on December 3, 1678
and was written by Henry Care and published by Langley
Curtiss, who lived at the sign of the " Goat " in Ludgate
Hill. Curtiss was soon nicknamed the " Mayor of
Gotham," and accordingly changed his sign to that of
" Sir Edmundbury Godfrey." This periodical was
licensed at first, and did not print news or comment upon
the news for some time to come. The year 1679, however,
saw a vast change.

On January 25 the King dissolved the Parliament.
It had sat ever since the year 1661, and was certainly
more entitled to the name of " Long Parliament " than
that of 1641, which only sat until the end of 1648, being
revived in 1660 in the manner already described. If
we exclude the Convention of 1660, Charles II's Long
Parliament was the first Parliament of his reign.

A new House of Commons soon assembled, composed
of violent supporters of the plot. On May 28, 1679, a
Bill for excluding the Duke of York from the throne was

[1] Duke of Beaufort's MSS., p. 72. The King, however, " turned
out " Williamson on February 10, when he delivered up the seals to
the Earl of Sunderland. On the 12th Williamson married the Dowager
Lady O'Brien.

read a second time. Charles II then entered upon the
greatest struggle of his life, for he was determined to
end the plot he had all along openly derided, and to punish
the plotters now plainly aiming directly at his brother
and indirectly at himself. He at once checked the Exclusion Bill by proroguing Parliament to the 14th of August,
and on the 10th of July, without allowing it to reassemble,
dissolved it and summoned a third Parliament. The
Whigs managed the elections well, and before the third
Parliament met, it was known that it consisted of even
more violent supporters of Oates and Shaftesbury.
On October 16, therefore, the King prorogued his third
Parliament before it had even met. This checked the
plot for some time and brought about the acquittal of
Sir George Wakeman, the Queen's physician, and of the
Benedictine monks, her chaplains. The rage at this
of the disloyal booksellers was unbounded, but for the
moment action was not taken against them. For libelling
Lord Chief Justice Scroggs in connexion with this trial
Henry Care was tried and convicted.[1] Little notice
need be taken of Care during this reign.

In the meantime, Shaftesbury's newspaper and pamphlet campaign on behalf of the Plotters had begun.
A commencement was made as early as April 1679, when
one Amy began to send out news-letters in opposition
to Muddiman. On the 28th the Privy Council cut short
his career by sending him to Newgate.[2]

Then the campaign of lies took a fresh form. Charles
the Second, when proroguing Parliament, had forgotten
that the " Printing Act " of 1662 fell due for renewal
in June 1679. Consequently, the Act lapsed and
Shaftesbury was enabled to set up presses everywhere.

[1] The indictment is set out in W. H. Hart's *Index Expurgatorius
Anglicanus*. See the Commons Journal of December 23, 1680, for the
debate on the cases of Care, Francis Smith and others, and compare
the actual indictments set out by Hart with the misleading quotations
made in the Journal.
[2] News-letter of May 1. Nothing more was heard of Amy.

Accordingly, on July 7, 1679, there appeared the first number of Oates and Shaftesbury's greatest newspaper, published by Benjamin Harris, an anabaptist bookseller living at the " Stationers' Arms," in the Piazza under the Royal Exchange in Cornhill.   This was at first entitled *Domestick Intelligence ; or News both from City and Country. Published to prevent false reports.* In the following year the periodical was renamed *The Protestant (Domestick) Intelligence,* and then lasted until April 15, 1681, when it was finally suppressed.   Throughout the Popish Plot the careers of the publishers of the newspapers (no longer pamphlets) are of greater importance than those of their writers, and since Benjamin Harris was to become the first American journalist and his career is of more than ordinary literary interest, I propose devoting some space to him.   The necessarily brief accounts of Harris that have yet appeared have been woefully inaccurate or incomplete.   Harris must have been a young man at the time when Oates's plot began, for nothing has been brought to light about him before the year 1679.[1]   Great confusion has been caused in the history of not only Harris, but also other seventeenth-century worthies, American as well as English, by the " Characters " of the late seventeenth-century London bookseller, John Dunton, who visited New England before the close of the century.   Until recently it has been the fashion to quote these " Characters " as if they had been seriously intended for biographies.   I must therefore commence my biography of Harris by pointing out that Dunton's " Characters " are utterly untrustworthy, by no means represent his own opinions, and have recently been exposed in America.[2]   The biography of Harris is a

---

[1] At first, in April, Harris seems to have contemplated a renewal of the " books of wonders," for he then wrote and published *Strange News from Lemster* (Leominster)—an account of an earthquake with supernatural details, for the truth of which he vouched.

[2] By Mr. Chester N. Greenough of Harvard, in the *Publications of the Colonial Society of Massachusetts,* vol. xiv. pp. 213-57 (March 1912).

stock instance of the unreliability of Dunton's "Characters," for Harris is the one man of whom Dunton, in 1706, wrote a full and vituperative account, several pages in length and partly in verse, in complete conflict with his "Character" of Harris in the previous century. I shall cite this later on.

One interesting fact about Harris is that he was an author as well as a bookseller. Muddiman says that he wrote his own *Domestick Intelligence*, but there are not wanting indications that Nathaniel Crouch, the "Richard Burton" of "Burton's books"—(of which Benjamin Franklin owned a set), was occasionally called in to assist in the editing of this periodical. The editing of the other Shaftesbury and Oates periodicals seems to have been the joint stock work of news-letter writers and of the booksellers who published them.

Little more than a month had elapsed after the start of Harris's *Domestick Intelligence* when an Irishman, Nathaniel Thompson, of the "Cross Keys," Fetter Lane, who was known to have printed Catholic books,[1] entered the lists against Harris, also with a *Domestick Intelligence. Published to prevent false reports*. The first number of this newspaper was "No. 15," and, until it changed its title (on September 6, 1679) to the *True Domestick Intelligence*, it can only be distinguished from Harris's paper by the imprints at the end, and, of course, the different items of news contained in it. A wordy war soon began between the two *Domestick Intelligences* and, as time went on, the plot continued, and other newspapers were added to support Harris, "Popish Nat," as he was nicknamed, was abused right and left. In obedience to the King's Proclamation against the newspapers, in May 1680, Thompson ceased to publish his *True Domestick Intelligence*, but later on was encouraged to reissue it. On

[1] See Hist. MSS. Commission's Eleventh Report, App., Part II., pp. 54–6.

March 9, 1681, therefore, Thompson recommenced journalism with No. 1 of *The Loyal Protestant and True Domestick Intelligence*. This lasted until November 1682 and was the last paper to be suppressed. By the middle of 1682 the whole of the Whig newspapers were stamped out.[1]

Harris's close connexion with Oates and Shaftesbury was quickly proved in 1679, by his publication of the most incendiary document of the whole Plot. This was the *Appeal from the Country to the City, for the preservation of his Majesty's Person, Liberty and the Protestant Religion.* Written by Charles Blount, the Deist or atheist (who, a few years later on, committed suicide), and signed " Junius Brutus," the exact date at which this document appeared has not hitherto been known. Muddiman, however, states expressly that it first appeared in the first part of October 1679,[2] and thus this tract was even more important than has been supposed. For the King had been in danger of death in the summer, and when the Duke of York, warned of this fact, had returned from his enforced exile, Charles II's illegitimate son, Monmouth, the " Protestant Duke," had been relieved of his command in the Army and exiled in turn. Had the King died, Monmouth was prepared to seize the crown by force. The " Appeal," therefore, was published in preparation for Monmouth's return (on November 29, 1679) in disobedience to the King's orders. A renewed struggle over the Plot then at once took place, in spite of the continued prorogation of Parliament.

---

[1] A catalogue of them was given in *The Times Tercentenary Hand-list* of 1920 (by the present writer). Very few appear to be missing in the Burney Collection.

[2] News-letter of October 14, 1679 : " There has lately been published a seditious pamphlet under the title of ' an Appeal from the Country to the City ' (The Council) have caused the dispersers to be seized and examined from whom they had it, and so they pursue it from hand to hand until at last they may come to that which writ it." Blount, the author of the tract, was never traced.

The object of the "Appeal" was to support the claims to the throne of the "Protestant Duke." In it Blount advised his readers to ascend the Monument to the great Fire of London and then to—

"Imagine you see the whole town in a flame, occasioned this second time by the same Popish malice which set it on fire before. At the same instant fancy that amongst the distracted crowd you behold troops of Papists ravishing your wives and daughters, dashing your little children's brains out against the walls, plundering your houses and cutting your own throats by the name of 'heretic dogs.' Then represent to yourself the Tower playing off its cannon and battering down your houses about your ears. Also, casting your eyes towards Smithfield, imagine you see your father or your mother, or some of your nearest and dearest relatives, tied to a stake in the midst of flames, where, with hands and eyes lifted up to Heaven, they scream and cry out to that God for whose cause they die, which was a frequent spectacle the last time Popery reigned amongst us."

Then the pamphlet attacked the Duke of York, as "one eminent great Papist, who, in the time of that Great Fire, pretended to secure many of the incendiaries, but secretly suffered them all to escape. Who this person was has already been mentioned by Mr. Bedlow." [1] The tract then wound up by advocating the claim to the throne of Monmouth, upon the King's "untimely death," and added that, "His" (Monmouth's) "life and

---

[1] The "depositions about the fire" were published by Bedloe as his own.

Up to the date of the Plot they were reissued at intervals with various titles, such as "London's flames," Elizabeth Calvert being the chief offender. She also issued a sequel in *Trap ad Crucem; or the Papist's Watchword*, published in 1670, apropos of the Southwark fire of that year (see Cal. of State Papers for 1670, pp. 422 and 433). The British Museum contains several copies of this latter tract, catalogued under "Papists."

Had Macaulay encountered this truly wicked little tract, he would have based pages of description upon it.

fortune depends upon the same bottom as yours. He will stand by you, and, therefore, ought you to stand by him. And, remember, the old rule is, ' He who hath the worst title ever makes the best King.' "

On October 16 Thompson's wife Mary (who had had nothing to do with the Appeal, but was arrested on suspicion, as her husband was printing an unauthorized newspaper) was arrested, together with the real vendors of the Appeal, Anne Brewster, widow of the Thomas Brewster convicted in 1664, and two clerks in the Letter Office, Murray and Rea or Ray.[1]

On the 5th February, 1680, Benjamin Harris was tried by Lord Chief Justice Scroggs for publishing the " Appeal." In fining Harris the large sum of £500 and sentencing him to the pillory, Lord Chief Justice Scroggs said :

" You can hardly read a more base and pernicious book, to put us all into a flame. It gives you such incitements and base encouragements, with such reflections upon all sorts of persons (for I have read it upon this account), that I think there can scarce be a worse made. He would set up another man that has no title to the crown. For, says he, the greatest danger accruing to your persons as well as to the kingdom, upon the King's untimely death, will proceed from a confusion, and want of some eminent and interested person whom you may trust to lead you up against a French and Popish enemy."

Harris stood in the pillory within sight of his shop, in front of which the " Appeal " was burnt by the common hangman. The Whigs stood in serried rows round the pillory, and he and they " hollowed and whooped and would suffer nothing to be thrown at him." But he was

[1] News-letter of October 16. Compare the Calendar of State Papers. Luttrell, in his Diary, asserts that Harris was not the first publisher, but Thompson, who was not punished, but " Harris bore all." This is a falsehood, taken from the Whig newspapers and news-letters from which his Diary was compiled. Harris was tried for the first edition, and it was not until *after* his trial on February 5, 1680, that the second edition, dated 1680, was published.

quite unable to pay the fine, nor would his own party subscribe the money. So he remained in Newgate until the end of the year. Nevertheless, he did not discontinue his newspaper, and it is probably at this time that Nathaniel Crouch edited it.

Six or more Whig newspapers appeared before the King issued his Proclamation of May 1680 forbidding their publication.[1]

To a certain extent this Proclamation was obeyed, but with the meeting of Parliament on October 21 the newspaper and pamphlet campaign on behalf of the Plot began again, with redoubled fury.

In the meantime, the least known portion of the Oates propaganda, that of the news-letters, had commenced. Henry Muddiman's monopoly had, for a time, been ended.

On December 13, 1679, Smallridge, Hancock and Combes were brought before the Privy Council " for writing seditious letters," [2] and in an intercepted letter of John Cotton, another newswriter, dated September 20, 1679, we have an interesting revelation of the fees charged.[3]

Cotton ended his letter by stating that he could not accept 10s. a quarter for his news-letter, but if his client would furnish him with another customer or two, he would send her three letters a week for £3 yearly, or two for 40s., or else 6d. a letter. This letter was addressed to Helperton, Salisbury, and since the postage to Salisbury amounted to fourpence,[4] this meant that Cotton would retain for himself the not very princely fee of twopence a letter. Nathaniel Thompson is the authority for the statement that in London the coffee-houses paid four or five shillings a week to the news-letter writers during the Plot.[5]

---

[1] Set out in *The Times Hand-list of English Newspapers*, p. 29.
[2] News-letter of December 13.
[3] Cal. 1679–80, pp. 245–6.
[4] See Hickes's list of Muddiman's correspondents in the Appendix.
[5] *Loyal Protestant*, No. 239 for March 1, 1682–3.

Information about Jasper Hancock—the principal Whig news-letter writer of the times—is very scanty, and it is quite impossible to identify his work, owing to the fact that all the news-letter writers of the day imitated Muddiman and did not sign their news-letters. All that we can say is that their letters are marked off from Muddiman's by the absence of the heading " Whitehall." Jasper Hancock was a " certain little shock Whig as fierce as a lion . . . this thing does so belabour them (his correspondents) with Queries by the Penny Post, a penny a week besides all the studying, he's at vast charge and pains, but the mischief on't is he cannot spell yet, he breaks Priscians head in English." [1] L'Estrange advised the Grand Jury who had in vain prosecuted his own publisher, Joanna Brome, to employ " little Hancock " to vent their " grievances." " He'll do't for pence a piece," said he, " And that is just eighteenpence for his reward." [2] And in 1683, when the ex-Lord Mayor, Sir Patience Ward, was tried for perjury, Thompson wrote : " The only divertisement the spectators had (who were almost crowded to death) was to see little H—ck the newswriter, who had planted himself in a window, with his sword erected in a corner and his bottle of the spirit of whiggism by him, now sipping it and anon fluttering out his fine cravat and wig, till an officer espying him commanded him down, at which he was hissed out of the Hall before the Court sat. So that he was forced to sneak away, without one tittle of news for his country customers." [3]

The Whig news-letters were longer lived than the newspapers, but hardly ever circulated outside London coffee-houses until the setting up of a Penny Post " within the contiguous limits of the Bills of Mortality." [4]   It

[1] *Heraclitus Ridens*, No. 39, October 25, 1681.
[2] *Dissenters Sayings*, Part II., Preface.
[3] *Loyal Protestant*, No. 235 for February 10, 1682–3.
[4] *The Practical Method of the Penny Post*, 1681.   By William Dockwra and others.

has been said of the Penny Post that William Dockwra, or Dockwray, sub-searcher in the Custom House, who, in conjunction with Robert Murray (the clerk in the Letter Office who had been discharged for circulating the " Appeal ") instituted the Penny Post, was really a benefactor of his times, and that Titus Oates denounced his plan, as a branch of the Popish Plot. These assertions have received the approval of Macaulay; and, on the face of it, they would appear to be reinforced by the pension of £500 a year granted to Dockwra in 1690. But in actual fact the Penny Post was set up solely in order to injure the Duke of York (Postmaster-General), to help the seditious newswriters, and with the express approval of Titus Oates, whose supporters actually prosecuted the publisher of the remark about Oates. The pension to Dockwra (who was anything but the " City merchant " he has been described as being) was awarded him for his great services in helping in Oates's campaign, and was on all fours with the pension granted by William III to Oates himself.[1]

[1] There are numerous references to the Penny Post in L'Estrange's *Observators*, from which the valuable services rendered by it to the run of lies and slander of the times can be gauged. The actual date of commencement of the Penny Post is stated in Thos. Delaune's *Present State of London* (1681), pp. 350–359. Delaune (who was a nonconformist minister) says that Dockwra was sub-searcher in the Custom House—rather lower in the social scale than Murray, who had become an upholsterer after his discharge.

It is one of Macaulay's defects that he *looked* at the Titus Oates newspapers but shirked the task of reading them. He possessed no critical knowledge of the tracts of the times, had not read L'Estrange's *Observators*, and, except for the collections of Sir James Mackintosh, knew nothing of the news-letters. He must have noticed Muddiman's name in Roger North's Life of Dr. John North, but, of course, knew nothing of his career. Macaulay glanced at *Smith's Current Intelligence*, No. 15 for March 30–April 3, 1681 (published by John Smith), saw that the paper said that Oates asserted that the Penny Post was " a device of Henry Nevil, alias Pain, who was known to be a great assertor of the Catholic cause," and read no farther among the papers of the times. But John Smith was not a Whig and wished to discredit the Penny Post. Thompson, in his *True Domestic Intelligence*, No. 77, for March 26–30, published a denial by Oates, who " owns the same to be very convenient for all men, and that the design would no more

The Penny Post made such a vast change in the distribution of letters that it is clear that there was an extraordinary reason for calling it into being.   In lieu of three posts a week it set up one for every hour daily, from seven in the morning to nine at night.   Such an extensive service could not then have been remunerative.

The Duke of York could have obtained no verdict against the promoters of the Penny Post until the City had been cleared of the dishonest sheriffs who packed the London juries, and therefore at first made no attempt to suppress the Penny Post.   But on November 22, 1682, he obtained a verdict for £100 against Dockwra.   With this the bulk of the news-letter campaign ended, and after the loyal Lord Mayor, Sir John Moore, finally put a stop to the seditious news-letters in June 1683, by forbidding " coffee-houses and other places to entertain them," [1] Muddiman once more reigned supreme in that branch of journalism.   On August 14, 1683, the King recognized the services of Sir John Moore " in delivering the City from the Whigs and restoring it to its Sovereign," by "recommending him to Posterity."   He ordered that Sir John Moore should, as an addition to his arms, bear " on a canton gules, one of the Lyons of England." [2]

Before continuing the history of the newspapers of the Plot, attention must be drawn once more to the danger of trusting either the newspapers or the news-letters of the times.   Even the imprints to the pamphlets and songs cannot always be accepted.   Harris, " Elephant Smith," and others invariably attributed seditious pamphlets to " Popish Nat," particularly if they had

---

serve the Papists to plot than the Protestants to counterplot them."
An unexpected piece of common-sense from Oates !   Nor was Macaulay aware that the Whigs actually prosecuted John Smith for his aspersion of Oates.   Their indictment is set out in W. H. Hart's *Index Expurgatorius Anglicanus*, pp. 268–9.
[1] News-letter of June 14, 1683.
[2] *Ibid.*, August 14, 1683.

printed them themselves, and Thompson often in sarcasm inscribed his songs and pamphlets " Printed for Benjamin Harris " or " Francis Smith," as the case might be.[1] The journal of Narcissus Luttrell, hitherto a chief authority on the times I am sketching, was composed almost entirely from the Whig news-letters and newspapers. It is thoroughly untrustworthy, therefore, and often exceedingly untruthful. When the remaining Calendars of State Papers for the reign of Charles II (now completed) are printed, research workers will be able to see in a moment that Luttrell is not to be trusted.[2]

Roger L'Estrange uttered a warning on this subject in 1682. " The history of this age," wrote he, " will come to be drawn from these papers, and will it not be worth while, think ye, to set after times right in a matter of this importance? " And " The celebrated heroes of this generation shall be either such as took their rise from alms-baskets or jayls. Or others, perhaps, whose hands shall have been double dyed in the sacred blood of Princes or Prelates. This will be the consequence undoubtedly of letting these licentious writings pass

---

[1] The songs printed by Thompson were re-published by him in and after 1685, as *Collections of Loyal Songs*, to which he prefixed his auto-biography, with an account of the indictments brought against him. In like fashion the other side printed " Collections " of their own songs, chiefly after the Revolution. Rarely, indeed, can the exact date of the publication of any individual song be stated. As one example of an intentionally misleading imprint, Thompson's " Let Oliver now be forgotten " may be mentioned. The imprint to this is " Printed for Benjamin Harris," with Harris's address, " and are to be sold by Langley Curtis," etc.

The best collection of the Whig songs is *Poems on Affairs of State*, 1640–1704, in three volumes, published in 1716.

[2] On such questions as the elections of the sheriffs from 1681 to 1683, Luttrell is in frequent conflict with the State Papers, from which Muddiman took his own accounts. The news-letters in the Greenwich Hospital collection, now being calendared, are almost entirely of Whig origin. How they came to Greenwich Hospital is not known. In the recently published Calendar for 1680–81 there is, I think, a special news-letter by Hancock to John Braman, M.P. for Chichester, dated May 10, 1681. Braman indorsed this " Mr. H. his letter." There was a signature to this, but it has been torn off. The first initial, however, still remains and is either " I " or " J."

unpunished. The Weekly Papers, whose office it is to
spread false news, traduce the King and his ministers,
misrepresent proceedings of State, improve all occasions
of making the officers and servants of the Government
ridiculous, and in a scurrilous way of buffoonery turn up
a crape gown man or a tantivy to make sport for the
multitude. . . . You shall find few dangerous libels
that come abroad . . . but you have either Curtis or
Janeway or Baldwin or (Francis) Smith, or, in short,
some of these weekly intelligencers for their vouchers." [1]

An extreme view, no doubt, but one with more than a
modicum of truth in it.

Roger L'Estrange says that he " contracted a horror
of the Plot " from its very inception, and up to 1681 he
had been firing off pamphlet after pamphlet against
its supporters. Muddiman, in a milder fashion, joined
him in his news-letters, putting forward the official views,
which, so he states, he was repeatedly ordered to give,
often, as he hints, by the King himself. But although
he never went beyond sarcasm at the expense of Oates
and Shaftesbury, and reserved his bitterest remarks
for the anabaptists, all his opponents feared to answer
him. No reply to him will be found in any of the newspapers or news-letters he denounced. It was far otherwise with L'Estrange, who was not attached to the office
of a Secretary of State, and had not the Privy Council
at his back. " Oliver's fiddler," " Dog Towzer " and
other epithets saluted him on all sides, until one phrase-
maker, in a delirium of vituperation, termed him " Tory-
Rory-dammee-Plot-shammee-younker-crape."

With the election of Bethel and Cornish for sheriffs
in July 1680 the struggle took on a new shape. The
sheriffs began to pack the juries, either themselves (as
when Shaftesbury was tried) or through the under-
sheriffs. City grand juries began to return " ignoramus "

[1] *Observator*, No. 152, June 10, 1682.

to indictments preferred against seditious writers and printers.[1]   When Sir Patience Ward was elected Mayor at the end of September 1680, the paralysis of justice was complete and the City was in a state of covert rebellion. The Lord Chief Justice Scroggs, who had sentenced most of the victims of the Plot, was impeached, solely because he had directed the acquittal of Sir George Wakeman and sentenced Harris.   Thompson was placed in the pillory and brutally stoned by a London mob, for publishing the *Letters to Miles Prance* of the Catholic barristers Farwell and Paine, contending that Godfrey had committed suicide.   When Parliament at last met, on October 21, 1680, there was every intention of impeaching L'Estrange and of trying him for his life.   So he prudently retired to Holland, remaining there until the King again dissolved the Parliament.

The Parliament of 1680, the last but one of the reign of Charles II, no more represented the nation than the Rump itself had done.   It was composed almost entirely of Whigs.   By dint of the ingenious but indefensible practice of splitting freeholds and thus swamping the loyal voters, the Whigs had succeeded in returning numbers of members who otherwise would not have been elected.   Bribery and other corrupt practices had taken place in the corporations, Whigs everywhere being intruded as returning officers.   Hence the subsequent forfeitures of charters during this reign.   An unprecedented number of the members consisted of City Whigs; others were involved in all the plots of this and of the next reign. Amongst them were Slingsby Bethel, the Shimei of Dryden's *Absalom and Achitophel*, City sheriff for this year, Dubois (Liverpool), a would-be sheriff, with his colleague Thos. Papillon (Dover), Pilkington, member

---

[1] A large number of these will be found in W. H. Hart's *Index Expurgatorius Anglicanus*, but this is by no means complete, as the newsletters prove.

for London, Sir William Waller (Junior, M.P. for West-minster) Brome Whorwood (Oxford City), George Speke (Somerset) John Speke (Ilchester), Sir Patience Ward (Pontefract), the Lord Mayor of this year, and a perjurer, and Sir Samuel Barnadiston, another City alderman and the foreman of Shaftesbury's " ignoramus " jury.[1]

The Commons soon proved their temper by electing William Williams, Recorder of Chester, their Speaker. Williams was counsel for Francis Smith, at his trials during this year. Emboldened by the results of the elections, Smith had issued a series of seditious tracts and must have amassed a small fortune by their sale. *A New Years gift for the Lord Chief Justice* (Scroggs), *Some Observations upon the trial of Sir George Wakeman*, and *An Act of Common Council*, were amongst those for which the Privy Council had ordered his prosecution— in each case with the result that a jury, packed by the under-sheriffs, had thrown out the bill.[2]   At Smith's trial, on September 16, 1680, for publishing the last-mentioned tract, Sir George Jefferies, Recorder of London, had expressed himself with justifiable indignation about the dishonest proceedings of the jury. Accordingly Smith printed an account of this trial, entitling it *An account of the injurious proceedings of Sir George Jefferies . . . against Francis Smith*.   At the end of this, Smith added his first autobiography, and told the story of his punish-ment for publishing the book of the Prodigies.   It has been described as a " piteous tale," and so it would be, were it not for the glib lies he had already placed on record.   Now, sure of the protection of the sheriffs and of the House of Commons, he actually took credit to himself for issuing the book.   " In August, 1661," wrote he, " a certain book was printed and published, entitled

---

[1] Luttrell's account of these men and of their machinations is extremely misleading and often untrue.
[2] Indictments in W. H. Hart's *Index Expurgatorius Anglicanus*.

Mirabilis Annus ; or, the Year of Prodigies. Then did a person of quality, yet living [Shaftesbury?] give me great encouragement for its publication, as a book grateful to the Authority (!) and of general caution to the Nation, both to behold and consider the works of God, and also to tremble for His judgements. But so it happened, contrary to my expectation, that the very day it was published, one of his Majesty's messengers came to my shop with a warrant, both to seize the book and my person."

The House of Commons then actually singled out this perjurer for honour. On October 30, the House, reversing for a brief period its order of June 1660, ordered its votes and transactions to be printed daily, and Francis Smith was appointed its printer. Next, on November 11, the Exclusion Bill was reintroduced, and on November 19, the House turned its attention to Benjamin Harris, who was still in prison, and petitioned the King to remit his fine of £500. The petition, was not granted [1] and, on December 23, the Commons petitioned a second time, with the like result. In the meantime the two Chief Justices, Scroggs and North, had been impeached, with two other judges of the King's Bench and Exchequer, and an address had been presented asking for the removal from all public offices of Sir George Jefferies. Worse was to follow, for when the Commons received no answers to their appeals for Harris, secret instructions were sent to the Marshal of the King's Bench Prison, ordering him to release Harris. After this Harris celebrated his release by publishing his *Triumphs of Justice over unjust judges*, " humbly " dedicating it to Scroggs, " from Westminster Hall, December 23, 1680." The tract itself is dated 1681, so that in all probability the 23rd of December, 1680, was the date of Harris's illegal release.

[1] On November 24 Harris petitioned the Lords. Hist. MSS. Commission's Eleventh Report, Part II., pp. 212–13.

On December 29 the venerable Lord Stafford was sent to his death by the House of Peers, upon the evidence mainly of other perjurers than Oates. But, on Saturday, January 1, Muddiman announced that "His Majesty doth neither give nor receive New Year's gifts." The reason for this was the open insult offered to the King by Sheriffs Bethel and Cornish. The sentence on Lord Stafford was that of drawing, hanging and quartering. The King, as was his right, commuted this to beheading. The sheriffs actually asked the Houses of Parliament whether they were to obey the King or carry out the original sentence. The Lords replied that the King's writ was to be obeyed, but from the Commons they received for answer the scandalous reply that the Commons were " content " that he should be beheaded. No wonder that there were no Court festivities for the New Year.

In the meantime, Francis Smith signalized his privilege as Parliamentary publisher by publishing the second important document of the Plot, entitled *The Speech of a Noble Peer*. Grossly insolent to the King and seditious in the highest degree, this explicitly stated that the King was "not to be trusted." This " speech " was universally understood to mean a speech by Lord Shaftesbury on December 23, and, though it was never delivered, there is every reason to think that it was his composition.[1] Satiated with the blood of Lord Stafford and perhaps a little afraid of the open anger of the King, the Lords then began to display more moderation. They had thrown out the Bill of Exclusion, and on January 4 they ordered *The Speech of a Noble Peer* to be burnt by the hangman and directed that Smith should be prosecuted.

---

[1] I do not quote this document, for it can be read in Christie's *Life of Shaftesbury*. Smith's third edition of this document, printed in 1689, after the Revolution, seems to prove that Shaftesbury really wrote it. Smith dedicated this edition to William III, and appended to it his second autobiography, entitled *The Case of Francis Smith*. No indication was given by him that the " Speech " was never delivered. The only copy of this edition appears to be that in the Guildhall Library, London.

Lord Macaulay draws attention to the fact that the most important debates in English history—the debates over the Bill of Exclusion—were passed over in complete silence by the *Gazette*, but he was not aware that the Goverment news-letters supplied this defect. Muddiman described the last days of the third Parliament of Charles II as follows :

" *Saturday, Jan.* 8, (1681) : I should have told you in the last that the Commons agreed with the Lords in their vote [about the Irish Popish Plot] with this addition : ' That the Duke of York being a Papist, the expectation of his coming to the throne hath given the greatest encouragement thereto, as well as to the horrid Popish Plot in this kingdom of England.' On the 7th, the House of Commons, upon debate of his Majesty's message [refusing to consider the question of exclusion] resolved that there can be no security nor safety to the Protestant religion, the King's life, or the well-constituted government of the Kingdom without passing a Bill for disabling the Duke of York to inherit the Imperial Crown of England. As also that until such Bill be passed they cannot give any supply to his Majesty, without danger to his Majesty's person and the Protestant religion and unfaithfulness to the Trust reposed in them. They resolved farther, that all persons who advised the message against the Bill for excluding the Duke of York have given pernicious counsel to his Majesty and are promoters of Popery and enemies to the King and Kingdom. And that the Earl of Halifax, in advising his Majesty to insist upon his last message against the Bill for excluding the Duke, hath given pernicious counsel. They voted an humble address to his Majesty to remove the Earl of Halifax from his councils and presence for ever, Mr. Lawrence Hyde from Council, presence and office of the Treasury, the Marquess of Worcester from Council and all office and employments of honour and profit, the Earl of Clarendon from Council and presence. And then voted whoever should lend money or advance upon any branch of the King's revenue, or accept or buy upon any tally of anticipation, should be judged to hinder the sitting of the Parliament, and be responsible to the Parliament therefore."

On Tuesday, January 11, 1681, Muddiman continued :

" On the 8th the House of Lords, as expedients, agreed that the Duke of York should be banished 500 miles out of the kingdom during the King's life, and that it should be treason for him to return, also to confiscate all his revenues, and that after the King's death a committee of forty-one persons from the Lords and Commons should appoint to all offices, military and civil."

The King gave his Parliament another day, and in the same news-letter, for Tuesday, January 11, our journalist gave his account of the result. It missed no point by the concise form in which it was stated :

" On the 10th, the Commons resolved that whoever shall advise the King to prorogue this Parliament to any other purpose than in order to pass the Bill against the Duke of York is a betrayer of the King, the Protestant religion and Kingdom of England, a promoter of Popery and pensioner of France. They resolved their thanks to be given to the City of London for their manifest loyalty to the King ! and their care, charge and vigilance for the preservation of the King's person and Protestant religion. And that it is the opinion of the House that, in 1666, London was burnt down by the Papists to introduce Popery and Arbitrary Power. They resolved that the Commissioners of the Customs and all other officers who shall break the laws against importation of French wines are promoters of the French interest and shall account for it to Parliament. They resolved that it was their opinion that the Duke of Monmouth was put out of all his places and commands by influence of the Duke of York, and that an address be made to his Majesty to restore him. They resolved that the prosecution of Dissenters on penal laws against Papists is at this time grievous to the People, a weakening of the Protestant religion and dangerous to the peace of the Kingdom. And were proceeding, when the Black Rod called them to the House of Lords, where his Majesty gave the Royal assent to the Bill against importation of [Irish] cattle, the woollen Bill, some private Bills, and then the Parliament was prorogued to the 20th."

Before the 20th arrived, Parliament, in spite of the threats of the House of Commons, was dissolved, and the King summoned his fourth and last Parliament to meet at Oxford, out of reach of the rebellious City of London. " Long live the King and the true Protestant religion as by law established," wrote Muddiman. When the City petitioned against the meeting of Parliament at Oxford, the King told them that " they should beware of such as advise them to such things as do not concern them." All the Shaftesbury and Oates journalists omitted this remark.

On the 9th of February, the Privy Council, finding that Harris had been set free, ordered the Marshal of the King's Bench to attend them " to give account how he came to be at liberty."[1] On February 11 the Marshal appeared, and was ordered to keep Harris in close custody.[2] At the same time, Council ordered Jane, the wife of Langley Curtiss (then in prison), to be prosecuted for publishing *A true copy of a letter intercepted, going to Holland to Mr. L'Estrange.* On the preceding day the

---

[1] News-letter of February 10.
[2] *Ibid.*, February 12.

Master and Wardens of the Stationers' Company had been ordered to suppress treasonable and seditious libels.

The final phase of the struggles between the King on one side, and the House of Commons and the City of London on the other, all caused by the " Popish Plot," then ensued.

CHAPTER XII

THE OXFORD PARLIAMENT—THE KING'S VENGEANCE BEGINS
—FATE OF THE PUBLISHERS OF NEWSPAPERS—DEATH
OF CHARLES II—DEATH OF MUDDIMAN—BENJAMIN
HARRIS, THE FIRST AMERICAN JOURNALIST—END OF
HIS CAREER IN THE FOLLOWING CENTURY

A T the commencement of the year 1681, the King
took the advice of his Chief Justice of the Common
Pleas, Francis North, first Baron Guildford, and
later on Lord Chancellor, as to what should be done
with the Whig newspapers he had been powerless to suppress. The Chief Justice's advice was most sensible.
He told the King not to continue prosecutions, which, as
we have seen, would be defeated by " ignoramus "
juries in the City, but to employ skilled writers to combat
them and issue papers on his behalf. The King did this
and, adds the Chief Justice's brother, the loyal journalists
" soon wrote " the others " out of the pit." [1]

Nathaniel Thompson presumably was one of the writers
employed, but of course the one man marked out for the
task was Roger L'Estrange. He descended into the arena
and fought Oates's journalists in their own way and in
their own language, with a vigour of expression and command of the English language that they could not hope
to imitate. He was capable of writing excellent English

---

[1] Roger North's life of his brother Francis.

when he chose, as his numerous translations from the
Spanish and of Æsop's fables and from Erasmus prove,
but he deliberately adopted the Whig style of invective,
in order to write them out of the field.   He told his readers
that he thought it might not be considered a fitting
occupation for " a gentleman and an old fellow of sixty-
eight," but pointed out that he had been compelled to
" descend into the kennel to lash a pack of curs." [1]

Lord Macaulay, fortified by his Whig prejudices, and
almost complete ignorance of the journals L'Estrange
wrote out of the field, has calumniated L'Estrange [2] in
terms which prove that he was a better partisan than historian.   He writes of L'Estrange's " mean and flippant
jargon, "but has nothing to say of the literary garbage
it was intended to counteract.   And his attribution to
L'Estrange of a " ferocious and ignoble nature " is in
direct opposition to all the facts.   The man who took a
leading part in bringing Oates to justice was not ignoble.[3]
The truth is, L'Estrange was the first Tory, just as Titus
Oates was the first Whig, and that has always been enough
for writers of Macaulay's school.   His life has yet to be
written.

No. 1 of L'Estrange's *Observators* appeared on April 13,
1681.   They did not contain news but commented on the
newspapers and pamphlets of the times, often with
extremely personal accounts of their writers and printers.
Throughout they were written in dialogue form and, for

---

[1] Preface to the fourth volume of the *Observators*.

[2] *History of England*, chap. iii. p. 593.

[3] The case of William Jenkyn by no means bears the construction
Macaulay put upon it from glancing at the two *Observators* for January
29 and 31, 1685.   L'Estrange makes out a very strong case against
Jenkyn in them.   It is not possible to follow up all the details given
in the *Observators* without going through all the pamphlets and papers
of the times and understanding the characters and history of their
writers and printers.   There is no evidence that the King "looked sad "
when he heard of the death in Newgate of Jenkyn.   It is more probable
that he had never even heard of Jenkyn's name.   And that the case
was of no importance is proved by the fact that the news-letters do
not even mention it.

Roger L'Estrange Esqr Ætatis suæ. 68.

P. Tempest ex;

From a print in the British Museum

all these reasons, are most difficult to follow nowadays. Before he sent the *Observators* to the press L'Estrange had them approved (probably by deputy) by both Secretaries of State.[1] This circumstance defeated the prosecution of himself set on foot by the Whigs in 1683.

"*Heraclitus Ridens; or, a Discourse between jest and earnest, where many a true word is spoken in opposition to all libellers against the Government*," preceded the *Observators* and commenced on February 1, 1681. Its author is generally considered to have been the poet and miniaturist Thomas Flatman. It was a running satire of some literary value and was reprinted in two small volumes in 1713. Dryden's *Absalom and Achitophel*, written by command of the King, also appeared in 1681.

Preparations for the Oxford Parliament commenced on February 11. Christchurch, Merton and Corpus Christi Colleges were set apart for the King and his Court. On the 19th, the Judges all attended the Council and were addressed by the King, who informed them that as he himself intended to govern by the laws, so he was determined that no one should break them. They were, therefore, to put the recusancy laws against Papists and *others* into execution, and were to direct grand juries accordingly on their circuits. This meant that the cumulative fines for not going to church were now to be inflicted, not merely on the Papists, as the last Parliament had wished, with a total exemption for Protestant dissenters, but on all without fear or favour. In the meantime, Francis Smith had entered the lists as a journalist. *Smith's Protestant Intelligence* began in February and was one of the most seditious and the most lying papers that had yet appeared. Tracts also poured from the presses. "Every day produceth a spawn of most villainous libels against his Majesty and the Government,"

[1] *The Observator*, No. 323, for April 20, 1683. See W. H. Hart's *Index Expurgatorius Anglicanus*.

wrote Muddiman, on March 5. " The ranker sort come generally from under a sister's apron or a brother's pocket, and are sometimes conveyed to parties in the country at the charge of the faction here."

Everyone thought that the session of Parliament at Oxford would be a long one. The five " Popish " Lords in the Tower, even, were sent there in order that they might be tried there by their peers. On the 11th March the King set out thither, and on the 17th the London members also departed for Oxford, accompanied by a cavalcade of some hundreds of armed men, amongst whom were Francis Smith, and the anabaptist Stephen College, the " Protestant joiner," and writer of most of the seditious songs of the times. For this occasion College had invented the " Protestant Flail." [1] The two were ringleaders in a design to seize the King, insufficiently described by Macaulay in his account of College. Macaulay is in error in asserting that the " Protestant Flail " was invented earlier than this.

The London cavalcade, although their direct route was up Holborn Hill, " by way of ostentation " went in a body down Fleet Street and the Strand to Charing Cross, within sight of Whitehall, before they turned north for the Oxford Road. The London Weavers, wrote Smith, had contrived a " very fine fancy " for the day—" that

[1] " Listen awhile and I'll tell you a tale
Of a new device of a Protestant Flail,
With a thump, thump, thump a thump,
Thump a thump, thump.
This flail it was made of the finest wood,
Well lined with lead and notable good
For splitting of braines and shedding of blood
Of all that withstood,
With a thump, thump, etc."

The song adds that the flail took its degrees at Oxford. It was pub-lished by Thompson in 1681. There is a copy of College's abominable *Ra-Ree Show* (too offensive to quote) in the British Museum, easily identified by L'Estrange's *Notes on Stephen College*, which the writers who have attempted to whitewash College do not seem to have read. Smith published the " Ra-Ree Show."

is, a Blew Sattin ribbon, having these words plainly and legibly wrought upon it, ' No Popery. No Slavery,' which being tyed up in knots were worn in the hats of the horsemen who accompanied our members." Carbines, pistols and "musquetoons" were in evidence in the bands accompanying all the members from all parts of England, according to Smith, and on March 17 he had informed his readers that the magistrates of the City of Oxford, " as we are credibly informed " (the old phrase of the book of wonders), " do not approve of quartering any troops within the walls of the city." This, of course, was untrue.[1] So confident was Smith that the King would be laid by the heels, that he waxed sarcastic in the issue of his paper for March 28, and wrote :

" Last week his Majesty was pleased to be present at the acting of a play—' Tamberlain the Great '—and upon Monday last [the day the Oxford Parliament met] his Majesty was to see a comedy called ' Plain Dealing.' " As the event proved, the titles of the supposititious plays were appropriate, but not quite so in the sense Smith intended. In the meantime he published another seditious tract, entitled *Vox Populi*, and, according to his second autobiography (of 1689), presented each member of the Oxford Parliament with a copy of it, at his own charge. The Oxford Parliament met on Monday, March 21, 1681 (the Lords in the Geometry School and the Commons in the Convocation House), and the House of Commons at once fell upon their old devices and brought in the Bill of Exclusion once more. On Monday the 28th, at ten o'clock in the morning, the King with dramatic suddenness dissolved Parliament for the last time. For the first time Charles II then publicly appealed to the nation.

---

[1] See Wood's *Life and Times* (ed. A. Clark), ii. 531, for a full description of the Oxford Parliament. Armour for the troops had been sent up by boat.

Announced by Muddiman on April 2, the " Declaration "
of Charles II was issued a few days later, and is the
most important document of the reign.   In it the King
summed up the offences of the House of Commons, " their
illegal and arbitrary orders, by which they had taken
Englishmen into custody for matters which bore no
relation to parliamentary proceedings, their declarations
that distinguished men were enemies to the King and
kingdom, made on bare suspicion, without proof or
hearing any defence, their unconstitutional votes against
lending the King money," and, in fact, all the points
Muddiman had evidently been instructed to report to his
correspondents in his news-letters.   This declaration was
read in every church and chapel throughout the land,
created a great sensation, and led to an outburst of loyalty
beyond precedent.   Addresses to the King in reply
poured in on all sides, and from this moment the King's
vengeance now began, and was only delayed until the end
of 1682 by the " ignoramus " juries of London.   For the
rest of his reign Charles II dispensed with a Parliament.[1]
The second and third cities of the kingdom, Norwich and
Bristol, led the way in addressing the King, and, in the
case of Norwich, extraordinary results followed.   Norwich
had for long been at cross purposes with London, and had
repeatedly prosecuted the dispersers of news-letters and
illegal newspapers and pamphlets.   But there was no
printing press in Norwich, or, indeed, anywhere out of
London, and the Mayor and Aldermen of that City desired
greater prominence to be given to their votes and proceedings.   So they encouraged a London bookseller,
John Smith of Great Queen Street, to issue a paper in
which all their documents should be printed.   John
Smith had already dabbled in journalism, and had printed

---

[1] " I will maintain my prerogative within its just bound; on the other
hand, I will not have my subjects give me the Law," said the King
(Ailesbury's *Memoirs*, i. 65).

the *Currant Intelligence* of 1680, already noticed, and he now commenced a fresh newspaper with the same title.

On the 17th May the Grand Jury of Middlesex presented John Smith for printing in his newspaper the petition to the King of the city of Norwich, presented on March 10. The sum of this petition, or, rather, address, was that " the burgesses of Norwich " prayed " for the preservation of his Majesty's person and government both in Church and State, as it is now by law established, as also his Grandeur by the punishing and suppressing all seditious and scandalous libels," and the granting to the King the supplies the Commons had refused. This was a blow in the face to the City of London, which had petitioned for a fresh Parliament, and was still doing its best to carry on the struggle, and, as the Grand Jury of Middlesex could not very well prosecute the city of Norwich, it attacked that city's printer and actually termed the loyal petition of Norwich " a scandalous libel."

The Mayor and Corporation of Norwich assembled in Common Council when they heard of the proceedings of the Grand Jury of Middlesex, resolved that they were illegal, and derogatory to the privileges of the subject, and at once ordered their address to be reprinted " with some additional reasons in justification of their actions, in vindication of their honour." They then ordered John Smith to print all this. Smith did so, in his *Currant Intelligence* for June 7–11, 1681. The additional reasons attacked the Grand Jury of Middlesex for stigmatizing their loyal address by the " frightful name of a libel," and accused its members of having been " engaged in the late horrid rebellion." John Smith's *Currant Intelligence*, therefore, is of considerable importance in the history of the city of Norwich. He must have been a Norwich man, though it is not possible to say more about him than that he commenced his last *Currant Intelligence* on March 9, 1681, and discontinued it towards the end of the year. It is curious that Macaulay should have committed so serious a blunder over John Smith's attack upon Oates.

On April 15 Francis Smith was brought before the Privy Council and sent to Newgate, with orders that he should be prosecuted. On April 11 he had printed a string of falsehoods, in his *Smith's Protestant Intelligence*, about the proceedings at the Privy Council, the object of which was to claim that the authority of the Commons was greater than that either of the Lords or Privy Council.[1]

Thus the number of his *Smith's Protestant Intelligence* published on April 15, was the last he ever issued. Muddiman's comment, on April 19, was : " The shutting up of Smyth put a stop to the *Protestant Intelligence* of yesterday, although those that know him do not believe it was altogether his. But it seems the Composer, now the Cat's foot is gone, is loath to put his own into the fire." Smith seems to have been discharged on condition that he printed no more newspapers, for the prosecution was dropped [2] and he never again issued a journal. He had undoubtedly rendered himself liable to a prosecution for high treason, if only because he published College's " Ra-Ree Show."

In 1681 Harris was the victim of a domestic scandal. His wife had been unfaithful, and the chief witness to the fact, apart from his journalist enemy, Thompson, is John Dunton, who, nevertheless, had termed her a " kind rib " when she stood by him in the pillory. Two satirical ballads celebrated this event.[3]

---

[1] News-letter of Saturday, April 16. The indictment and passage in question are set out in W. H. Hart's *Index Expurgatorius Anglicanus*, pp. 260–7.

[2] *Currant Intelligence*, July 9–12, 1682.

[3] See page 44 of " Dunton's Whipping Post; or, a Satyr upon Everybody. To which is added A Panegyrick on the most deserving Gentlemen and Ladies in the three kingdoms. With the Whoring-Pacquet or news of the St—ns and kept M—s's. Vol. I. To which is added the Living Elegy; or, Dunton's letter to his few Creditors. With the character of a Summer friend. Also the Secret History of the Weekly Writers. In a distinct challenge to each of them," etc. The sub-title

Step by step, beginning in the autumn of 1681, the King now retaliated upon his enemies. On August 31, " about eleven o'clock," Charles II ordered Titus Oates to be removed from his lodgings in Whitehall, and thus rid himself of the presence of this fellow in the Royal palace. " Those who have observed his deportment," wrote Muddiman, " have long stood in admiration that his Majesty (if anything of clemency can be admired in so gracious a Prince) could so long endure him under his roof. He was insolent, ungrateful and inconstant, sometimes an evidence for, sometimes an evidence against, the King, and both where his sacred life was concerned."

Dissenters were now harried all over the kingdom; at Yarmouth (for instance) the Grand Jury presented two or three Papists (all they had), but also forty-one nonconformists, for not coming to church. Conventicles were suppressed, pulpits being pulled down and benches torn out of them and burnt. The news-letters are full of details of all that went on, and depict a stern and determined King who rose at five in the morning to direct prosecutions at the Privy Council. Only in London the King had not yet conquered, and was not master for another year or more, thanks to the disloyal sheriffs. On July 2 (the greatest step the King had yet taken) Shaftesbury was sent to the Tower.

On September 19, therefore, Smith thought the time an appropriate one for reissuing his *Speech of a Noble Peer*,

to the (separately paged) last section is " The Living Elegy; or, Dunton's letter to his few creditors, with the character of a Summer friend. To which is added, The Lives, Religion, and Honesty of the ' Moderator,' ' Wandering Spy,' ' Rehearsal.' ' London C–D ' (alias ' Post '), Interloping ' ' Whipster,' and the other attachers of my person and Goods." " Printed in the year 1706." This is a rare book, and the British Museum contains only one copy. Pages 41 to 46 of the last section are devoted to Harris. The two songs published in 1681 (with the fictitious imprints of Smith) were " ' The Saint ' turn'd curtezan," and " The Protestant Cuckold. Being a full relation how B. H., the Protestant news-forger, caught his beloved wife Ruth, in ill circumstances." Dunton's book is very scurrilous, but contains a great deal of valuable information, particularly about newspapers of the year 1706.

and, therefore, had it cried about the streets, "about ten at night." For this he was again indicted—the passage in the "Speech" set out in the indictment [1] commencing with the following words : " My lords, tis a very hard thing to say that we cannot trust the King . . . he is such a one as no story affords us a parallel of; how plain and how many are the proofs of the design to murder him, how little is he apprehensive of it," etc. Bail was refused to Shaftesbury, who was later on released by an " ignoramus " jury, in face of an overwhelming amount of evidence against him. Shaftesbury remained in England until the following year, when all his arrangements in the City for a rebellion were broken by the election of Sir John Moore as Lord Mayor. On February 8, 1682, Langley Curtiss was sent to Newgate for publishing false news about the Grand Jury of Middlesex.

On May 16, 1682, Richard Janeway was tried at Guildhall, for a passage in his *Impartial Protestant*, and brought in " Not Guilty " by a packed jury. This disgraceful proceeding was countered by the Court of Exchequer, to which Janeway had formerly given bail to be of good behaviour. So, on June 1, the Exchequer estreated the recognizances. Then, wrote Muddiman, on June 3 : "Janeway finding himself and his bail clapped up in gaol upon his misdemeanour without the hope of being released by a London jury, and knowing by the experience of Ben Harris how slow the Party are in redeeming the Brotherhood from tribulation, made his application to the Attorney General, and so far prevailed as to gain his and their liberty upon engagement to trade no more in the publishing seditious or treasonable pamphlets. And upon that account it is that you want the *Impartial Protestant Intelligence.*" The " authors " of the *Impartial Protestant* were Henry Care, Thomas Vile, George Larkin

[1] Indictment in W. H. Hart's *Index Expurgatorius Anglicanus*, pp. 221–2.

(its printer), Hancock and " a certain bookseller near the Royal Exchange," according to the *Loyal Protestant* for June 13, 1682.

On June 10, Muddiman wrote that " The Whigge party are quite down in the mouth.   They do not open in coffeehouses as formerly, and the thinking men do now desert them."   Shaftesbury, he added, had absconded.   Shaftesbury died in Holland a few months later on.

In 1683 attempts were made on both sides to set up newspapers once more.   Nathaniel Thompson was the first offender, and revived his *Loyal Protestant*.   But on March 14 he was haled before the Privy Council for asserting in his paper that Lord Dumbarton had been appointed General of Scotland, and the Marquess of Huntly Governor of Stirling Castle, and was sent prisoner to the Gate house.[1]   This finally ended his journalism. On March 22 Benjamin Harris tried to revive his *Domestick Intelligence* by the trick of publishing it gratis,[2] but this of course was at once stopped.

In March 1684, towards the end of the Great Frost, when oxen were roasted whole upon the Thames, and a regular fair was held above London Bridge, we find the last notice of Francis Smith in this reign.   Writing on Tuesday March 4, Muddiman said, " On the 3rd Frank Smyth was taken.   He is best known by the name of ' Elephant Smith,' a bookseller who lives at the Elephant in Cornhill, and was in his time the prime disperser of all sorts of the most lewd and seditious pamphlets.   He had practised a long time in that way, till the Law laid claim to him and had imposed several fines to which he was liable.   Upon that account, he quitted his house, fled first to Holland, and since has wandered about the country in England under several disguises, till the City Marshal picked him

---

[1] News-letter of March 15, 1683.
[2] Transcript of the Stationers' Registers, under date of March 22, 1682/3.   No copy is known to exist.

up, and he now stands committed to make the Law satisfaction."

But the seditious booksellers and printers were treated mercifully. No one was tried for high treason, for the Government's object was to put a stop to the flood of lies and sedition rather than to be vindictive. Smith's fines eventually were remitted by James II,[1] a piece of clemency which, of course, he rewarded by publishing his last false account of his trials and sufferings. And Benjamin Harris's fine of £500 was remitted by King Charles II upon promise of better behaviour. He, too, requited the Government in similar fashion to Smith, and on August 7, 1683, was reported to have been selling at Bristol fair the seditious pamphlets he no longer dared to expose in London. His pamphlets were seized, but he himself seems to have been permitted to escape.

By the end of the reign of Charles II the press was " in order " again. Dissent was all but stamped out and the King supreme. The sorrow of the nation at the King's death was deep, and if only for the dead King's sake every welcome was given to his brother. We have no better witness to these points than the nonconformist historian Calamy. In his *Historical Account of My Own Life* Calamy wrote :

" Never did I see so universal a concern as was visible in all men's countenances at that time. I was present upon the spot, at the proclaiming of King James II at the upper end of Wood Street in Cheapside (which is one of those places where proclamation is usually made upon such occasions), and my heart ached within me at the acclamations made upon that occasion, which as far as I could observe were very general. And it is to me a good evidence, that all the histories that fall into our hands are to be read with caution, to observe that Bishop Burnet

---

[1] *Public Occurrences truely Stated*, No. 1, February 2, 1687/8.

positively affirms that ' few tears were shed for the former
nor were there any shouts of joy for the present King.'
Whereas I, who was at that time actually present, can
bear witness to the contrary. The bishop, indeed, who
was then abroad, might easily be misinformed; but methinks he should not have been so positive in a matter of
that nature when he was at a distance."

Muddiman retained his monopoly of issuing the written
news until the end of the year 1687, when James II also
employed one or two writers of his own faith. Parliament renewed the Printing Act of 1662 in 1685, and the
Act was not finally suffered to lapse until the year 1695,
when William III also abandoned the claim to the Royal
prerogative in printed news, and licensing of books came
to an end as well.

At the end of 1688, Muddiman was clearly Jacobite in
his sympathies, so that it is improbable that his privileges
were continued by William III. In October 1689 he ceased
writing, and in March 1692 died at his house " at Coldhern,"
and was buried by the side of his wife in Kensington
parish church. In the almost total absence of State Papers
for the reign of James II, his news-letters are one of the
most valuable records of that reign.

After the accession of James II, Benjamin Harris was,
of course, heartbroken at the failure of Monmouth's
rebellion and attempted to "improve" it by more
seditious prints. Accordingly, on November 11, 1685,
Lord Middleton issued a warrant to the Stationers' Company "to damask ' English Liberties; or, Freeborn
subjects inheritance,' and to deface a copper-plate for
printing off seditious figures or emblems, entitled ' A
Scheme of Popish Cruelties; or what we must expect
under a Popish successor,' which were issued at the House
of Benjamin Harris, near the Royal Exchange, London,
Victualler." So that Harris had abandoned the open

sale of books, and was now carrying on a coffee-house, where, beyond a doubt, those like-minded to himself might meet and plot fresh treason.

Thus England became no place for Benjamin Harris. Where he then hid himself is uncertain, but probably he went to Holland and, finding that he was not safe there, embarked for Boston in New England. Here at first he opened a coffee-house. It has long been known that the first American newspaper was *Publick Occurrences, Both Foreign and Domestick*, published on September 25, 1690, and that this bears the imprint of " R. Pearce, Boston," who published it " for Benjamin Harris, of the London Coffee House," but the only known copy of *Publick Occurrences* is that in the Record Office at London. It goes without saying that it was at once suppressed, for " containing reflexions of a very high nature." This is probably the reason why a copy was sent to the English Government. Thus, as the wheel of chance would have it, Benjamin Harris became the patriarch of the press in a country which nowadays boasts more newspapers than any other in the world. Nor do his claims for remembrance in the United States end here.

In 1679 Harris published a tiny spelling-book for children, entitled *The Protestant Tutor*, stating in it that he was its author, as well as its publisher, and advertised it extensively in his *Domestick Intelligence*. Quite by accident, the book filled a long-felt need, for there was no spelling-book for children in existence, and thus ran through many editions, which differ very much. But Harris had no intention of doing a public service by issuing his book. His sole aim and object was to train up children to hate " Popery," and apart from the nature of the catechism of negation in the book, the children were taught by it that it was their bounden duty to "hate the Pope." When Harris went to America he took with him, or had sent to him, copies of his *Protestant Tutor*. Whether he simply

FRONTISPIECE OF THE FIRST EDITION OF THE
"PROTESTANT TUTOR"

(From the copy at the British Museum)

Dr. Titus Oats.   Captain William Bedloe.

S. Edmondbury-ged free-strangle

Sir Edmondbury Godfrey ftrangled.

ILLUSTRATIONS TO THE "PROTESTANT TUTOR"

sold these or had them reprinted there is nothing to show, for no copy of an American seventeenth-century edition of the book has survived, and very few of those printed in the eighteenth century. Children have a habit of destroying their school-books. But the book, under varying titles and with varying contents, became the school-book of the dissenters of America for the next hundred years, and for yet another hundred was frequently reprinted. It became the famous *New England Primer*, whose historian and bibliographer [1] tells us that Franklin and Hall printed over 37,000 copies of the book between 1749 and 1766, and that as the former began to print it in 1735, it is probable that at least double the number existed. " An over conservative claim for it is to estimate an average annual sale of 20,000 copies during a period of a hundred years, or total sales of 3,000,000 copies."

Harris was consoled for the suppression of his American newspaper by being appointed " Printer to his Excellency the Governor, Sir William Phips . . . and Council." Mr. Pearce's feelings when this appointment was made have not been recorded, but there was very little printing to be done in the colony at this time, and he must have suffered financial loss by the appointment. In 1692 Harris printed the Laws of Massachusetts, reprinting them in 1694, so that it is fairly evident that it was not quite safe for this supporter of Monmouth to return to England when William and Mary came to the throne at the end of 1688. By 1695 he thought it safe to return, set up in business in London once more and issued a fresh paper, entitled *Intelligence Domestick and Foreign*, from his shop in Fore Street. This failed, and ended with the eighth number, published on June 7, 1695. He then moved to Bartholomew Lane, near the Royal Exchange, and commenced a fresh newspaper, *The Pacquet-boat from Holland and Flanders*. This

[1] Mr. Paul Leicester Ford : *The New England Primer* (New York, 1897).

also failed.   In 1699 another newspaper was commenced by Harris, entitled *The London Slip of News, both foreign and domestick* (No. 1, June 6).   He was then living in " Maiden Head Court, Great Eastcheap," but a few weeks later on moved once more to the " Golden Boar's Head, against the Cross Keys in Gracechurch Street."   These frequent changes of address do not betoken prosperity. With its second number, Harris's *Slip of News* became *The London Post*, and was the longest lived of all his newspapers.

Hitherto the career of Benjamin Harris had been one rather of tragedy than of comedy.   It was well, therefore, that it should have ended on a note of broad farce, contributed, as usual, by an Irishman, no less a person than the author of *Gulliver's Travels*—Dean Swift.   Harris's *London Post* never was a success, and in the year 1705 had dwindled down to a tiny sheet of only two pages, of which one was devoted to " Resolutions upon the present position of affairs.   By Truth and Honesty."   It goes without saying that " Truth and Honesty " was Harris himself, but by this time the public had heard quite enough of Harris and would not buy his paper.   John Dunton unkindly remarked that Harris " scandalized truth, by pretending to write for it," and bluntly termed him a " knave," adding that his " useless and thievish paper " was suppressed in that year " for want of receivers."   Harris, therefore, was compelled to seek for other ways of earning a living, and adopted expedients which led up to Dunton's denunciation in the following year, 1706.

An old friend and ally of Harris was the Whig almanac maker, John Partridge, a shoemaker who had set up in business as an astrologer in 1678.   This prophet got into trouble over the Rye House Plot, and at the trial of the Rye House conspirators in 1683 evidence was given that he had been one of those willing to kill the King, but had been unable to join the others at the Rye House because

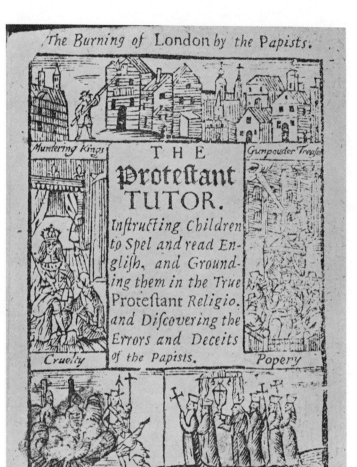

The Burning of London by the Papists.

Murtering Kings

THE
Proteſtant
TUTOR.

Inſtructing Children
to Spel and read En-
gliſh, and Ground-
ing them in the True
Proteſtant Religio,
and Diſcovering the
Errors and Deceits
of the Papists.

Gunpowder Treaſon

Cruelty

Popery

London. Printed for Ben Harris under the Piazza
of the Royal Exchange in Cornhil, 1679

TITLE-PAGE (ENLARGED) OF THE FIRST EDITION OF THE
"PROTESTANT TUTOR"

(The original measures 2 13/16 in. by 2 1/16 in.)
(From the copy at the British Museum)

he could not ride.   Partridge, therefore, thought that
he would be safer in Holland when his friends were tried
and executed, took refuge at Amsterdam, and remained
there until William and Mary came to the throne.

Following the example of the Reverend Dr. Oates, who
had returned from the University of Salamanca with the
degree of D.D. conferred on himself by himself, John
Partridge brought back with him the degree of M.D. of
the University of Leyden, obtained in like fashion.   In
and after 1690 Dr. Partridge issued his almanacs again,
dealing in misty predictions and carrying equivocation
to its finest point in them.   At the end he always advertised his celebrated pills.   In this year he also married,
his bride being Jane, the widow of Kirkman, the Duke of
Monmouth's tailor.   The two set up housekeeping at
East Sheen, between Richmond and Mortlake, some distance out of London.   One peculiarity of the astrologer's
almanacs of the times is that when the original writer
was dead, another succeeded to his mantle and carried
on his almanac.   Thus, " Wing's " Almanac was still
being carried on, although he had died in 1668.   So also
was " Poor Robin " (Henry Care) although " Poor
Robin " died in 1688.   And as for Francis Moore " M.D.,"
then alive, are not his almanacs still with us under the
name of " Old Moore "?   One astrologer, living until
1704, was the Jacobite Gadbury, with whom Partridge,
naturally, had an annual quarrel in prose and verse.
Dreadful predictions abounded in Partridge's *Merlinus
Liberatus*, interspersed with signs of the zodiac and
symbols of the planets and their aspects (Swift terms them
" Pot-hooks ") by way of proof of all that he said.   Nobody knew what he meant, nor did Partridge himself at
the time when he wrote, but his predictions were so carefully
worded that he was always able to claim that he had
prophesied an event *after* it had happened.   Naturally,
therefore, his almanacs were in great demand, and, in

his own eyes, Partridge was a personage of national importance.

Dunton, in the Appendix to his *Whipping Post*, sympathized with Partridge in the quarrel with Harris that now took place, and in all probability his pamphlet fell into Swift's hands and led him to purchase Partridge's almanac. For Benjamin Harris had a son who dabbled in astrology, and failing anything else to print, the pair testified their real regard for " truth and honesty " by pirating the almanacs of the highly important Partridge, who, in his *Merlinus Liberatus* for 1706, also styled himself " John Partridge, a lover of truth."

" I have been abused and the countrey also," wrote Partridge in this, " by a supplement added to my almanack, forged and contrived by Benj. Harris and his son, tho' I knew nothing of it till it was printed." In order that he might prevent " the abuse of the World " by such " knavish tricks," he went on, he had printed a " hand " at the end, and, as for anything beyond that hand, " it is a cheat and he is a knave, that did it ! So says your friend J. Partridge."

Harris then placed his additions in the body of the almanac. Accordingly, *Merlinus Liberatus* for 1707 contained another denunciation :

" If there is anything added to this Almanack by B. Harris, either in the middle or the end of it, besides these three sheets [*i. e.* 48 pages, octavo], it is a piece of knavery and not mine. Likewise, if there is anything in my name, called a prophecy or prediction, it is done by a Pack of Rascals, contrary to my will or knowledge. I am also informed that there is in the countrey an almanack sold, said to be done by Dorothy Partridge, as my wife; there was never any such thing pretended to by her, nor is it her name, and he is a villain that writes it, and it is a cheat put upon the countrey, and this I do to prevent it and to advise you not to buy it. John Partridge."

ILLUSTRATIONS TO THE "PROTESTANT TUTOR"

The spectacle of two "lovers of truth"—Whigs too—falling out in this manner was irresistible to the witty Tory Dean of St. Patrick's. October was the month in which the Stationers' Company published all the almanacs for each ensuing year, and when October 1707 arrived, a sensation was caused, not only in London, but all over Europe, by a new prognostication, which was not in the least misty or indefinite, but quite precise in all its prophecies. This was entitled :

"Predictions for the year 1708. Wherein the month and the day of the month are set down, the Persons named and the Great actions and events of next year particularly related as they will come to pass. Written to prevent the people of England from being further imposed upon by the vulgar Almanack makers. By Isaac Bickerstaff, Esq."

Swift had seen the name of Bickerstaff over a blacksmith's shop in Long Acre, and selected it as being uncommon. The pseudonym was afterwards used by Steele and Addison, in the *Tatler*, by Swift's permission.

In his preface Bickerstaff solemnly declared that there had been a gross abuse of astrology, for which he could not blame the "noble art," but the few "mean illiterate traders " who degraded it. " I wonder," he added, " when I observe gentlemen in the country, rich enough to serve the nation in Parliament, poring in Partridge's almanack to find out the events of the year at home and abroad." And as for Gadbury and the rest, " What have we to do with their advertisements of pills or their mutual quarrels in verse and prose of Whig and Tory ? "

Mr. Bickerstaff then announced that he himself would proceed in a " New Way," and that " Partridge and his clan may hoot me for a cheat and an impostor if I fail in any single particular of moment. . . . My first prediction is but a trifle, yet I will mention it to show how ignorant those sottish pretenders to astrology are in their own concerns.   It relateth to Partridge the Almanack maker.   I have consulted the Star of his Nativity by my own rules; and find that he will infallibly die upon the 29th of March next, about eleven at night, of a raging fever.   Therefore I advise him to consider of it and settle his affairs in time."

Other predictions followed, calculated to excite the interest of the haters of France.   Cardinal de Noailles, Archbishop of Paris, would die on April 4th, the Prince of the Asturias on April 11, and the Pope himself on September 11.

East Sheen was somewhat inaccessible in those days, owing to the absence of bridges, so that it was not easy to find out what really happened to Partridge on March 29.   So Swift issued another pamphlet within a day or two of that date, and entitled it, " The accomplishment of the first of Mr. Bickerstaff's predictions; being an account of the death of Mr. Partridge, the almanack maker," in a letter dated March 30, purporting to be " from a Revenue officer to a Lord."   By way of affectation, Partridge occasionally omitted the first " r " in his surname, so Swift improved upon this, intentionally mis-spelt Partridge's name " Patrige," and in describing the death-bed scene with great detail, made Partridge acknowledge that " all pretences of foretelling by astrology are deceits," and that he himself was " a poor ignorant fellow."   Then " Patrige," with two London quacks by his side and " a fanatic preacher " for his spiritual guide, expired " about five minutes after seven.   By which it is clear that Mr. Bickerstaff was mistaken almost four hours in his calculation.   In other circumstances he was exact enough. . . . I shall wait .with some impatience, and not without expectation, the fulfilling of Mr. Bickerstaff's second prediction, that the Cardinal de Noailles is to die upon the 4th April, and if that should be verified as exactly as this of poor Patrige, I must own I shall be wholly surprised

IOHN PARTRIDGE B.

Fatis agimur: Cedite Fatis.
Sen:

Engraved by S: Crignand.

(From a print at the British Museum)

and at a loss, and infallibly expect the accomplishment of all the rest."

This was not all. An " Elegy " on the death of Mr. " Patrige " followed a little later on :

> " Here five feet deep lies on his back
> A cobbler, starmonger and quack,
> Who to the stars in pure goodwill
> Does to his best look upward still.
> Weep, all you customers that use
> His pills, his almanacks, or shoes."

Attention has already been called to the credulity of the times. What followed is almost beyond belief. The first two pamphlets were translated into nearly every European language, and the Portuguese Inquisition solemnly burnt them, probably because of the forecasted death of the Pope. This incident is too well authenticated to permit of any doubt about it. Partridge was at his wit's end to know what to do, and actually advertised that he was " not only now alive, but also alive upon the 29th of March in question." The absurd manner in which this advertisement was worded increased the popular conviction that he was dead. The indignant astrologer then turned, unluckily for himself, to a witty literary man, Dr. Thomas Yalden, for aid, and, with the help of Steele and Congreve, Yalden concocted a defence for Partridge entitled *Squire Bickerstaff detected ; or, the Astrological Impostor convicted.*

" It is hard, my dear Countrymen of these United Nations," began this tract, " it is very hard that a ' Britain ' born, a Protestant Astrologer, a man of Revolutionary Principles, an assertor of the liberty and property of the People, should cry out in vain for justice against a Frenchman, a Papist and an illiterate pretender to science."

Under the pretence of exposing false reports the writers then went on to tell the story of the sexton tolling the passing bell, the undertaker arriving to measure Partridge for his coffin, and so on. The whole wound up with an Advertisement of an " Appeal to the Learned " about to be issued by Partridge, and addressed to the " Literati of the Whole World." " France and Rome are at the bottom of this horrid conspiracy against me," Partridge was made to wind up, and Bickerstaff, " the culprit afore-said, is a Popish emissary, has paid his visits to St. Germains and is now in the measures of Lewis XIV." " In attempting my reputation there is a general Massacre of Learning designed in these Realms; and through my sides there is a wound given to all the Protestant Almanack makers in the Universe."

In October 1708, the Stationers' Company published Partridge's almanack for 1709, in which also appeared a denial, but after this actually refused to issue any more of his almanacs on the ground that he was dead !

Swift then closed the controversy with a " Vindication of Isaac Bickerstaff, Esq. against what is objected to him by Mr. Partridge in his Almanack for the present year 1709."

This " Vindication " gravely expostulated with Partridge for his ungentlemanly conduct in calling " Bickerstaff " a " fool," " villain," and " impudent fellow," at the end of his almanac, and with matchless irony then went on to prove that he was *not* alive—the chief proof of this, of course, being the fact that Dove, Wing, Poor Robin and Gadbury, although they were all dead, still published almanacs. As for the assertion of a Frenchman that Cardinal de Noailles was still alive, " notwithstanding the pretended prophecy of Monsieur Biquerstaffe," how far was " a Frenchman, a Papist," and an enemy to be believed " in his own cause against an English Protestant *who is true to the Government* " ?

Partridge was not able to recommence his almanacs until 1713, when he issued *Merlinus Redivivus* for 1714. At the end he threatened " to oblige the world " with the nativity of Swift—" that notorious cheat," and went on, " I doubt not but that these beggarly villains that have scarce bread to eat without being rogues, two or three poor printers and a bookbinder, with honest Ben, will be at their old trade again." [1] This is the last reference discoverable about Harris.   His will, if he made one, was not proved in Canterbury Prerogative Court, but he probably died before 1720, about which time the last edition of his *Protestant Tutor* appeared.

[1] The cause of Partridge's renewed wrath seems to have been a small tract of twelve pages, entitled, " The Right and True Predictions of Dr. Patridge's [*sic*] prophecy for the year 1712. . . . Together with . . . Mrs. Dorothy Patridge's Speculum . . . By J. Patridge.   Student in Physick and Astrology. . . . London.   Printed by J. Read, near Fleet Street."

At the end there are the words " Licensed according to Order," but licensing came to an end in 1695.

APPENDIX A

To the King's most Excellent Majestie.

The Humble petition of James Hickes, Clerke in ye Lre. Office. Sheweth

That the pet. sent the first lre. by the post from Namptwich unto London in 1637 and hath been the principall instrument in the management of that road, which brings in att present att least £4000 p. annum cleere, and in 1640 was sent for theire, by Mr. Burlimachie to be clerke in the office in London for that roade.

That in 1642, by order of the right hon^bl Secretarie Nicholas to the said Burlimachie, the petitioner settled postages betwixt Bristoll and York for your late father's service (of blessed memorie) in the beginning of his troubles & likewise carried and conveyed all ye Pacquettes from beyond ye seas unto his said Majestie to Kennelmeworth Castle before Edgehill fight and until Aprill following unto Oxford.

That yor pet^r in Aprill 1643, for writeing to the Right Honb^le Secretarie Nicholas certain passages of Parliam^t against his late Matie (the lre. intercepted) was by Miles Corbett committed to prison, and about Michas. following being released, repaired to Oxford, where he was for divers years imployed by the right honb^le the then Secretaries of State in divers businesses and particularly att Weymouth for the dispatch of his Maties lres. to and from foreign parts (as by their Commissions under hand

and seale more at large may appear). And was also confirmed therein under the Royal Signett Manuall, & there remained until the Earle of Essex possessed the same.

That the petitioner is the only Clerke that was ever turned out of his imployment in the said office, cast into prison and went to Oxford to service his Matie, wherein he hazarded life and spent his whole estate to the ruyne of himselfe wife and childeren, & in his Maties service also was slaine his aged Father att 74 yeares, under the Command of the Right Honble the Earle of Northampton att Edgehill, to the great griefe, losse, and dammage of y^r petitioner.

That yor pet^r (after 8 years experience in his Maties service & losse of his employment) by means of friendes gott into the said office againe, wherein wth great paines & difficulties he hath continued for the space of 9 yeares and contracted many infirmities of body, and much impared his health being altogether uncapable of any other imploym^t.

The premises considered

He most humbly praies yor most sacred Matie to grant the continuance of yor pet^rs imployment in the said office during his life under the accustomed sallaries, proffitts and priviledges allowed and paied unto him for severall yeares past by the Farmer and govern^r of the said office, for the preservation of himselfe and familie from utter ruyne.

And yor pet^r (as in duety bound) shall ever pray &c.

(No date and no endorsement. S.P Dom. Chas. II, Vol. VI, No. 104.)

APPENDIX B

(Taken by James Hickes of the Letter Office.)

A List of Mr. Muddiman's correspondance taken yᵉ 27 and 29 Novʳ and yᵉ first of Decemʳ 1665 and yᵉ due post sett at yᵉ end of them as the [sic] ought to have bin paid. (S.P. Dom., Vol. 138, No. 23, I.)

Monday Dec. yᵉ 27. 65. For yᵉ Cittye and Kent.

	d.
John Burroughs, yᵉ Citty rememʳ.	2
Cornett Billing, Horseferry Westmʳ.	2
Sir Nathanil Lowell, near Maidstone.	4
Cornett Devonshire, Bishopsgate St.	2 x
Minheer Vanduisen, Antwerp.	4 x
Monsieur Puffendorffe,¹ à Parris.	4 x
Sir William Clerke, at yᵉ Cockpitt.	2
Countiss of Thanet, Tunbridge.	4 x
Mr. Anthony Cowley, at yᵉ Rose Tavern in Canterbury	

Wensday yᵉ 29. 65.

John Burroughs, Citty Remembʳ.	2
Sir William Clerke, at yᵉ Cockpitt.	2

¹ Monsieur Puffendorf was interviewed in Paris in 1668. See Robert Francis's letters to Williamson of April 8/18 and 11/21, 1668. He was evidently a writer of some importance and one of the editors of the Paris *Gazette*. There are a number of references to Puffendorf, and in the Calendar for 1668 Puffendorf has been misread " Puttendorf," and is thus entered in the Index.

Mr. Beale, Talbott in Fleet Street.   2
Sir Ralph Vernon, Russell Street.   4
Mr. Jacobson, Stillyard.   2
Countis Devonshire, Bishopsgate street   2 x
Mr. Watts, in Deale.   4 · ·
Sir John Griffith, at Gravesend.   4
Mr. Smith, deputie clerke of the passage, at Margate 4 x
Mr. Dallet, in Rye.   4 x
Mr. Carlisle, Dover.   4 · ·
Mr. Coney, Chirurgion at Chatham.   4 x
Monsieur Puffendorffe, à Parris.   4 x

Fryd. Dec. ye 1. 65.

Mr. John Burrough, Citty Remem^r.   2
Mr. Hewiett, Castle Tavern Fleet St.   2
Countiss of Devonshire.   4 x
Sir William Clerke.   4
Sir William Swann, Hamborough.   8 · ·
Minheer Vanduisen, Antwerp.   8 x
Mr. James Harrison.   4
Sir Nathaniel Powell, near Maidstone.   8 x
Mr. Anthony Cowley, Canterbury.   4 x

Tewsday, Nov. ye 28. 1665.
Chester Road and Ireland.

Sir John Packington, nere Droytwich.   5 x
Daniell Flemington Esq, [sic, Le Fleming], Kendall. 5 · ·
Jo. Adams, Esq, at Istod Hall, nr. Whitchurch.   5 x
Rich Warnesley Esq, at Duckenhall Lanca .   5 x
Samuel Bathurst Esq, Dublin.   8 x
Lord Arch. Bishopp of Cashill, Ireland.   8 x
Capt. Marke Davis, at Tripleton, Ludlow.   5 x
Lord Leigh, at Stoneley, nere Coventry.   4 x
Lord Herbert of Cherbury, at Lyssen Mon^r.   5 x
Tho. Page Esq, in Dublin.   8 x

Sir Roger Bradshaw, Wigann. 5 . .
Sir Jeffery Shackerley, Chester. 5 . .
Francis Lord Angar [Aungier], in Dublin. 8 . .
Earle of Clanrickard, Gallaway. 8 x
Robert Leigh Esq, in Dublin. 8 . .
Coll. Talbot, in Dublin. 8 . .
Robert Johnson Esq, at yᵉ Minim Dub. 8 x
John Digby Esq, Stony Stratford. 4 x
Mr. Chaplin, at How, nere Tocester [Towcester]. 4 x
Sir Brian Broughton, at Beaudsert.
    [Beaudesert, Leighton Buzzard?] 5 x
Sir John Hanmer, nere Whitchurch. 5 x
Major Thorp, Chester. 5 x
Jo. Digby Esq, nere Stony Stratford. 5 x
Owen Feltham Esq, at Billing. 4 . .
Lady Mary Carew, near Coventry. 4 x
Lord Cholmondeley, nere Namptwich. 5 x
Mr. Bernard, in Bridgenorth. 5 x
Jo. Adams Esq, nere Whitchurch. 5 x

Satturday yᵉ 2 Decemʳ 65.
Chester and Dublin.

Jo. Adams Esq, nere Whitchurch. 5 x
Lord Herbert of Cherbury at Lyssen in Muʳ. 10 x
Earle of Clanrickard, in Ireland. 4 x
Lord Windsor, at Kitterminster. 5 x
Mr. William Wright, in Darby. 5 x
Coll. Talbott, in Dublin. 8 . .
Sir Jeffery Shackerley, Chester. 5 . .
Robert Leigh Esq, in Dublin. 8 . .
Lord Angire, in Dublin. 8 . .
Robert Johnson Esq, Dublin. 8 . .
Jo. Digby Esq, nere Stony Stratford. 4 x
Sir Roger Bradshaw, Wiggin. 5 . .
Mr. Ralph Hope, in Coventry. 4 x

Mr. Samuel Bathurst, in Dublin.	8 x
Tho. Page Esq, in Dublin.	8 x

Tewsd. Novr ye 28. 65.
North and Scotland.

His Grace ye Earle of Rothes, High Com^r.	1 fr. 6 x
Mr. Fras Lumley, Marchant in Hull.	5 x
Sir Jo. Munson K^{nt} Bartt. Lewton Lincoln^r.	5 x
Sir Roger Langley, Yorke.	5 x
Walter Walsh Esq, Houghton Hall, Fairbridge.	5 x
Doctor Tho. Smith, Cockermoth Carlisle.	5 x
Sir Francis Cobb, Beverley.	5 ..
Dr. John Sudbury, Deane of Durham.	5 x
Lord Allington, Horseheath, Newmarket.	4 x
Sir David Jenkins, Rippon.	5 x
Mr. Brookes, Chirurgion, Bridlington.	5 x
Sir Phillip Musgrave, Carlisle.	5 x

Thursday ye 30 Nov^r .65.
North and Scotland.

His Grace ye E. of Rothes, High Com^r.	1 fr. x
Lord Fanshaw, Ware Larke.	4 x
Jo. Davis, in Yorke.	5 x
Dr. Jo. Sudly, ye Deane of Durham.	5 x
Sir Will. Hickman, Newmarket.	4 ..
Jo Hatcher Esq, nere Stamford.	4 ..
Dr. Guy Charleton, Prebend. Durham.	5 x

Sattered. ye 2d. Decem^r. 65.
North and Scotland.

George Stirling Esq. Glovat, nere Glasco in Scotland.	6 x
His Grace E. Rothes.	1 fr. x
Lord Allington, nere Newmarket.	10 x
Do^r Sudbury, Deane of Durham.	10 x

Tewsdy. Nov. 28. 65.
Bristoll & Gloustʳ & South Wales.

Sir Edward Stradling, St. Donat's Castˡᵉ Glor.	5 x
L. Col. French, Hereford.	5 x
Sir Willm Aumont, Reading.	4 x
Sir Willᵐ Backhurst, at Swallowfield Bridg.	4 x
William Conane Esq, Recorder, Wells.	5 x
Capt. Jo. Morgan, Rupeire, Glamorganshr.	5 x
Sir Edward Mansell, Glamorganshr.	5 x

Thursd. 30 Novʳ. 65.
Bristoll, Gloucester & South Wales.

Sir Baynham Throgmorton, at Chase Hall in the Forest of Dean.	5 x
Jo. Price at Wistaton, nere Hereford.	5 x
Tho. Lloyd Esq, of Whitminster, Gloucestrsh.	5 x
Robert Atwood Esq, Bristow (Bristol).	5 x

Satturday 2 Decmʳ 65.
Bristoll, Gloucester. & South Wales.

Sir Will. Backhouse, Reading.	10 x
Sir Edw. Stradling, Glamorganshire.	10 x
Coll. Morgan, Rupere, Glamorganshr.	10 x
Lt. Coll. French, Hereford.	10 x
Jo. Hall Esq, at Usely.	10 x
Sir Edw Mansell, Glamorganshr.	10 x
Willm. Duckett Esq, Chipenham.	5 x
Mr. Fannen, at Tillerts, Maydenhead.	4 x
Sir Edward Poole, Cirneister [Cirencester].	5 x
— Stonor Esq, at Henly.	4 x

Tewsd. Novʳ. 28. 65.
Plymouth & Cornwall.

Mr. David Grosse, Plymouth.	5 d
Sir Francis Roles, at East Witherby, Sarum.	4 x

Sir Walter Yonge, Colleton, nere Hampton.	5 x
Mr. Will Symonds, Lanceston.	5 x
Mr. Staplehill, Dartmouth.	5 ..
Sir Willm. Portman, Orchard Portman.	5 x
Mr. Arrman (?) Exon.	5 x

Thursd. 30 Novr. 65.
Plymouth & Cornwall.

Mr. David Grosse, Plymouth.	5 ..
Mr. Courtney, in Salisbury, Bookseler,	4 x
Major Henshaw, Isle Jersey.	5 x

Satterday 2 Decemb. 65
Plymouth & Cornwall.

Sir Willm Portman, Orchard Portman.	10 x
Sir Francis Rolles, at Thetherley.	8 x
Mr. David Grosse, Plymouth.	10 ..
Mr. Knightbridge, Minister, Dorchester.	10 x
Sir Will. Windham, nere Taunton.	5 x
Mr. Henry Newle, at Tanton.	5 x

Those persons y^t are pricked at the end " .. " I see you write unto, those that are at ye end " x " I have wrote unto, and those not pricked nor crossed at ye end I suppose are out of use at present.

Second List by Jas. Hickes of the same dates.
(S.P. Dom., Vol. 138, No. 23, II.)

This list contains the same names and postage prices, but is without the dots and crosses.

At the end of this second list he has written " I owne 28."[*]

" For his own acc^t at least 76."

The back is indorsed " This is a list for your owne perticular and observation." The second list was probably sent to Williamson on December 2.

The list transcribed was probably sent after Hickes had sent out his circular in February 1666.

These lists were not annexed to Hickes's petition and appear to have been kept secret between Williamson and himself.

APPENDIX C

To the Right Hon. Henry, Lord Arlington, & Sir William Morice of his Ma^ts most Honble Privy Councill & Principall Secretaries of State &c.

The Humble Petition of James Hickes sen^r of the Letter Office, in London.

Sheweth.

That yor pet^r being advised of Mr. Henry Muddiman's dismission from any future service to your hon^rs and Mr. Williamson yor Hon^rs Secretarie and particular charge given yor Pet^r and the rest of the Officers in the Letter Office not to admitt any of the said Henry Muddiman's letters for the future to pass ffranck upon that account, as formerly they had done. Upon wch yor Pet^r considered it necessarie to give advise by L^r. to those Persons with whom Mr. Muddiman had under yor Hon^rs held correspondance and to acquaint them soe much. Which yor Pet^r accordingly did, by sending the letters unto them a copye of which is hereunto annexed. Which the said Mr. Muddiman understanding, hath in his several letters sent to all parts of this Kingdome endeavoured by his Calumnies and ill language to impair the creditt and good name of yor Pet^r, therein accusing yor Pet^r as detected of forgery. Which imputation if just would necessarily rendre yor Pet^r unfit for any place of trust or continuing the imploym^t in which he hath been a most paine full labourer since the first establishing the conveyance of Letters.

Now, for as much as yor Pet^r hath bin a member of this office for 28 yeares and imployed in many great trusts, as may appear by divers commissions and orders under the hands and seals of the Right Honble George Lord Digby and Sir Edward Nicholas his M^{ts} (of ever blessed Memory) Principall Secretaries of State. And since by the Postmaster General, deceased, in severall extraordinarie services, and since yor Hon^{rs} enterance unto these great affaires of State now managed by you. In all which God hath made him so happy as to receave your honours commands from tyme to tyme. In Order and Obedience to all which he hath justly, faithfully and diligently to the best of his judgm^t & skill as in the presence of Almighty God, discharged his duties therein, as a loyall, faithfull and obedient subject and servant.

May it therefore please yor Hon^{rs}

To consider yor Pet^{rs} condition

And as his Creditt and Reputation in matters of trusts in his said employment is the only estate and fortune for himselfe and familly to subsist by, That you will be in Mercie and Justice pleased to Command the said Henry Muddiman before you to justify his allegations secretly [sic] transmitted by him up and down the Kingdom to the wounding and blemishing yor Pet^{rs} good name and happiness, and soe farr as in him lyeth to destroy the same and if proved by him yor Pet^r submitting to yor Hon^{rs} judgment & punishment.

If not, that your Hon^{rs} will please to cause the said Henry Muddiman to repayre yor Pet^r in such manner and ways as yor Hon^{rs} shall thinck most fitt.

And for yor hon^{rs} long life and happiness yor Pet^r shall dayly pray."

———

NOTE.—This petition is calendared under the conjectural date of December 2, 1665, in the Calendar for 1665–6, p. 85, and is there asserted to annex the two lists of

Muddiman's correspondents. The petition clearly does *not* annex either of these lists but, as it states, Hickes's circular, and its date must have been March 1666, according to Hickes's own statements. The circular is set out in full in the text (*supra*, p. 187).

APPENDIX D

A Narrative of the discourses betwixt Mr. Henry Muddiman & James Hickes sen.r concerning his Correspondence, &c. May it please y.r Hon.rs.

1. I conceave it to be nere six yeares since Mr. Williamson gave me order from Mr. Sectr.y Nicholas for Mr. Muddiman's letters passing ffree. Which I diligently observed during Mr. Muddiman's sending to my hands for my care and dispatch.

2. That in August last the said Mr. Muddiman grew very strange and jelious in all his deportments towards me. And having an Oportunity of drincking accidentally with him, I took notice of his strangeness. Upon which hee said to me I had wrot to his correspondants and instanced Mr. Bowers in Yarmouth. To which I answered him it was true I had wrot to him, but it was in answer to one he wrote to me. Mr. Bowers his first and last letters I have to show to clere the same

3. That about Michaelmas last Mr. Muddiman sending his letters, barren of news, but the weekly intelligence of two sheets inclosed to helpe out. And as many as would have come near 30 shls. a night should they have been paid for, upon which I had some discourse with him about it, telling him the officers took notice of them and questioned their going ffree. Soe discoursing of the greatness of his letters and numerousness, telling him his sending the Common News-books to his correspondants might be of prejudice to the officers upon the severall

268

roads whose only perquisite is to send ye common printed news. And the (y) might judge my complying with him to be their prejudice they passing all my hands. At which hee huffed and said " What was that to me? " Where hee sent one he would send 20, the Office lost not by him nor them for they went upon the King's account. I told him we weare and so ought to be as careful in contracting the account upon the King as we were to see the Office not suffer loss. Soe we parted.

4. Mr. Muddiman complayning one post day for want of news, that he swore by his fayth hee had now or never to make a letter. Uppon which I took occasion to take notice unto him of the great number of letters hee sent and the few returned he had. To which he answered me that hee had order'd all his correspondants to address his letters to my Lord Arlington & Mr. Williamson and that was the reason.

5. It hath clearly appeared all along, his constant intelligence hath come from Yarmouth, Deale, Dover, Plymouth and Norwich. Soe it's playne the numerous-ness of his letters were not for the Kings service. But his great advantage, having yearly stypends for the same from the greater number, from forty shillings to above forty pounds a person. And his charg of his letters to the King have come to many hundreds of pounds since he was intrusted in that service. Yet never appeared to my Lord Arlington, or Mr. Williamson, until his coming to Oxford, of the great numbers of letters he weekly sent. Then his Ma^{tys} service, committed to the care and order of Mr. Williamson requiring the largest and most exactest account of intelligence, found not one letter in answere to most of the letters hee sent. Soe this discovering, it settled in this manner. Hee was in short tyme dismissed from any future service therein. And if I am not mis-informed, he hath addressed and sent letters of other business, in which neither the King nor himself was

concerned, to the end they might goe free, to the prejudice
of the office & charge of the King, &c.

6. That Mr. Muddiman in Decm^r last transmitted all
his letters under cover to one Mr. Edmund Sawtell in the
Letter Office, for him to dispose of, not in the least giving
notice thereof to me, that had so long faithfully served
him therein. And contrary to Mr. Williamson's knowledge, or order for the same.

7. That Mr. Muddiman, about 16 or 17 of February
last, coming to enquire whether his letters went free as by
order of the Right Honble Sr. William Morice, by Mr.
John Cooke, upon direction of his pacquettes, I tould
him yea.   Well, he said, now my letters will goe and come
free as formerly. I answered, " not by that Order,"
for that Order related only to that pacquett.   Soe no
more would goe by that order, for what letters came for
him he must pay for, that Order took noe notice of them.
He then said hee would hand Mr. Secretarie Morice, his
generall order for all.   Which as yet is not come to the
office.

8. After this discourse I friendly desired of him the
reasons of his dismission from my Lord Arlington & Mr.
Williamson.   A discourse wee had, the substance of
which was as followeth.   First, hee did not believe my
Lord knew anything of it.

Secondly that Mr. Williamson had little correspondance
but what hee had gott for him.   Thirdly that Mr.
Williamson had in designe for a yeare past or more to
gett the publick Intelligence into his hand.   And the
better to accomplish the same, Mr. Williamson had
several tymes desired a list of his correspondants names
Which hee refused, and that caused him to stay the longer
with him, knowing hee could but send to the office and
have it.   Otherwise hee had left him long before.   And
now Mr. Williamson haveing got his desires in the Gazett.
It was much better for him now with Mr. Secretarie

Morice then before. To the first I answered him I did
believe Mr. Williamson dismissed him, not without my
Lord's knowledge. To the second I knew Mr. Williamson
had correspondance before him and without him. To
the third that I believed he had never designed or desired
to get the Publick Intelligence into his hands. But I
did believe it was by the King's command & my Lord
Arlington's that putt him upon it. To which Mr. Muddiman replyed he believed the King knew nothing of it.
Then I answered, " It seems strange to me and I could
not believe hee would medle into such a thing when an
other Person had a Pattent for it, except by speciall
command & authoritie."

9. Then the said Mr. Muddiman tould me I had noe
correspondance but by his letters. I answered him I
had four weekely from him by Mr. Williamson's order, to
pleasure 4 correspondants, which they before were
constant in writing to me and that formerly I had a
general correspondance, before I thought he was capable
of writing a letter, and what he had long wrot, was but
from the sight of the letters of my Lord's, Mr. Williamson's, their friends and servants, and not by the product
of his own intelligence and that I conceived he would
want much to write. Hee answered mee he would write
as full and large in all respects, with as much freedom as
before. And before the Gazett, I tould him that hee
should not do, except by the Satturday's post and that
would not signifie much. For coming to a conclusion
hee wished there were noe news printed, for it was against
his interest, I tould him I did believe as much.

10. And lastly, some few days after hee came in a very
great huff and heat and tould mee hee understood I had
wrote to his correspondants, that hee was putt off from
my Lord Arlington and Mr. Williamson, and that he
could not write much now, and pressed me to write to
them all, to recall the same, for that hee would write as

formerly. I answered I should not write to recall anything. Nor had I wrote anything but that I would owne
to any persons that were in authoritie to require the same.
Hee tould me then hee would write. I desired him to
let me know what he would write and I would write too.
Soe in this heat we parted and I have not seene him
since, but heard of him, by those scandalous lines which
occasions my humble petitioning your hon^rs.

Indorsed " Narrative of severall discourses betwixt
Mr. Muddiman and James Hickes Senr."

The Summary of this document on page 484 of the
Calendar for 1665–6 is as follows :

" Statement by Jas Hickes of *his correspondence* [*sic*]
with Hen. Muddiman. Had orders six years since from
Sec. Nicholas to let Muddiman's letters pass free and
attended carefully to them, but Muddiman grew cold in
August, and said Hickes had written to his correspondents,
reproached him with abuse of his privilege of sending
free. He received few letters back and therefore, though
he sent so many letters, receiving from 40s. to £40 each
from his correspondents, the King was little benefited.
This was found out when the Court was at Oxford and he
was dismissed from further service. He still tried to
get his letters passed free and pretended he was dismissed
because Williamson wanted to get the Gazette into his
own hands, that the chief correspondence both of
Williamson and Hickes was gained through him and
declared though he was *no longer able to see private letters*
[*sic*] he would write as good news as before." [2¼ pages.]

APPENDIX E

Hickes's Letter to Williamson, dated June 30, 1667

This letter is occasioned by some rules offered by S^r. John Benett, Saturday night, to ye officers in the Inland letter office.

S^r. I wrot you two or three lynes ffryday morning and then hoped to have wayted upon you Satturday morning, but business and Sr. Johns commands prevented and when I shall have such an opportunitie I am not yet certaine of, though ye sight of you, and ye oportunitie of halfe (an) hower's discourse is desired by me, as a woman in travail for safe deliverie. Sr. Satturday night, Sr. John Benett, about 10 or 11 a clock, declared to my selfe and ye rest of ye officers that wee must pay for all our letters and that wee must not send any more news bookes, for that by their passing their letters free they might give conveyance to what letters they pleased to ye damage of the office. And for ye news books, it was of great value and not to be suffered, saying hee would have every one to give account of what hee sent and to whom and hee would take care of them. S^r upon this I tooke the boldness to answer him that it was ever to this tyme the only priviledge the clerkes and Postmas^{trs} had for their single letters free, but what letters were posted inclosed was for ye more safe and quick delivery and not in the least to the damage or losse to ye office.

273

And for my part I did believe I had many for one, in respect (to) what the other clerks had, but not one of particular service to myself but concerned yᵉ office or some correspondents of yoᵣₛ, *of whom you instructed me to manage* 30 *or* 40 *twice weekly* (Italics mine) and for my part I would not pay for any single letter to my selfe whatsoever. They should lye undelivered as unanswered. Neither should I decline my newsbooks, for as my principalls was if I served for sixpence to serve as justly as for thousands and I should as in yᵉ sight of God and not as an eye servant. But if I must be reduced in my sallary and lose yᵉ advantage of my newsbooks, I would rather withdraw my selfe and live with salt and watter. And that it seemed strange to me to hear of such a prohibition from the governor of this office (the former persons, governors, rather blaming the clerkes for remissness in not writing and corresponding with yᵉ postmasᵗʳˢ to redress and set things right, & freedom for what books or postage they desired from yᵉ clerks). And further tould him that from the beginning to this daye the correspondance betwixt the clerks and Postmasᵗʳˢ had bin the only cause of directing and maintaining yᵉ settlement of Correspondance into all parts of yᵉ Kingdome from yᵉ Crown roads and how their correspondance should now bee a damage I understood not. However hee insisted still upon his owne will, but heard me with patience. Sir John was pleased to suggest to the officers hee took notice they had not aplyed themselves to him and hee was not obliged to seeke them, or to comply with their desires. I answered him, Sr. if they failed in applying themselves possibly I was to blame, telling them it never was the custom of the officers, & that it would not signifie more than to render them some wayes defective. And that it was Sir Phillip Frowd's last part to have acted to (have) surrendered to Sʳ John a clere and free possession of these offices and officers, but in these particulars he failed (going out like the snuff of a candle, never saying to his officers, farewell, nor to any one of us that he was going). I tould Sr John soe farr as ever I could and might deserve they (would) be my last words unto him, I knew not one officer there but he was a just and an honest man and discharged his trust accordingly, and did justly deserve the continuance of his imployment, and encouragement rather then to be reduced in sallary or any of his news books, &c. And I tould Sr John I sent ye first letters that were sent and kept ye Chester road, and knew from y^t seed ye cropps now gather and humbly desired that hee would not take away or obstruct his officers in their common ordinarie and usual perquisites least it may secretly create a worme in the body, which may prove a destruction as well as all former encouragement and advantages had proved prosperous. Indulgence and support draws just actions, miseries and poverty creates carelessness. And if the security declared be carried on here and abroad, let me speake my thoughts, and says, the prosperity and in course of this office is at best; and, as I tould Sr John, had hee not a heart of stone and considred the services his eyes beheld was done him, hee would rather advance and incourag them then to reduce them. But with all I tould him, I wish your security, destroy not your prosperity, for I believe that ye course you take is destructive. Sr John said he could have 40 officers y^t wanted imployments. I tould him I did believe so and more. But I tould him, it was not his class, with swords at their sides (and) velvet jacketts of their backs that would doe their business. From such as from favour to great friends or persons might be admitted. Of which kind we had such as proved as very rogues & cheats as ever Newgate had inside. And, as God had made me an instrument of rooting them out and soe as to see this office settled soe as at present I thinck to the view of Sr John, Mr. Ellis and others concerned, if they please, it will appear the office cannot be wronged one penny nor hapeny—of which small sums we have to account with.

Sr, I might say more to our Satturdayes discourses, but I shall not venture farther, fearing I might be to troublesome. Sʳ, how far I have been judged serviceable to my Lord and you, you best know, as farr as I may be usefull at present and future tyme must make out. And as I am deprived by business and attendance of such oportunities as might be most convenient to wayte upon you, let me humbly pray and desire your favour in making known my condition to my Lord, and of us all. And that you will please to take notice to Sr. John of what I here write if you think fitt. And when you have soe done as to honʳ mee with two lynes what will come of mee and my [sic] myne and of us all—Sʳ yet one passage may not be forgotten. Sr. John hearing me patiently and kindly and came to me and tould me hee intended not that to my sallary as to others and that hee would not doe anything without my advise. But for the news-books, hee must not suffer to pass. To which I returned him most humble thanks for any favour or respects, but if hee took away my bookes he might please alsoe to take my sallarie. And soe God bless him and yᵉ Office. But soe long as I was concerned there I would send the news untill it pleased him to take them up and burne them. And how he could put an obstruction upon them for this six months I knew not, without violating my Lord's settlement with the postmasᵗʳˢ in generall for six months, beg-ing June 25 and ending December yᵉ 25, 1667. Which settlement is that they have to stand upon the same termes and sallaries as before. Soe abridging them of their news books and making them paye for their letters will prove of sad consequence and be an obstruction to their future settlement, if not absolute destruction. (It) cannot be thought men will work themselves day and night and spend their substance for those that will screw them soe close and noe incouragement. I desired Sr. John as he wished my Lords honor and happiness to consider well the prosperity of this office. Hee tould mee I could not but knowe my Lord gave great rent and more than ever and how hee must take care to improve all things towards it. I answered I was not altogeather a stranger (to) what was to be paid, nor was I all together a stranger in knowing how it should be paid. And as I was a servant I hated and scorned to eat my master's bread and doe him the least damage in the world knowingly. Soe I should say no more to that but leave all to his consideration.

While I am a servant I am comanded by God Almighty to doe fayr and faithfull service, and soe by his gratious helpe & assistance I will (But when at libertie I am to seeke a lively hood honestly), Sr. as I have ever served his Matie, my Lord (and) you. And most of all the ministers of State in ye kingdome in ye tymes of danger and sickness & in tymes of health. Let me not want your favour I beseech you, to acquaint my Lord with my condition. And Sir John alsoe (to whose desires I have to the best of my judgment given my judgment in relation to all their affairs, and shall as farther requested). And that you will be pleased to move them here, for my settlement and my favour. And some few lynes from your hand to-morrow night with your letters if possibly that I may know my Lord's and Sir John's pleasure, that by the same I may studdey a cheerful proceeding as in my business, or seeke prudently out for myne and my family's future preservation. Which I must take care to provide for or else I am worse than an infidel. Sr. As I ever took delight in ye receipt of your commands and observing them justly and quickly, soe I beseech you once more pardon all the trouble of these lines and as you desire my Lords honr. in the concernes of this office, soe favour me, his honr^s most humble & most obedient servant, grting his will and pleasure to my humble and earnest desires. Soe the Lord of his infinite mercie keepe you (in) it.   I am

Sr.

Yor most obliged and obedient servant

JAMES HICKES.

Lond. June 30, 1667.

(S.P. Dom. Chas. II, Vol. 207, No. 123.)

APPENDIX F

Honor'd Sʳ.

I cannot rest quite silent, but intimate to yoᵣˢᶠ chiefly the rendition used by Sʳ John Bennet as to settlement of postmasters here, hee resolving to bring yᵐ to yᵉ rate of twentie shillings per mile. Which reduceth postmasters from £40 per annum to £20, and soe proportionably, more or less. And (he) soe harshly treats them that if they do not imediately comply, they must with harshness out of his sight and not (be) farther treated with. Severall are settled so but with much disgust. So with others, making one contract one night and flying from it next day, that makes men doubt so farr that they are to be removed at pleasure. For our own poore porters, being two, who sitt dayly and night weekly, their sallaries formerly 10 and 11 shillings per weeke, and had sixpence for sending expresses coming to Whitehall, must now, they understand, have but six shillings per weeke & nothing for forwarding yᵉ expresses. For all our letter carriers, in number above 30, which had 8 shillings a week, this morning are informed by Sʳ John and Mr. Ellis and by me, from him, that they must have but 6 shillings a weeke. What all things will come unto as to my Lord's and his advantage tyme must produce, but those that wish yᵉ preservation of my Lords honour

279

and his interest herein are at a stand, yet upon all occasions have declared themselves against these severe proceedings, as judging them inconsistent with hon^r and interest. Of which I shall say little more.

This month I have been concerned in the forreign office as well as the inland, spending my mynd and strength in both 5 nights in the week, which service hath been exceedingly severe upon me. Especially (as) to my dyet. I have putt ye forreign office cleerly into ye method of ye inland, that they may clerely see what they have and how. Which by former Governors included and positively said were impossible. I am certain it will turn to account many hundreds of pounds per annum if not more. And though I am, and my wife, (which troubles mee now) are tould I am designed to ruine for my progress, when I have served their turne, rather than to be countenanced and preserved, yet I value it not. It shall never be said while God gives me strength and abilities but I will spend my spiritts in the faythful discharge of my trust ; y^t when I am cast off as useless, yet enemitie it selfe shall not saye its own eye servant or unjust.

I have one thing more to saye, that I understand Sr Phillip Froud hath soe recommended to Sr John his boye, that wayted upon him & served him. Which some few months since, hee put into ye office to receive letters at the window. To be of these singular parts and knowledge of the affaires of the office farr beyond Mr. Parsons, our accountant & my selfe (I must confess it's a correction to make a boye steward, but of noe honour for himselfe, otherwise hee would have putt him to doe that which hee omitted and left others to doe). And I suppose last night hee made use of him, for after my Chester maile was made up and the Northerne maile made up, fit for conveyance, Sr John caused them (to be) carried up into his chamber and this young gentleman, Mr. Leeson, with him, opened the mails and baggs, to what end or purpose

they best know nor I gather not. It may be to see what
gazetts I send on my roade, but if I have any taken
away or obstructed I shall heare of it. And if I deserve
not from my Lord the sallaries and those perquisites, as
my Gazetts, for the preservation of his Maties revenue in
ye violent tyme of contagion and his hon^{rs} interest to this
day, as formerly I injoyed them, from ye most nearest
and savingest grounds and masters interest, I hope my
Lord will signifie his pleasure and if hee shrink my
services (and I) deserve not what I have, I shall submitt.
But upon my word as a just and honest man where [*sic*]
it not for the duties and service I owne and shall ever
acknowledge to be due to my Lord from mee and yourselfe
alsoe, these proceedings and dayly discouragements
would make me desist and others alsoe. For my owne
part I shall say little. Those that I have served may
speak truth if they please; justly to the contrary of my
paynes and integritie they cannot. But for Mr. Parsons,
I shall say, here is the ablest, most dilligent and payne-
fullest accountant that ever sett penn to paper here,
transcending all former as to his method and generall
knowledg in both offices or (few) is now to be (nosed?) by
a boye. I hope Sr John will not need any other advise
then soe great a proficient in parts and knowledge (as
Sr Phillip hath presented him to be) can afford. All this
that I have wrote is onely for your own sattisfaction,
make what you please of it, and though I am not soe well
as to wayte upon you my self now, nor doe I know ever
or never, yet be pleased to know that there is not a man
that lives, hon^{rs} my Lord more justly. Nor shall more
faythfully improve his interest then
                              Sir
Yo^r most humble & faythfull servant for ever
                                    JAMES HICKES.

Lond. July ye 2, 1667.

Sr,   My sallarie is and hath bin £100 p. annum. The gazetts upon Tuesdays, 15 dussen and 3 or 4 odd ones, the gazetts upon Thursdays, 17 dussen some odd ones. Some to particular friends that never paid a penny. Some paye 2d a gazett, & the most but threepence. Sent into Ireland 2. For which I humbly crave my Lords favour and allowance, under his honors hand if you thinck fitt, to support me against all dayly discouragements, other wise my last days wilbe needfull.

(S.P. Dom. Car. II, Vol. 208, No. 36.)

APPENDIX G

NEWS-LETTERS OF HENRY MUDDIMAN IN THE STATE
PAPERS, WRONGLY ASCRIBED TO OTHER WRITERS, OR
NOT IDENTIFIED HITHERTO

NOTE.—The following news-letters by Henry Muddiman
can be traced in the Calendars of State Papers by their
dates. Those to which no comment has been added
have not hitherto been identified. Those asserted in the
Calendars of the late Mrs. Green to be the work of Robert
Francis or other writers have been identified by comparison with Henry Muddiman's original draft. News-
letters correctly attributed in the Calendars to Henry
Muddiman have not been included in this list.

Date.		*Address.*
July	27, 1666.	
July	30, ,,	(Haarlem.)
Sept.	29, ,,	Mr. Nowell, Stationer, Norwich.
Oct.	11, ,,	George Powell, Pembroke.
Aug.	15, 1668.	(Wrongly stated to have been sent by Francis to Williamson.)
Aug.	18, ,,	(Wrongly stated to have been sent by Francis to Williamson.)
Aug.	18, ,,	(Wrongly stated to be by Rob. Francis.) To Dr. Ludkin, Ipswich.
Aug.	20, ,,	To Mr. Warner, Winchester. (Wrongly stated to have been sent by Francis to Williamson.)
Aug.	25, ,,	

Aug.	27, 1668	To Mr. Saunders, Scarborough. (Wrongly attributed to Francis.)
Aug.	29, ,,	To Sir Edward Hungerford, M.P., Bath. (Wrongly attributed to Francis.)
Sept.	3, ,,	To Hugh Hodges, Sherborne (Wrongly. attributed to Francis.)
Sept.	5, ,,	To Rich. May (M.P.) Chichester. (Wrongly attributed to Francis.)
Oct.	17, ,,	To Sir Edward Hales, M.P., Sittingbourne.
April	4, ,,	(Calendar of 1670 Addenda.) To the Mayor of Bodmin, Cornwall. (Wrongly ascribed to Francis.)
Jan.	13, 1670.	Robert Aldworth, Town Clerk of Bristol.
Feb.	26, ,,	Mr. Scawen at Molenack, Plymouth.
April	16, ,,	Wm. Coward, Recorder of Wells.
April	19, ,,	H. Norman.
April	23, ,,	Sir Philip Honeywood, Governor of Portsmouth.
April	26, ,,	Wm. Ducket, M.P.
April	30, ,,	Jacob Layfield, King's Searcher at Harwich.
May	3, ,,	John Gauntlett of Salisbury.
May	5, ,,	Thos. Hill, Prebendary of Salisbury.
May	12, ,,	Francis Buller, M.P.
June	9, ,,	Thos. Bard, Haberdasher, Hereford.
June	14, ,,	Sir Walter Moyle of St. Germans.
June	27, ,,	Gilbert Staplehill, Dartmouth.
July	2, ,,	Wm. Coward, Wells.
July	5, ,,	Mr. Smyth, Clerk of the Passage, Deal.
July	12, ,,	Gilbert Staplehill.
July	14, ,,	Thos. Cole, Custom House, Southampton.
July	28, ,,	— Eldred, Colchester.
Aug.	16, ,,	Kirk, Cambridge [the Coffee-house].
Aug.	23, ,,	W. Symonds, Launceston.

Aug. 25, 1670	Mr. Cole, Custom House, Southampton.
Aug. 30, ,,	W. Symonds, Launceston
Sept. 3, ,,	Edw. Berkeley, Dorset.
Sept. 27, ,,	Sir Phil. Honeywood.
Oct. 27, ,,	Rob. Aldworth, Town Clerk, Bristol.
Oct. 29, ,,	Wm. Scawen, Molenack, near Plymouth.
Nov. 3, ,,	Mr. Warner, White Hart, Winchester.
Nov. 17, ,,	*Ibid.*
Nov. 19, ,,	Hen. Newte, Tiverton.
Dec. 8, ,,	Mr. Worth, Collector, Falmouth.

(NOTE.—The heading " Whitehall " is omitted in the Calendaring of the following letters.)

May 6, 1671.	To Samuel Goodwyn, Woodbridge, Suffolk.
May, 9, ,,	To Mr. Kirke (Coffee-house), Cambridge.[1]
May 13, ,,	Robt. Stanton, St. Edmunds Bury.
May 11–18 ,,	Robt. Aldworth, Town Clerk of Bristol.
May 23, ,,	Earl of Exeter, Burleigh.
May 27, ,,	Robt. Stanton, Bury St. Edmunds.
May 30, ,,	Earl of Exeter.
June 1, ,,	Capt. Welsh, Rye,
June 3, ,,	Sir William Wyndham, Orchard Wyndham.
June 6, ,,	William Symonds, Launceston.
June 8, ,,	Mr. Mawson, Postmaster, Hull.
June 10, ,,	Sir Ed. Hungerford, Farley Castle, Chippenham.
June 13, ,,	Mr. Norman, Under-sheriff of Devon.
June 15, ,,	Mr. Coles, Customs House, Southampton.
June 17, ,,	Robt. Stanton, Bury, Suffolk.
June 22, ,,	Mr. Courtney, Bookseller.

[1] See Roger North's *Life of Dr. John North*, in reference to the letters to Kirke.

June 24, 1671		Thos. Stonor, Watleton Park, Henley.
June 29,	,,	Mr. Warne, The White Hare, Winchester.
July 1,	,,	John Davies, Hereford.
July 4,	,,	Thos. Bampfield, Dorchester.
July 6.	,,	John Dawes (*sic* Davies), Excise Office, Hereford.
July 8,	,,	Thos. Wall, near the Tolzee, Bristol.
July 18,	,,	Gilbert Staplehill, Dartmouth.
July 20,	,,	John Celey, Orchard Portman, Taunton.
July 22,	,,	Wm. Scawen, Molenack, Plymouth.
July 25,	,,	Walter Tucker, Lyme.
July 27,	,,	John Davies, Excise Office, Hereford.
July 29,	,,	Sir Edward Poole, Kemble, Cirencester.
Aug. 1,	,,	Gilbert Staplehill, Dartmouth.
Aug. 3,	,,	Geoffrey Daniell, Marlborough.
Aug. 5,	,,	Wm. Scawen, Molenack, Plymouth.
Aug. 8,	,,	Walter Tucker, Lyme.
Aug. 10,	,,	Sir Rich. Everard, Newhall, Essex.
Aug. 12,	,,	Robert Stanton, St. Edmunds Bury.
Aug. 15,	,,	Sir Ed. Hungerford, Farley Castle, Bath.
Aug. 19,	,,	William Scawen.
Aug. 24,	,,	Mr. Worth, Collector, Falmouth.
Aug. 25,	,,	William Scawen.
Aug. 31,	,,	Mr. Saunders, Scarborough.
Oct. 26,	,,	,, ,, ,, ,,
Oct. 28,	,,	William Scawen.

(After this date the thefts apparently ended.)

INDEX

ABERIN, Major, 127
Adultery Act, of the Rump, 28 *n.*
Albemarle, Duke of (*see* Monck, George).
Alleyn, Sir Thomas, Lord Mayor, 67, 79, 101, 103
Amy, ——, news-letter writer, 213
Anabaptists, and baptists, 21; and Fifth Monarchy, 22–27; denounce their own followers, 25–26
Annesley, Arthur (Earl of Anglesey), 37, 40 *n.*; President of Council of State, 106
Appeal, the, 216–218
Apprentices, of London, petition of, 78; five killed by Hewson, 79; rising of, 96
Arlington, Lord (*see* Bennet, Sir Henry).
Army, the, 18–22; pay of, 18 and *n.*; mutinies, 80; second mutiny, 96; address to Monck, 115
Ashton, Colonel, 58
Atkins, Alderman Thomas, 16 *n.*
Aubrey, John, 88, 90

Ball, Henry, 194, 201–202
Barebone, Praise-God, petitions Rump, 102, 129; and seditious tracts, 109
Barebone's Parliament, 15; and civil marriage, 27
Barkstead, John, 44
Barnadiston, Sir Samuel, 226
Bate, George, 135 *n.*
Bath, Earl of (*see* Grenvile, Sir John).
Bedloe, William, 217
Belasyse, Lord, 55 *n.*, 123
Bennet, Sir Henry (Earl of Arlington), 144, 162, 163; Post-

master, 173; letter to L'Estrange, 174; ignorance of office affairs, 178, 181, 195
Bennet, Sir John, Deputy Postmaster, 196; takes Hickes to a tavern, 196; stops abuse of free postage, 197; Hickes's insolence to, 198–199; turns Hickes out of Office cellars, 200
Berkenhead, Sir John, 124
Bethel, Slingsby, 224, 225, 228
Bickerstaff, Isaac (*see* Swift, Jonathan).
Blount, Charles, 216
Booth, Sir George, 62, 63
Bradshaw, John, 61; death of, 71; his iron hat, 71; his perquisites, 71; Charles I's contempt for, 72; songs about, 72 and *n.*, Nedham's eulogy of, 72. 75 *n.*
Brathwaite, Richard, 31
Brewster, Anne, 218
Brewster, Thomas, 142, 143, 158, 159; conviction and death of, 171, 218
Bristol, 2 *n.*, 238
Brome, Joanna, 220
Bromhall, Thomas, 203 *n.*
Brook, Peter, 65
Brookes, Nathan, 158; conviction of, 171
Browne, Sir Richard, Lord Mayor, 136–141
Butler, Samuel, and Fifth Monarchy, 22; ridicules Rump, 70; character of Shaftesbury, 106, 107

Calamy, Edmund, 244
Calmady, Josias, M.P., 127
Calvert, Elizabeth, 158, 169, 170; death, 171, 217 *n.*
Calvert, Giles, biography of, 142, 158, 159; death of, 161 *n.*, 169

287

Canne, John, 32, 33; official journalist, 45; his manifesto, 46; supplanted by Nedham, 66; resumes journalism, 76; his periodicals, 77; journalist of the Rump, 84, 112, 126; attacks Muddiman, 128; is suppressed, 130

Care, Henry, 211, 212, 213

Catherine of Braganza, Queen of Charles II, 86, 212

Chapman, Livewell, 108, 109; proclamation for his arrest, 110, 142, 143, 169

Charles I, murder of, 15, 18 n.; statue of, 107

Charles II, Willys's plot to murder, 61–62, 87; his Declaration from Breda, 117; proclaimed King, 119–120; return of, 121; his reception of Monck, 121; and the Solemn League; his annoyance about a newsletter, 205–207; dissolves first Parliament, 213; dissolves second Parliament, 213; and third Parliament, 213; appeals to the Nation, 237–238; dispenses with a Parliament, 238; retaliates on whigs, 241; death of, 244

Child murder, 28

Clarges, Sir Thomas, 64; delivers message to Rump, 68; advises Committee of Safety, 75; disbands Army, 123

Cleiveland, John, 14

Clubs, origin of, 89; the Commonwealth and Rota clubs, 89

Cobbet, Colonel, 68, 74

Cobbett's "State Trials" (see "State Trials").

Coffee, first advertised, 14 n., 89 n.

College, Stephen, the Protestant joiner, 211; his Ra-Ree Show, 236 and n., 246

Combes, ——, 219

Committee of Safety, 41; reconstituted, 71, 75; attacks the City, 76, 78; its proposals, 79; collapses, 80

Commons, House of, 17, 18; members of Rump, 17 and n.; secluded members of, 38; character of Rump, 40; the "Representative," 42; vote of, 65; ejected by Lambert, 69; second restoration of, 81; roasting of the Rump, 104; Long Parliament restored, 105–106; Convention Parliament of 1660, 107, 117, 119, 120, 127; Long Parliament of 1661, 142, 148, 149; dissolved, 212; Parliament of 1679, 212; dissolved, 213; of 1679–1680, 225; corrupt, 225–226; insults the King, 228; dissolved, 231; Oxford Parliament, 231, 235; dissolved, 237 (see also Lords, House of).

Conservators of Liberty, 80

Cook, John, Under-secretary of State, 186, and n.; repeats order in Muddiman's favour, 190

Cooper, Anthony Ashley (Earl of Shaftesbury), Butler's character of, 106–107; foments Oates's plot, 210–211; conducts Press campaign, 211; The Speech of a Noble Peer, 228 and n.; indictment against thrown out, 242; absconds and dies, 243

Corbet, Jeffery, 35

Corney, Peregrine, 170

Cornish, Henry, 224, 228

Cotton, John, news-letter writer, 219

Council of Six, the, 153, 169, 170

Council of State: of the Rump, 41; of the Long Parliament, 106

Coventry, Henry, Secretary of State, 203

Coventry, Sir William, 204, 205, 206, 207

Creake, ——, seditious printer, 143

Cromwell, Oliver, and beer, 20 n.; his monument destroyed, 44 and n.; his cruelty, 58

Cromwell, Richard, 48

Crouch, Nathaniel, 215, 219

Curtiss, Langley, 212; his wife imprisoned, 231, 242

Darby, Michael, 107 and n.

Davenport, John, 157

Delaune, Thomas, 5 n., 221 n.

Desborough, John, 20, 68; presents petition to Rump, 68; Commissary-General, 70
" Divil of Dewsbury " (see Oldroyd, Robert).
Dockwra, William, 220 n., 221 and n., 222
Door of Hope, the, 136-139 and n.
Dover, 121
Dover, Simon, 171
Downing, Sir George, 184, 185
Duckenfield, Colonel, 69
Duckett, William, M.P., 147
Dunton, John, his characters, 214 and n.; his " Whipping Post," 240 and n.
Dury, Giles, 87 and n., 111

Earl's Court, 3, 167 n.
England at Restoration, 2
Etherege, Sir George, his Man of Mode, 205
Evans, Elizabeth, 169
Evelyn, John, translation of a Character of England, 6
Exeter College, Oxford, 52, 53

Fairfax, Lord, 55; and Monck, 63; in arms, 80, 140
Fairford, prodigies at, 132-133
Farnley Wood conspiracy, 168-171; tract on, 169 n.; predicted in " Panther Prophecy," 170 n.
Feake, Christopher, his hymn, 29 n.; his Beam of Light, 34
Fergusson, Robert, 211
Fifth Monarchy, and the anabaptists, 22-32; and a projected massacre, 34-35; rising in 1661, 136-141
Flatman, Thomas, 235
Fleetwood, Major-General Charles, 20; commissioned by Speaker, 47; petitions Rump, 67, 68; commission revoked, 68; one of the Nine Worthies, 68, 76, 81
Frowde, Sir Philip, Deputy Postmaster, 165, 196, 197, 198

Godfrey, Sir E. B., 209, 210, 225
Goodwin, John, 14
Goodwin, Thomas, 22 n.

Green, Mrs. M. A. E., her bad calendaring and mistakes, 174 n., 181, 184 n., 189 n., 192 n., 200 n. (see also summary on p. 272 in Appendices).
Grenvile, Sir Bevill, 51
Grenvile, Sir John (Earl of Bath), 52, 63; his interview with Monck, 114-115; sent to the King, 115; created Earl of Bath, 117; his reception by Parliament, 119
Grenvile, Sir Richard, 51, 52

Hacker, Francis, regicide, 89
Hackney coaches, 5 and n., 98
Haddock, Sir Richard, 205
Hall, Mr., Letter Office clerk, 182
Hall, John, Poet, 39 n.
Hancock, Jasper, news-letter writer, 219-220
Harby, Richard, 93 n.
Harrington, James, 89, 90
Harris, Benjamin, 211; his Strange News from Lemster, 214 n.; biography of, 214-215; publishes the " Appeal," 218, 223; Commons petitions for, and illegal release of, 227; his insult to the Lord Chief Justice, 227; is sent back to prison, 231; his domestic scandal, 246 and n.; revives his paper, 243; fines remitted by Charles II, 244; renewed plots of, 245; becomes first American journalist, 246; issues a Protestant Tutor, 246-247; prints Laws of Massachusetts, 247; fails as a Revolution journalist, 247-248; his London Post, 248; Dunton on, 248, 250, 255
Harrison, Thomas, Regicide, his biography, 25 n.; executed, 134
Henshaw, Thomas, of Kensington, 131
Henshaw, Thomas, Major, 61, 131, 139, 140
Herbert of Cherbury, Lord, 148
Hertford, Marquess of, 55
Hesilrige, Sir Arthur, 41, 68; opposes Lambert, 69, 89, 101; a quaker's remark to, 103; death of, 140

Hewitt, Rev. Dr., 58; petition of his widow, 58 *n.*

Hewson, John, Colonel, 19; kills City apprentices, 78, 79; indicted for murder, 92; song about, 92; dies from starvation, 93

Heyden, van der, 9

Hickes, James, Clerk in the Letter Office, 8, 145; biography of, 181 and *n.*; obtains list of Muddiman's correspondents, 183; sends list to Williamson, 183; Muddiman stops letters for, 183; attacks Sawtell, 184 and *n.*; his circular, 187; falsehoods of, 188, 189 and *n.*; his narrative, 190, 193; malpractices stopped, 196–197; complaints to Williamson, 197–200; steals Muddiman's newsletters in the post, 200–201 (*see also* his letters and documents in the Appendices).

Hill, Rev. William, informer, 152, 153 and *n.*

Hills, Henry, biography of, 91 *n.*

Hinton, Sir John, 53, 54, 104

Hobbes, Thomas, the philosopher of Malmsbury, 15, 16, 67, 94

Holles, Colonel Gervase, 40

Hopton, Sir Ralph (Lord Hopton of Stratton), 51

Hungerford, Sir Edward, 147

Innes, Captain Robert, 13

Intelligencers, 10 and *n.*, 11 and *n.*

Ireland, census of in 1659, 3 and *n.*

Ireton, John, Lord Mayor, 67

James, John, Fifth-Monarchy man 141–142

Janeway, Richard, seditious publisher; bail estreated, 242; his *Impartial Protestant* and its writers, 242–243

Jefferies, Sir George, Recorder of London, 226, 227

Jenkins, Sir Leoline, 203

Jenkyn, William, nonconformist, 234 and *n.*

Jessey, Henry, 33, 132, 133; and *Mirabilis Annus*, 154; his letter, 154 *n.*

Kiffen, William, 25, 49 *n.*

Lambert, John, Major-General, 20; date of his death, 21 *n.*; presented with deer, 46, 63 *n.*; returns to London, 67; petitions for a General, 68; ejects the Rump, 69, 70; marches against Monck, 75; his men disappear, 94; escape and capture of, 116, 117; Muddiman buys his wife's house, 166

Leicestershire, Gospel spirit of ministers of, 65, 152, 158

Lenthall, Speaker William, 38, 64, 69; excluded by Lambert, 69

L'Estrange, Sir Roger, his pamphlets, 109 and *n.*, 125; his biography, 130; Surveyor of the Presses, 151; his services 161; supersedes Muddiman, 162; his views about printed news, 163, 164; his "Relations," 164 *n.*; refused free postage, 165; price of his news-books, 165 and *n.*; letters to Lord Arlington, 175–178; imitates *Gazette*, 180; appeals to the King, 180, 193, 202; warning against whig papers, 223–224; attacks the Plot, 224, 231; his *Observators*, 233–235

Letter Office of England, 7, 8; burnt down, 193

Leyden, John of, 23

Lichfield, Leonard, Oxford University printer, 178

Life-guard of the Rump, 43

Lisle, John, 58 and *n.*

Lister, Sir William, 166

Lloyd, Owen, 29 *n.*

London, at Restoration, 2–5; refuses to pay taxes, 67; taxed £100,000 by Rump, 101; gates and posts of, 101; fire of, 161, 193

Lords, House of, 105, 109; prosecutes Francis Smith, 228; at Oxford, 237 (*see also* Commons, House of).

Ludlow, Edmund, regicide, falsehoods about the Rump, 17 *n.*, 68; falsehoods about Tonge's plot, 153 *n.*

Luttrell, Narcissus, 223, 226 n.

Macaulay, Lord, errors of, 1, 203, 221, 229, 234 and n., 236 and n., 246
Macock, John, printer, 90, 91, 92, 192, 193
Manton, Thomas, D.D., 151 and n.
Marten, Harry, 38 and n., 40, 89
Marvell, Andrew, 90, 211
Maxwell, David, bookseller, 125
Medley, William, 31
Middleton, Sir Thomas, 62, 63 n.
Miles, Mr., " intelligencer," 37, 48, 49
Milton, John, 38, 39, 90, 107, 108
Mirabilis Annus, 153 and n., 154–157, 161, 226–227
Monck, General George, his peremptory letter to the Rump, 47; biography and character, 50–54, 63, 68; action against English Army, 73–75; addresses Scots, 77; " Iter Boreale," 94; petitions to, 95, 96; and Devon, 96–97; enters London, 98; speech to Rump, 99; plot against, 100; destroys gates of City, 101–102; letters to Rump, 103–104; restores Long Parliament, 105–106; " Victor sine sanguine," 118 and n.
Monck, Nicholas, 53, 63, 68
Monmouth, Duke of (James Scot), 216, 217
Monson, William Viscount, 38 and n., 40
Moore, Sir John, Lord Mayor, 222, 242
Morice, Sir William, Secretary of State, 53, 97 and n., 113, 114–115; his motion in the House, 119; first Secretary of Charles II, 122; his paper, 181, 186; retains Muddiman, 187; aspersed in the preface to the Calendar of State Papers of 1665–1666, 189 n., 191, 192; resigns secretaryship, 202
Morland, Sir Samuel, 59 n., 60–61
Mortality, Bills of, 5 and n.
Muddiman, Alice, 85

Muddiman, Edward, 85, 86
Muddiman, Henry, 11, 12; birth of, 85; education of, 86; his first periodical, 87; and Dury, 87 n.; Pepys's mistake about, 88; and Macock, 90, 91; official journalist, 110–111; and Canne, 112; Monck's orders to, 115 and n.; description of Restoration by, 120–122; publishes the King's letter, 122; his Apologia, 129; attached to Secretary of State, 130; his offices, 145; his correspondents, 145–148, 149 and n., 151 and n.; and L'Estrange, 165; sends out the news-books, 166; his fee for news-letters, 166; his country house, 166, 167 and n.; does not trust Williamson, 172, 173; summoned to Oxford, 174–175; precautions against Hickes, 183; and Secretary Morice, 185; his seals, 186; his circular, 188, 190; writes Secretary Morice's paper, 191 and n.; and Current Intelligence, 193; writes down Gazette, 194–196; removes his offices, 203; and Sir George Etherege, 205; and the King, 206; and Sir Richard Newdigate, 207, 209, 224; describes debates on Exclusion Bill, 229–231, 235–236, 243, 245; dies at Coldhern, 245
Muddiman (or Muddyman) John, 85 n.
Muddiman, Sir William, 85 and n., 86
Münster, anabaptists of, 13, 14
Murray, Robert, 218, 221

Nedham, Marchamont, 14, 34 n., 45, 66 and n.; eulogy of Bradshaw, 72 and 75 n.; falsehoods of, 78, 80, 85, 109, 110; ejected, 111, hue and cry after, 111–112; pardoned, 112
Newcombe, Thomas, printer, 178, 193
Newdigate, Sir Richard, 207
News-books, 9–14; profits of, under Cromwell, 125; at Restoration, 125, 178

News-books, Titles of :
  Mercurius Politicus, 12
  Publick Intelligencer, 12
  The Weekly Information, etc., 13
  The Publick Adviser, 13
  Mercurius Britanicus, 14
  Faithful Intelligencer, 77 *n.*, 78
  Mercurius Britannicus, 77 *n.*
  An exact Accompt, 84
  The Parliamentary Intelligencer, 86, 87
  Mercurius Publicus, 87
  Mercurius Politicus (1660),112
  Publick Intelligencer (1660), 112
  Mercurius Aulicus (1660), 125
  Mercurius Democritus (1660), 125
  Mercurius Veridicus (1660), 125
  The Kingdom's Intelligencer (1661), 131
  Mercurius Caledonius, 131
  Nouvelles Ordinaires de Londres, 131
  The Newes, 163
  The Intelligencer, 163
News-letters, 10 and *n.*, 11 and *n.*, 130–131, 165 and *n.*, 166, 173 and *n.*, 185 and *n.*, 186–189, 219–221, 245
Newspapers, List of :
  Oxford Gazette, 178 ; date of, 178 *n.* ; is the first paper, 179 *n.* ; becomes *London Gazette*, 186
  Publick Intelligence, 180
  Current Intelligence, 191
  Domestick Intelligence (Harris) 214
  Domestick Intelligence (Thompson), 215
  Loyal Protestant, 216
  Observator, 234
  Heraclitus Ridens, 235
  Smith's Protestant Intelligence, 235
  Currant Intelligence, 239
  Impartial Protestant, 242–243
  Publick Occurrences (of Boston, America), 246
  London Post, etc., 248
Nicholas, Sir Edward, Secretary of State, 49, 122, 144

" Nine Worthies," the, 68, 93
North, Sir Francis, Lord Chief Justice of the Common Pleas, 227 ; his advice about libels, 233
North, Roger, 3, 221 *n.*, 232
Norwich, City of, 3 *n.*, address to the King, 239 ; attacked by Middlesex Grand Jury, 239
Norwich Post, the first country paper, 10

Oates, Samuel, 20 *n.*, 152
Oates, Titus, 35, 152 ; origin of his Popish Plot, 208–209 and *n.* ; 221 and *n.* ; the first whig, 234 ; expelled from Whitehall, 241
Okey, John, Colonel, 19, 89
Oldroyd, Robert, the " Divil of Dewsbury," 168
Oudart, Nicholas, Latin Secretary, 144, 186 *n.*
Overton, Colonel, 32, 44
Oxford, Parliament of, 235–237

" Panther Prophecy," the, 29, 170 *n.*
Parker, Martin, 4 *n.* ; his famous ballad, 84
Parliament (*see* Lords, and Commons).
Partridge, John, 248–250 ; denounces Harris, 250 ; Squire Bickerstaff detected, 253, 254 ; believed to be dead, 254 ; attacks Swift, 255
Patience (Patient) Thomas, 25 and *n.*
Paule, George, 60, 61
Payne, Anthony, 52 and *n.*
Pecke, Samuel, 10 and *n.*
Pembroke, Lord, 30
Penny Post, 220 and *n.*, 221 and *n.*, 222
Pepys, Samuel, 205, 206 ; imprisoned, 211
Perrot, Charles, second editor of *Gazette*, 186 and *n.*, 195
Peters, Hugh, executed, 134 ; his biography, 135 *n.*
Petty, Sir William, 90
Phelipps, Edward, M.P., 146
Phenix, the, 143, 169
Plague, the, 5

Plunket, Oliver, Archbishop, executed, 210; the King's retort to Lord Essex, 210

Polygamy, 28

Poole, Captain, 64 *n.*; imprisoned, 76

Post Office (*see* Letter Office).

Price, John, Monck's chaplain, 64, 118

Pride, Thomas, Colonel, 18 *n.*, 19

Printing Act, the, 123, 124 and *n.*, 149, 150 and *n.*, 213

Prodigies, Book of (see *Mirabilis Annus*).

" Protestant Flail," the, 236 and *n.*

Prynne, William, 37, 81, 82 *n.*, 105

Quakers, 27, 140

Qualifications for Parliament, 99, 100

Ranters, the, 27

Ray (Rea), Charles, 218

Regicides, execution of, 134, 156

Representative, the (*see* Commons, House of).

Richter, Georg, *Epistolæ Selectiores*, 26 *n.*, 28 *n.*

Robinson, Luke, 95 and *n.*

Rolle, Mr., 96

Rolle, Captain, 127

Rolle, Sir Francis, 127

Rossingham, Captain Edmund, 10 and *n.*

Rota club, 89, 90

Rump Parliament, origin of term, 16 *n.* (*see* Commons).

Rushworth, John, 106, 206 *n.*

St. John's College, Cambridge, 86

St. John, Justice, 30

St. Paul's Cathedral, 4

Sawtell, Edmund, Clerk in the Letter Office, 183; warns Muddiman, 183; attacked by Hickes, 184, 185

Scot, Thomas, 41; character of, 44, 45; his plot with Willys, 58–62; suppresses news-books, 84; meets Monck, 95; order to Monck, 96; first plot against Monck, 100; assassination plot, 104; ejected from Secretaryship, 106, 126

Scot, Thomas, junior, 100

Scotland, population of, 3

Scroggs, Sir William, Lord Chief Justice, 213; impeached, 225, 227

Sealed knot, 55 and *n.*

Secluded members (*see* Commons, House of).

Seven Principles, 79

Shaftesbury, Earl of (*see* Cooper, Anthony Ashley).

Skinner, Cyriac, 90

Skippon, Major-General, 21, 49 *n.*, 76

Slingsby, Colonel, 148

Slingsby, Sir Henry, 58

Smallridge, ——, 219

Smith, Francis, 132; his nickname, 153; his biography, 158–161; his examination, 160 *n.*; anabaptist teacher, 161; 169, 211, 223; his first autobiography, 226–227; his *Speech of a Noble Peer*, 228; his second autobiography, 228 *n.*; his newspaper, 235–236; his falsehoods about the King, 237; his falsehoods in his newspaper, 246 and *n.*; reissues *Speech of a Noble Peer*, 241–242; again arrested, 243, fines remitted by James II, 244 and *n.*

Smith, Sir James, 126

Smith, John, bookseller, and Oates, 221 *n.*; employed by Mayor and Aldermen of Norwich, 238–239

Speeches and prayers of the regicides, 135, 170; termed a cheat, forgery and imposture, 171

Spittlehouse, John, his *Rome ruined by Whitehall*, 24

Stafford, Lord, 228

State Trials, false and mutilated documents in, 142 *n.*, 153 *n.*, 171 *n.*

Stationers' registers, 124 and *n.*

Streater, John, his biography and periodicals, 90 and *n.*; Comptroller of the Artillery, 91; helps capture Lambert, 116; honoured by Parliament, 116 and *n.*

Swan, Thomas, 146

Swan Alley, meeting-house, 31, 34, 136, 141

Swift, Jonathan, 251; predicts Partridge's death, 252; Elegy on Partridge, 253; his "Vindiction," 254
Sydserf (St. Serf), Thomas, 131

Temple, Sir Richard, 95
Temple, Sir William, 145
Thompson, Mary, 218
Thompson, Nathaniel, biography of, 215–216, 218 *n.*, 220, 223, 225, 232, 243
Thurloe, John, 12, 44, 56, 106
Toleration, meaning of in 1659, 33
Tonge, Ezerel, 208
Tonge, Thomas, plotter, 152, 153
Trap ad Crucem, 217 *n.*
Trapnell, Anna, 29, 30, 142
"Treatise of the Execution of Justice," 169
Trevor, Sir John, Secretary of State, 87 *n.*, 202
Twyn, John, plotter, 169 and *n.*; executed, 170

Vane, Sir Henry, junior, 42; plots with Willys, 58–62; his axiom, 67; song about, 93, 94
Venner, Thomas, 31; sermon and rising of, 136–141

Wakeman, Sir George, 213
Waller, Sir William, 52, 55
Waller, Sir William, junior, 226
Ward, Sir Patience, Lord Mayor, 220, 224–225

Watermen, petition of, 97 *n.*, 98, 129
Westenhanger Castle, 61
"When the King enjoys his own again," 84 and *n.*
Whitton, Colonel, 97 *n.*, 98
Wildman, John, 89
Williams, Oliver, 13, 76–77, 112–113, 126–128, 130
Williamson, Sir Joseph, Secretary of State, 144; his character, 145; and Muddiman, 172; warned by Downing, 185, 189; defeated by Muddiman, 191; his news-letters, 200; Ball's report to, 201–202, 205, 206, 207; imprisoned and released, 211–212; turned out, 212 *n.*
Willys, Sir Richard, 55 *n.*; posting of, 56; a traitor, 57, 59; his plot against the King, 61, 62, 94
Wolfamcote, 85
Wonders, Book of (See *Mirabilis Annus*).
Wood, Major, on Fifth-Monarchy men, 35

Yalden, Dr. Thomas, 253
Yard, Robert, 194, his presumptuous news-letter, 206
Yarmouth, Grand Jury of, present dissenters, 241
York, Duke of (James II), 207, 210, 212–213; obtains verdict against Penny Post, 222, 229–231